KIERKEGAARD AND THE LIFE OF FAITH

INDIANA SERIES IN THE PHILOSOPHY OF RELIGION

Merold Westphal, *editor*

KIERKEGAARD AND THE LIFE OF FAITH

The Aesthetic, the Ethical, and the Religious in Fear and Trembling

Jeffrey Hanson

Indiana University Press

Bloomington and Indianapolis

This book is a publication of

Indiana University Press
Office of Scholarly Publishing
Herman B Wells Library 350
1320 East 10th Street
Bloomington, Indiana 47405 USA

iupress.indiana.edu

♾ The paper used in this publication meets the minimum requirements of the American National Standard for Information Sciences—Permanence of Paper for Printed Library Materials, ANSI Z39.48–1992.

Manufactured in the United States of America

Library of Congress Cataloging-in-Publication Data

Names: Hanson, Jeffrey, author.
Title: Kierkegaard and the life of faith : the aesthetic, the ethical, and the religious in Fear and trembling / Jeffrey Hanson.
Description: 1st [edition]. | Bloomington : Indiana University Press, 2017. |
Series: Indiana series in the philosophy of religion | Includes bibliographical references and index.
Identifiers: LCCN 2016042293 (print) | LCCN 2016045061 (ebook) | ISBN 9780253024701 (cloth : alk. paper) | ISBN 9780253025029 (e-book)
Subjects: LCSH: Kierkegaard, Søren, 1813-1855. Frygt og bæven. | Christianity—Philosophy. | Abraham (Biblical patriarch) | Sin—Christianity.
Classification: LCC BR100.K523 H36 2017 (print) | LCC BR100.K523 (ebook) | DDC 198/.9—dc23
LC record available at https://lccn.loc.gov/2016042293

1 2 3 4 5 22 21 20 19 18 17

Dedication

For the ones who taught me the little mystery:
My father, George
My mother, Danielle
My sister, Jamie
And the ones who taught me the great mystery:
My wife, Roxene
My son, Tristan

The true religious existence is to be as if demolished for this life—but still to consider oneself blessed.

Kierkegaard, *Journals and Papers*

Contents

Acknowledgments

PORTIONS OF THIS book have appeared in print before as "The Shipwreck of the Aesthetic and Ethical," *Graduate Faculty Philosophy Journal* 32, no. 2 (2011): 371–405, reprinted by permission of Philosophy Documentation Center; "'He Speaks in Tongues': Hearing the Truth of Abraham's Words of Faith," in *Kierkegaard's* Fear and Trembling: *A Critical Guide*, edited by Daniel Conway (Cambridge: Cambridge University Press, 2015), 229–46, reprinted by permission of Cambridge University Press; and "The Phenomenon of the Good: Reconstructing Religion in the Wake of Deconstruction," in *Reexamining Deconstruction and Determinate Religion: Toward a Religion with Religion*, edited by J. Aaron Simmons and Stephen Minister (Pittsburgh, PA: Duquesne University Press, 2012), 131–54, reprinted by permission of Duquesne University Press.

KIERKEGAARD AND THE LIFE OF FAITH

Introduction

FEAR AND TREMBLING was famously recognized by its author as being sufficient among his writings to secure his everlasting fame as an author,[1] but the text has arguably proven to have a captivating power beyond even what Kierkegaard himself imagined. It has been read and reread and puzzled over and argued about in countless languages and in numberless papers and books. So why presume to write yet another book on *Fear and Trembling*? Because while many books have recently appeared in English that seek to clarify this text (and indeed many of them have done a marvelous job), none has sought to interpret it anew. And such an interpretation is required today because many of the interpretations that have been lately offered are incomplete in scope or woefully off the point. Some are both.

The current interpretation takes in the whole of *Fear and Trembling*; in fact, it is the argument of this book that Problema III, which has in some interpretations been wholly ignored and in none has received pride of place, is in fact a key portion of the text, containing the final elaboration of all of its most important points. A convincing reading of *Fear and Trembling* can no more afford to truncate the text in this way than Plato's *Republic* can be properly understood by stopping at the end of Book VII. By downplaying or even discounting Problema III many interpreters fail to see that the life of faith not only suspends and reinvents the ethical but also suspends and reinvents the aesthetic, providing a complete picture of how the knight of faith realizes in a new way the demands of both goodness and beauty. The current interpretation likewise seeks to place *Fear and Trembling* in direct relationship with the most important references that Kierkegaard himself made to his own work, chief among these a long footnote in the introduction to *The Concept of Anxiety* that provides an indispensable Ariadne's thread for the course of this book.

Furthermore, the current interpretation dispenses with a proliferation of misunderstandings of this text that are united by their central conviction that *Fear and Trembling* involves at its core a conflict between religion and ethics, between the good and the holy, or between an absolute and a generalized responsibility. The argument of this book is that this conflict, which has been the presupposition of pages and pages of commentary on *Fear and Trembling*, is—at best—a subordinate concern of the text. Insofar as there is a central conflict thematized in this book, that conflict is between the rigorous demand of faith that comes from God and the humanly devised ethical systems that are usually considered sufficient (by both pre-Christian and "spiritless" pseudo-Christian cultures) to secure "the good life." More interesting to Kierkegaard in the end, however, is not the conflict between these modes of life but the manner in which the demand of faith necessarily transforms the ethical vision while overcoming it; in short, his interest is in the way in which our vision of the Good is broken by, and then rebuilt by, our encounter with God. Kierkegaard has almost no interest whatsoever in how or whether the apparently unethical can be explained or excused by recourse to "faith"; what he is trying to do is alarm a complacently Christian audience of readers into recognizing what their faith actually requires of them and the extent to which real adherence to that faith should alter the entirety of their lives.

Fear and Trembling is very simply principally about how faith changes the whole of life and does so in ways that are often elusive and difficult to discriminate as distinct from the style of life pursued by many nonfaithful (but nonetheless admirable) people. The life of faith nevertheless can be described and, more important, can certainly be lived out. Faith changes the whole of life in three principal manners that *Fear and Trembling* concerns itself with.

First, it changes the faithful person's response to the world, especially her response to life at its most challenging: faith is a means of coping with the inevitable losses, heartbreaks, and difficulties presented by life and enables an appreciation of life as a gift without discounting the very real and legitimate sense in which life remains deeply objectionable on humanly constructed ethical and aesthetic terms.[2] This aspect of faith's work is consistently opposed, both by Johannes de Silentio and by Kierkegaard's authorship as a whole, to the pagan conception of fate and stoic resolve in the face of fate. Fate remains forever ambiguous and unreconciled to life's goodness, which only faith wholeheartedly, and not naively, affirms.

Second, faith changes the faithful person's relationships with others: faith deepens our relationships to degrees of intimacy that a life lived without faith cannot recognize and intensifies the communication between persons that is the hallmark of their relationships' endurance amid transformation. As we will see, faith contents itself not with the maintenance of relationship but enjoins by necessity the deepening of relationship even while acknowledging the fragility and ultimately the impermanence of such relationships.

Third, faith changes the faithful person's understanding of herself: faith inculcates in us simultaneously an awareness of our own profound proclivity toward evil and an openness to being loved and forgiven despite our own wickedness. This final aspect of faith's effort educates the faithful about the need to steer clear of their own worst possibilities and prepares them for the healing that is needful when the wrong possibilities have been enacted. As Silentio will say, though, faithful acting for one's own sake is tantamount to acting for God's sake as well,[3] so we also should be aware that the relation of the self to the self can never fully develop in faith without also being in relation to the divine. *Fear and Trembling*, though, is often more elliptical on this subject than one might expect.

My way of addressing this lacuna will be to draw on other writings from Kierkegaard in brief codas to each of the chapters I devote to the three Problemata sections. In each case what I aim to do is to go beyond the letter of the text and engage in some speculation (though not unwarranted speculation, I hope) about how the implications of *Fear and Trembling* might be more fully fleshed out. In each case the coda will try to envision how a more specific set of Christian categories would extend the message of *Fear and Trembling*, a message that is compatible with Christian conceptuality but does not necessarily have to assume it for the text to succeed. I think Kierkegaard himself would say that faith is incoherent without a revelation from God but that once that revelation has been given, the nature of faith can be retrospectively reflected upon, even by one who has not, like Silentio, accepted that revelation. His account, then, will not be fundamentally awry or suspect but simply not the last word on the matter; the codas to chapters 6, 7, and 8 will try to say more than Silentio can.

It is these dimensions of faith's effect on the life of the faithful person—world, others, self, and God—that will structure subsequent readings of each of the sections of *Fear and Trembling*; as they are embroidered throughout the text with one another, so too is the treatment of them necessarily interwoven. For the sake of structure, I proceed through the text section by section in what follows, but these dimensions of faith should be kept in mind as the primary concern of each chapter. Again, the chapters build in intensity toward the key, final problem, as I maintain is the case for *Fear and Trembling* itself.

Haufniensis and Silentio on the Ethical Ideal

A new interpretive path into *Fear and Trembling* is opened through a perhaps unusual point of entry: the introduction to *The Concept of Anxiety*. It goes without saying that these two texts are composed by different pseudonymous personae—*Fear and Trembling* by Johannes de Silentio, and *The Concept of Anxiety* by Vigilius Haufniensis—and this is a distinction that Kierkegaard himself would have his readers respect. The case prosecuted by this book does not depend on complete agreement between the two authors. All that is required is a recognition that the same concerns were forefront in Kierkegaard's mind during the writing of both texts (which were in the end published only a year apart) and the granting of a certain hermeneutical privilege to a metatextual moment in the introduction wherein Haufniensis speaks *about* Silentio's effort in *Fear and Trembling*. No such comment can have sole interpretive authority any more than the author of a text can be the only interpreter of its meaning. The meaning of *Fear and*

Trembling, like the meaning of any text, outruns Kierkegaard's own purposes. However, Haufniensis's retrospective gloss on Silentio cannot be ignored either. So far, much critical literature has treated *Fear and Trembling* as a hermetically sealed whole, whereas the footnote in the introduction to *The Concept of Anxiety* suggests that Kierkegaard himself had not altogether stopped thinking about what he had offered the reader in *Fear and Trembling*.[4] Throughout the reading that follows in this book, evidence from within *Fear and Trembling* will constantly be educed to support the possibility that the introduction to *The Concept of Anxiety* is relevant to *Fear and Trembling*.

The longest footnote in the introduction to *The Concept of Anxiety* is in part a commentary on *Fear and Trembling* and establishes a stronger connection between these two works than is usually observed. It reads as follows:

> In his work *Fear and Trembling* (Copenhagen: 1843) Johannes de Silentio makes several observations concerning this point. In this book, the author several times allows the desired ideality of esthetics to be shipwrecked on the required ideality of ethics, in order through these collisions to bring to light the religious ideality as the ideality that precisely is the ideality of actuality, and therefore just as desirable as that of esthetics and not as impossible as the ideality of ethics. This is accomplished in such a way that the religious ideality breaks forth in the dialectical leap and in the positive mood—"Behold all things have become new"[5] as well as in the negative mood that is the passion of the absurd to which the concept "repetition" corresponds. Either all of existence comes to an end in the demand of ethics, or the condition is provided and the whole of life and of existence begins anew, not through an immanent continuity with the former existence, which is a contradiction, but through a transcendence.[6]

The thematic link between *Fear and Trembling* and this footnote from *The Concept of Anxiety* is not obvious at first. In the complex introduction to the latter, Haufniensis embarks on an elaborate discussion of the confused state of science. In the epigraph to the work, Haufniensis writes, "The age of making distinctions is past. It has been vanquished by the system,"[7] and his introduction, with its veritable thicket of distinctions, seems directly intended to combat the system's confusion of distinctions, particularly the confusion between metaphysics and dogmatics perpetrated by the deployment of speculative concepts like mediation and reconciliation.[8] And while this polemic against the confusion of the sciences may seem "extraneous," it is nevertheless, Haufniensis insists, essential to the topic at hand.

That topic is obviously anxiety, but inasmuch as "the present work has set as its task the psychological treatment of the concept of 'anxiety,'" he writes, "it must also, although tacitly so, deal with the concept of sin. Sin, however, is no subject for psychological concern."[9] In fact, not only is sin not a subject for psychology, Haufniensis claims it has "no place, and this is its specific nature."[10] Sin in fact is altered in both its concept and mood when any particular branch of science—aesthetics, metaphysics, psychology, ethics, and dogmatics—attempts to take it up.

The most surprising such distortion would probably be the failure of ethics to deal with sin; this is the last and most extensive treatment Haufniensis provides, and as he himself says, "ethics should be a science in which sin might be expected to find a place."[11] But there is here a great difficulty, and that is that ethics "develops a contradiction" inasmuch as it both imposes infinite demands and recognizes the impossibility of fulfilling them. Like the harsh disciplinarian (and here Kierkegaard echoes Saint Paul's critique of the law in the epistle to the Galatians[12]), ethics crushes without uplifting, a consequence of what Haufniensis calls its ideality. "Ethics points to ideality as a task and assumes that every man possesses the requisite conditions,"[13] chief among these conditions being as Haufniensis reports three pages later, "the presupposition that virtue can be realized."[14] Ethics never observes, according to Haufniensis, but is "always accusing, judging, and acting";[15] "it is a disciplinarian that demands, and by its demands only judges but does not bring forth life."[16] The ideality of ethics is peculiar to it, inasmuch as unlike the other "ideal" sciences, ethics tries to make its ideality *actual* and in so doing assumes that every individual has the capacity to meet its inflexible standards, expectations that cannot be disappointed or altered.[17] As Haufniensis says pithily, "The more ideal ethics is, the better."[18] Because ethics is an ideal science, it cannot incorporate the actuality of sin; sin is proof positive that human beings *don't* possess the requisite condition, virtue cannot be realized, we do not have the capacity to meet the ethical demand that is imposed upon us. "Sin, then, belongs to ethics only insofar as upon this concept it is shipwrecked with the aid of repentance."[19]

To speak of ethics as being shipwrecked on the rock of sin and repentance means that the careful expositor must be prepared to reinvent ethics on the basis of the destruction of the ethical ideal, to transform it in an entirely new way without recourse to the established categories of science; when the actuality of sin is truly acknowledged, it is recognized as no mere incidental intrusion upon the ethical ideal but as a fundamental feature of human reality. "In the struggle to actualize the task of ethics, sin shows itself not as something that belongs only accidentally to the accidental individual, but as something that withdraws deeper and deeper and as a deeper and deeper presupposition, as a presupposition that goes beyond the individual. Then all is lost for ethics."[20] Once sin has been recognized as pervasive and operative at the core of the human person, Haufniensis concludes, "it is, therefore, impossible for anyone to write an ethics without having altogether different categories in reserve."[21]

What is thus required is a new ethics, one that builds from the ground up, so to speak, on the shipwrecked ruins of the old ethics, the one that sin does not belong to and which if it were to try to incorporate sin would find itself "lost."[22] This is particularly true, apparently, of pagan ethics, as Haufniensis asserts that "sin's skepticism is altogether foreign to paganism. Sin is for the ethical consciousness what error is for the knowledge of it—the particular exception that proves nothing."[23] The same could be said however of any ethical consciousness that remains "pagan" in its alienation from revealed truth.[24] Paganism, and by extension any ethical consciousness that remains broadly pagan in its defining outlook, simply cannot cope with the actuality of sin, and for such a consciousness repentance is an equally fruitless gesture. All pagan or spiritless ethics can do is judge; it cannot "bring forth life," for it is incapable of providing the means of regenerating the repentant. All it can do is restate, more emphatically if necessary, its inflexible demands, even in the face of willful and contrarian flaunting of those demands.

The new ethics, which would draw on dogmatic inspiration, is built up from the ruins of the first ethics and proceeds by a reversed movement. "Ethics will have nothing to do with bargaining; nor can one in this way reach actuality. To reach actuality, the whole movement must be reversed."[25] The old ethics imposes an ideal from the top down on the facts of the human condition and concedes nothing to those facts. The new ethics accounts for the facts of the human condition and raises them from the ground up to a chastened but life-giving revised ideal. "With dogmatics begins the science that, in contrast to that science called ideal *stricte*, namely, ethics, proceeds from actuality. It begins with the actual in order to raise it up into ideality. It does not deny the presence of sin."[26] Having accepted the actuality of sin, and depending on the presupposition of hereditary sin that dogmatic theology posits, this "second ethics," as Haufniensis comes to call it,[27] "does not ignore sin, and it does not have its ideality in making ideal demands; rather, it has its ideality in the penetrating consciousness of actuality, of the actuality of sin."[28] Second ethics acknowledges the reality and abandons ideality only to reinvent it; second ethics insists on an ideal, but its ideal quality does not consist in the purity of its demands and its inflexibility with respect to accommodating failures to meet those demands, but in its acute awareness of the fallen human condition and its preparedness to insist on a transformed ideal that the human condition can nevertheless be empowered and ennobled to meet.[29] It is in this respect that its movement is reversed: "The new ethics . . . sets ideality as a task, not by a movement from above and downward but from below and upward."[30]

Part of what I want to argue in this book is that *Fear and Trembling* addresses the same set of concerns that I have identified in the introduction to *The Concept of Anxiety*. In particular, there is a thematic connection between sin as it is treated in the two works, indirectly in both but perhaps significantly nonetheless, and the disruptive effect that the actuality of sin has on the ideal status of the ethical. As we will see, the teleological suspension of the ethical can be successfully understood as another iteration of the need for "second ethics." The whole reason why the ethical as universal is even subject to suspension in the first place is a function of its ideal status: It makes demands, but because of the reality of sin, its demands can never be met. Faith alone, Silentio will argue, can establish a new ideal that in turn makes possible a specifically religious ethics that incorporates the pervasive reality of sin at its basis. I will argue further that correlate to the actuality of sin at the basis of the new ethics (toward which *Fear and Trembling* gestures by means of the teleological suspension of the ethical) is the possibility of the forgiveness of sin; faith, the religious ideal, the ideal of actuality, thereby brings forth life, that is, establishes an ethics that can actually be lived, because it can actually offer—through the power of forgiveness—the moral perfection for which the ethical ideal originally aimed.

One reason why my interpretation stresses Problema III is that the issue of sin comes up with particular force in that section of *Fear and Trembling.* Ultimately, the argument about Problema III will be that while the context of Haufniensis's speculations differs from Silentio's, there is in the latter's text an enactment, we might say, of the principles that the former puts forward. Specifically, Haufniensis's diagnosis of the problem that sin poses to any attempt to treat it either as a matter of aesthetic interest or ethical deliberation is operative in Silentio's text. Silentio accepts before the fact the validity of Haufniensis's claims and brings them dramatically to life by his reworked deployment of the key narratives in Problema III—the story of the Delphic bride and groom, the folk tale of Agnes and the merman, the apocryphal story of Tobias and Sarah from the book of Tobit, and the legend of Faust and Margaret.

With escalating clarity, these vignettes actually illustrate in an imaginative and lively manner the same point Haufniensis makes in a more theoretical and methodologically technical way. For both authors sin is a problem for ethics inasmuch as the idealized rules put forward by classical ethics cannot cope with the actuality of sin but can only inveigh impotently against it. Likewise for both authors, faith alone, a religious ideal, can save the ethical by reconstructing its ruins on a new basis.

Haufniensis and Silentio on the Aesthetic Ideal

A comparable case can be made with respect to aesthetics. For both Haufniensis and Silentio, sin is also a problem for aesthetics inasmuch as it thwarts an aesthetic ideal, the "rules" that govern what makes for an artistically satisfying story; actual sinful human lives are neither tragedies nor comedies and resist description by such aesthetic conventions. Haufniensis's remarks on this subject are not as extensive or detailed as his analysis of ethics, perhaps unsurprisingly: *The*

Concept of Anxiety is not preeminently about an aesthetic issue but (among other things, of course) about the transformation of ethics when it is refounded on a dogmatic presupposition. But the warping effect of an aesthetic treatment of sin is targeted by Haufniensis in a significant paragraph:

> Thus when sin is brought into esthetics, the mood becomes either light-minded or melancholy, for the category in which sin lies is that of contradiction, and this is either comic or tragic. The mood is therefore altered, because the mood that corresponds to sin is earnestness. The concept of sin is also altered, because, whether it become comic or tragic, it becomes in any case something that endures, or something nonessential that is annulled, whereas, according to its true concept, sin is to be overcome. In a deeper sense, the comic and the tragic have no enemy but only a bogeyman at which one either weeps or laughs.[31]

When subjected to aesthetic treatment, sin becomes either the object of comic laughter or of maudlin hand-wringing. In neither case is earnestness attained. Earnestness, as we learn from a later section of the same text, is a wholly self-reflexive attitude, an "acquired originality of disposition" that allows the self to return again and again to the same activities with originality each time rather than out of uninspired habit.[32] It is not merely an immediate feeling but a disciplined manner of keeping the self's activities ever new, even when, or perhaps especially when, those activities have to be repeated. This is not the same as enthusiasm, which waxes and wanes; nor is it the same as pedantry, which obsesses over some definite area of fixed interest.[33] What earnestness is "about" is itself. Before one can be earnest about anything, one must first be in earnest about oneself.[34]

The self-reflexive structure of earnestness supplies a clue as to why it is the proper mood for sin. Daily recommittal to the ethical task cannot be sustained by mere enthusiasm, which inevitably burns out. Such a recommittal must be undertaken with self-seriousness, the earnestness that is recommitment to the self in its fullest development before it is recommitment to any particular course of action, even a course of action as apparently obviously compelling as "today I will do what is right." Enthusiastic resolve to avoid specific sins or perhaps even to avoid sin in general is not enough. One must commit to oneself, and in so doing, live that commitment through the daily task of vanquishing sin.

This is why Haufniensis asserts that earnestness is the appropriate mood that corresponds to the correct concept of sin as something to be overcome, that is actively vanquished, rather than being cancelled.[35] If earnestness is not attained, and the mood is either tragic or comic, then sin is wrongly understood as something that "endures," that is, simply persists without being willed, or something "inessential," an accident. Haufniensis itemizes a number of ways that sin can be misconstrued: "Whenever the issue of sin is dealt with, one can observe by the very mood whether the concept is the correct one. For instance, whenever sin is spoken of as a disease, an abnormality, a poison, or a disharmony, the concept is falsified."[36] The only way to overcome sin, as we learn from *The Sickness unto Death*, is to conquer it again and again, inasmuch as every moment we are in despair we are sick by our own willing, and mere acquiescence to this state of affairs is tantamount to actively prolonging it.[37]

Earnestness about sin rejects the misconstrual that nothing can be done about sin and the equally false apprehension that it can be flippantly evaded. This is why the comic and tragic have no real enemy, only an object for their scornful mocking or self-pitying weepiness. In both cases sin becomes a spectacle that can solicit what are only superficially opposed reactions.[38] It is surely important that tragedy and comedy, the two traditional modes of classical theatrics, are singled out here as inappropriate means of relating to sin. The classical world, as we have already seen and is consistently reiterated by Kierkegaard throughout his authorship, has no fit concept of sin. We will see in the course of this book's argument how part of what faith entails is the rejection of these inadequate traditional aesthetic genres and their attendant falsifying moods. The right aesthetic register for describing faith, as we will see in the discussion of Problema III, will have to surpass both tragedy and comedy.

It is clearer in the case of the ethical how the "rules" that govern the ideal are shattered and reconstructed again on the basis of dogmatic presuppositions. Less clear is how this is true for the aesthetic as well. George Pattison has observed that Kierkegaard's use of the term "aesthetic" as a label for a form of life that other thinkers in his line of descent were content to call "inauthentic" or afflicted by "bad faith" is somewhat idiosyncratic.[39] Arguing that Kierkegaard's thinking on art was much of a piece with the thrust of German idealism generally, Pattison points out that "there are three areas which highlight the way in which Kierkegaard used the idealist concept of art in formulating his own judgement on the limitation of art *vis-à-vis* religion. These are: the ideal nature of art, the synthetic character of aesthetic experience and the timelessness of art."[40] Because these characteristics define what art can be, they mark out limits both to what art can accomplish and to the sort of life that is lived "aesthetically" or the aesthete's life. I will accordingly in this book talk about "aesthetic ideals," or "rules" that govern both how an aesthetic work and an aesthetic life are constructed. We know that the aesthetic life is not the highest capable for a human being, according to Kierkegaard, but we must also recognize that despite its limits it has an inherent "logic,"[41] and it is this logic that Silentio appeals to implicitly and explicitly at various points in his argument, especially when he is seeking to contrast the life of faith with the aesthetic life. As I will argue in this book, the life of faith of course is not reducible to either the aesthetic or ethical life, but it will exhibit features of both, since the religious wholly dismisses neither the aesthetic nor the ethical.

Returning to the characteristics of the aesthetic that Pattison identifies, it is easy to see how the ideal nature of art is also the aspiration of the aesthetic life: art on the idealist view is meant to productively project a world of meaning out of the ego's inner resources, principally the infinite potentiality of its creative freedom and will. As Pattison goes on to show, "the world of ideality is given a quite different ontological status in Kierkegaard's view than that which it had held in idealist thought. From a Christian point of view which presupposes the fall, man's alienation from both God and his own essential being, the human subject cannot determine reality as such solely on the basis of his own inner freedom."[42]

This basic objection is lodged by Kierkegaard against the Romantics from the very beginning of his authorship in *The Concept of Irony* and, as we will see, is reasserted in *Fear and Trembling* as well. Part of why the aesthetic life is deservedly called "aesthetic" is that it seeks to model within itself the "rules" of idealist aesthetic production, according to which "imagination projects a world in which the essential interests of the self are reflected and realized."[43] We know that for Kierkegaard, exclusive devotion to such a project is doomed to failure, but I will argue its logic persists in transformed fashion even within the religious life.[44]

Continuing with Pattison's analysis, now with respect to the "synthetic" character of art, according to the idealist conception, external forms that result from the deployment of unfettered creativity are just expressions of the Idea.[45] Art thus aims to provide a kind of unity and harmony that real life never affords. In Pattison's words, "Aesthetic experience gives to sensuous, material life a unity and ideality which is not immediately apparent in other dimensions of experience."[46] This again however is a limit, inasmuch as art thereby is thwarted by any subject matter that proves intractable: "Art cannot deal with any subject-matter that is inherently discordant or incomplete and it will only be able to deal *artistically* with ugliness or pain where these are seen in the light of a final resolution which brings everything to a good end. Art therefore reconciles us to life by presenting a harmonious and pleasing image of what life is like which anaesthetizes any sense of outrage we may feel in the face of suffering."[47] I will argue that this exact dynamic is explored and questioned by Silentio, especially in his treatment of the story of the lad and the princess.[48] Once again, this characteristic of aesthetics is also mirrored in the aesthetic life, which if at all possible evades any genuine confrontation with pain, boredom, or difficulty, and if not possible stylizes these setbacks to its own ideal self-conception: "Life can only be admitted into art when it has first been tamed, filtered through the reconciling spirit of the artist,"[49] a maxim that holds true not just for the formal practitioner of the fine arts but for the aesthete as well. Yet here again there is a limit that prevents the aesthetic life from being entirely squared with the religious; the aesthete avoids the wound or covers it over, while faith alone binds up every wound. Once again, I will show that this critique is Silentio's as well, and that once it has been prosecuted, the aesthetic is nevertheless reinstated in regenerated form at the end of his book.

The final point that Pattison identifies as key to understanding the coincidence of aesthetic properties and artifacts and the style of life that Kierkegaard dubs "aesthetic" is the shared aspiration to timelessness. Common to the nineteenth-century Romantics was the thesis that "by virtue of its harmonious perfection, its completeness, art lifts us out of the dispersion of temporal existence. The barriers of separation which time imposes are broken down."[50] Here again though there are limits to this project and to the style of living that models itself on the aesthetic ideal. As Pattison quotes Judge William writing in *Either/Or*, "If I wish to portray a hero who conquers kingdoms and countries, this can be done very well in the moment, but a cross-bearer who takes up his cross every day can never be portrayed in either poetry or art, for the point is that he does it every day . . . Courage can be concentrated very well in the moment; patience cannot, precisely because patience contends against time . . . long-suffering cannot be portrayed artistically, for the point of it is incommensurable with art; neither can it be poetized, for it requires the protraction of time."[51] This timelessness is of course for Kierkegaard illusory; the aesthetic life seeks to freeze time in a static idealized manner, to escape from the vagaries of individual existence in favor of a flight to the unreal. The religious life is by contrast fully reconciled to time and lives through and within it.[52]

Recall, as I argued above, earnestness is the proper mood for sin, and earnestness in the face of sin, like patience and daily taking up of one's cross, is another phenomenon that cannot be easily poetized. Once more this thematic point will be re-echoed in my reading of *Fear and Trembling*, a text that in my view also rejects the consolations of resignation and its attendant escapism in favor of an embrace of the fragility of life and its goods, which are dispensed within time over the course of an individual lifetime touched by both pain and beauty.[53]

I delineate these qualities of aesthetics and the aesthetic ideal now because the life of faith will be shown to emerge from the collision of the aesthetic ideal with the ethical ideal. Both of these ideals are shattered by reality in such a way as to make possible the religious ideal, the only ideal that is also actual. As such, the religious ideal embodies the aesthetic's aspiration to idealization, synthetic unity, and timelessness, concretely expressed in the "rules" that secure a beautiful, holistic, and eternal ideality, but does so in a real, lived life, not a fantasy realm. This complete development of the life of faith will become clear in the treatment of Problema III, which completes the itinerary of faith by recapitulating the aesthetic as well as the ethical. It does so by satisfying the demands of the aesthetic in surprising ways; that there are such demands is clear from the third

Problema, which often speaks of what aesthetics, in adherence to what I am calling its internal logic, demands, contrives, or insists upon in order to maximize the dramatic effect, emotional resonance, or other ideal qualities of the situations of life that it influences and interprets.

As we will see, Silentio argues that such aesthetic ideals contradict themselves when they are applied to reality—that is, the conventions that make for aesthetic satisfaction are rarely realized in the course of actually lived life. The religious life, though, achieves a broken aesthetic integrity. For reasons we have already seen, the aesthetic ideal, if it is paramount in the individual's life, cannot be reconciled to the religious life. But the religious life does successfully achieve rebuilt aesthetic satisfactions, in much the same way that it lays the foundation of second ethics. I will attempt to show that there is an isomorphism between the resignation of the ethical ideal and the resignation of the aesthetic ideal. In the case of the latter, the knight of faith has to surrender the classic consolations of aesthetics: escape from actuality in favor of flight to the ideal, tidy and seamless unity of projects and purposes, and evasion of time, suffering, and the difficult and protracted cultivation of human character. The knight of faith resigns the Romanticist illusion of the merely aesthetic life, but she fully expects to get these satisfactions back again, inasmuch as she actually lives out the beautifully restored existence that Romantic longing aims for but can never achieve on its own. Thanks to dogmatic presuppositions (like the revelation of sin and the possibility of its forgiveness)[54] that are lacking in the narratives that Silentio examines in Problema III in order to set off their differences from the story of Abraham, the aesthetic ideal, as much as the ethical, can be made new. The life of faith will therefore be beautiful as well as good, demonstrating the synthetic unity and integrity, the aspiration to timelessness and authorial originality, and culmination in the proverbial happy ending that normally are realizable only in the fictive world of art.

Haufniensis on Silentio

Returning to our analysis of the introduction to *The Concept of Anxiety*, let us revisit Haufniensis's claim in his footnote that "Silentio makes several observations concerning this point. In this book, the author several times allows the desired ideality of esthetics to be shipwrecked on the required ideality of ethics, in order through these collisions to bring to light the religious ideality as the ideality that precisely is the ideality of actuality, and therefore just as desirable as that of esthetics and not as impossible as the ideality of ethics."[55]

It is odd given the highly technical context of the introduction of *The Concept of Anxiety* that *Fear and Trembling* should come up at all. There has been no reference to the extraordinary trial of Abraham and little discussion of faith.[56]

Even in this footnote faith does not come up explicitly; instead, as we have seen, *Fear and Trembling* is parsed by Haufniensis in terms of its accomplishments with respect to ideality and actuality.

Haufniensis claims that Silentio has made "several observations" concerning "this point." This point can only be the one he has just made, namely, that "sin, then, belongs to ethics only insofar as upon this concept it is shipwrecked with the aid of repentance."[57] The strange thing is that Silentio mentions sin only in passing in *Fear and Trembling*, very obliquely at the beginning of each of the three Problemata sections[58] and again in a footnote in Problema III, and even then he mentions sin only as a topic that he is specifically *not* speaking of. In that note Silentio writes, "Up until now I have assiduously avoided any reference to the question of sin and its reality. The whole work is centered on Abraham, and I can still encompass him in immediate categories—that is, insofar as I can understand him. As soon as sin emerges, ethics founders precisely on repentance; for repentance is the highest ethical expression, but precisely as such it is the deepest ethical self-contradiction."[59] The logic here plainly echoes the articulations that Haufniensis put forward in the introduction to *The Concept of Anxiety*, and insofar as Haufniensis credits Silentio with having made his point for him many times, we need to read *Fear and Trembling* with a view to identifying precisely how Silentio accomplishes this feat. The entire exegetical project that follows in this book is therefore directed toward identifying the various moments in *Fear and Trembling* where Silentio dramatizes Haufniensis's point.

I therefore read *Fear and Trembling* with a view to ferreting out the various ways in which Silentio "several times allows the desired ideality of esthetics to be shipwrecked on the required ideality of ethics." Likewise I will try to draw attention to the many points at which Silentio shatters two kinds of ideality—the ideality of aesthetics against the ideality of ethics—in order to give rise to a new ideality, the ideality of actuality that is dubbed the religious.

To conclude these thoughts, and to anticipate the spirit in which I will read *Fear and Trembling* in the rest of this book, it may be helpful to think of the interplay of aesthetic and ethical ideals in pedestrian terms that can nevertheless be fully supported by Kierkegaardian conceptuality. As Kierkegaard famously said, "Philosophy is perfectly right in saying that life must be understood backwards. But then one forgets the other clause—that it must be lived forwards."[60] We understand backward by means of strategies that can be associated with "recollection" in Kierkegaard's parlance, while we live forward by means of "repetition." Despite the fact that repetition deserves a certain pride of place in Kierkegaard's thinking, recollection is not slighted by him but is on the contrary indispensable to the task of navigating life. By recollection we gather a sense of ourselves on the basis of our past experiences, the circumstances of our given place and time, and the roles and positions we occupy vis-à-vis our neighbors and loved ones.[61] These elements of the self's existence shape ideals on the basis of which the self attempts to live forward.

As we have seen, there are two principal ideals relevant here: the aesthetic ideal and the ethical ideal. The aesthetic crystallizes our sensible and artistic preferences: just as a story has a coherent logic to it, so too we think of our own lives as a story we are writing for ourselves with a certain organic development to it, an almost fated necessity of one inevitability leading to the next, and finally a happy ending. The ethical ideal gives expression to a moral demand: we seek to define and think of ourselves in terms of the roles we occupy and the responsibilities we faithfully discharge; one is a conscientious citizen, a devoted spouse, a loving parent. The reason we cannot live forward wholly on the basis of such recollective ideals is that life is also mined with actualities that hinder their realization, and most especially the actuality of sin prevents either ideal from being readily implemented. Life does not unfold as a series of fortuitous eventualities that lead smoothly to a happy conclusion, and we prove ourselves to be indifferent citizens, inconsiderate spouses, and careless parents. Given that this is so, that the life we imagine for ourselves does not come to pass, that our expectations are disappointed by reality, that we do not turn out to be the people we hoped we would become, the question that *Fear and Trembling* and *The Concept of Anxiety* are meant in large part to address is how we go on after the ideal has broken down.[62]

The religious ideal, the ideal of actuality, is fashioned after these harsh realizations have been made and furnishes a way to move forward with a guiding vision, though one that is tempered by an acquaintance with actuality. The self would like to live a story that has a happy ending, but sin prevents this. The self would like to be morally responsible, but sin prevents this. Faith acknowledges that actuality defeats our original plans and preferences and moves us toward an ideal that does not pretend that sin, loss, and even death are not serious hindrances to the happiness and moral aspirations for which we originally aimed; faith, then, also gives us back our original desires in reconstituted, and indeed improved, form. This is how faith grasps that God, in the words of Saint Paul, "is able to do exceeding abundantly above all that we ask or think";[63] we strike out in life to live forward on the basis of what we ask or think. We are invariably disappointed. We can remain with that disappointment, or we can open ourselves in faith to something we did not ask or think, something that on the other side of disappointment and loss will prove to be greater than what we could ask or think, because God knows that we don't know what we really want and gives it to us without our having asked for it.[64] This gift of God, beyond what our own ideals can anticipate, is the meaning of the religious ideality. The religious ideal is not a precarious ideal susceptible to the vagaries of life and its setbacks but is the ideal that is at the same time actual, and as we will see, it unites the aesthetically desirable and the ethically required. The religious ideal is as lovely as the aesthetic ideal and not as impossible to realize as the ethical ideal; it is the marriage of the beautiful and the just.[65]

It is this marriage that is at the heart of *Fear and Trembling.* Abraham's trial is first and foremost not to be understood as an alleged conflict between the "right" and the "holy" or between general duties and an exceptional, extravagant, or absolute duty. His trial is at once uniquely his own, as each of us will have to face a trial that is uniquely our own, but it is at the same time analogous to anybody else's: to negotiate the terms on which his life can go forward once his ideals have been ruined by actuality. Having received the miracle of fatherhood in his advanced age, Abraham is bound to his son in an ethically charged relationship and seeks to live his life out as a dutiful husband and father. The command to then sacrifice Isaac poses a palpable threat to his ability to perform these ethical roles. Similarly, the aesthetic ideal by which he seeks to live is placed in jeopardy: There can be no happy ending to his story if he is compelled to execute the task that is apparently before him. Proceeding on the basis of faith will uproot Abraham from the security and consolation of both the ethical and aesthetic; on the terms of either, his action will be incomprehensible. But to proceed on the basis of faith is to recover on the far side of the ruins of the ethical and the aesthetic a life that is both morally renewed and beautifully restored.

At the Crossroads of the Ideal and Actual: Consciousness and Its Transformations

The content of *Fear and Trembling* therefore involves a complex association of the ideal and the actual, and I maintain that the style of the work too mirrors this structure. Despite controversies in the critical literature over whether Silentio is trying to stress the shocking actuality of Abraham's situation or deduce from it a more broadly applicable lesson or symbolic value, both of these positions are off the mark.[66] The truth is that Kierkegaard through Silentio is interested in the transformative truth of Abraham's example, which itself can be treated neither only by a brute recitation of the historical facts of the case or as a fairy tale didactically presenting a straightforward "moral"—"Be like Abraham and everything will turn out all right in the end!"

The sort of transformation that is aimed at by the retelling of Abraham's story goes by many names in Kierkegaard's corpus—imitation as opposed to admiration, upbuilding, appropriation, subjective truth—all familiar to his genuine readers and students, who understand that the aim of the authorship was always to change the self rather than merely reflect upon it. To secure this aim it is vital for Kierkegaard to write in such a way that the story speaks directly to the reader and places demands upon her.[67] Patrick Stokes presents a fine discussion on the power of story to speak directly to the reader in his discussion of *For Self-Examination*'s use of the parable told by Nathan to King David. Stokes comments:

> David is to *see himself in* the story even though there is nothing in the objective conceptual content of the narrative that resembles or alludes to him . . . It takes a not inconsiderable stretch of imagination to read Nathan's parable of a rich man slaughtering a poor man's lamb as an analogy for adultery and murder. Once again, the *meaning* conferred by the image is nowhere to be found in its direct content, but in the "viewer's" engagement therewith. This is not, however, to say that David simply imports a meaning into the story that "properly" doesn't belong there; rather, he uncovers a meaning that is only accessible if he engages with the story in the self-referential attitude of *interesse*.[68]

Stokes refers here to the intended effect of opening the eye of moral vision. The king does not at first perceive that the story is about him until Nathan prophetically concludes with the damning words "Thou art the man." Thus the requisite direct identification with the subject matter on the part of the listener is attained. Undue focus on what Stokes calls "the objective conceptual content" and hasty generalization of the story into a putatively broadly applicable moral are both to be avoided if the story's real force is to be felt. In this sense I suggest that the form of many of the vignettes in *Fear and Trembling* embroiders the actual and ideal together in a fusion of content to its appropriate mood. As Stokes convincingly argues, that Kierkegaard is able to effectively elicit the reader's personal identification and transformation with this kind of writing is itself a result of the structure of the self who is doing the listening to the story in the first place.

Drawing on the unfinished material at the conclusion of *Johannes Climacus*,[69] we can with Stokes identify an idiosyncratic perhaps but nonetheless potentially relevant definition of consciousness.[70] As Stokes observes, it is somewhat strange, given the central importance of consciousness to both *The Concept of Anxiety* and *The Sickness unto Death*, that this topic does not receive more concentrated attention from Kierkegaard and that readers of Kierkegaard don't pay more attention to the *Johannes Climacus* material, if only because it is such a comparatively sustained thematic engagement.[71] My interest in this material has to do with the isomorphism between consciousness described by Climacus as a collision of the ideal and real and the same collision that Haufniensis describes as definitive of the religious ideal, a dynamic I perceive to be at work in both the content and form of *Fear and Trembling*.

The question posed at the outset of the last section of *Johannes Climacus* is "What must the nature of existence be in order for doubt to be possible?"[72] We perceive from the beginning then that the inquiry is in a way an attempt to "reverse engineer" the experience of doubt, the possibility of which has been engaging Johannes's semicomic attention. Since doubt is something Johannes is determined to do, what sort of being is he such that doubt is possible for him? We are told straightaway that an "empirical answer" is impossible, because life offers "a multifariousness that would only hide a perplexing diffusion over the whole range of extremes. In other words, not only could that which evokes doubt in the single individual be extremely different, but it could also be the opposite, for if someone were to discourse on doubt in order to arouse doubt in another, he could precisely thereby evoke faith, just as faith, conversely, could evoke doubt."[73] On the basis of this observation it would seem that we can read *Johannes Climacus* as in accord with Vigilius Haufniensis, who also is keenly aware of the fundamentally ambivalent nature of experience. Because the self is always situated in a historical environment, Haufniensis observes that "the most dissimilar things may produce the same effect. Freedom's possibility announces itself in anxiety. Consequently, a warning may bring an individual to succumb to anxiety . . . although of course the warning was intended to do the opposite. The sight of the sinful may save one individual and bring another to fall. A jest may have the effect of seriousness, but also the opposite. Speech and silence can produce an effect opposite to what was intended. In this respect there are no limits."[74]

The point of these observations is that experience is fundamentally ambivalent; it lends itself to completely opposed interpretations. *Fear and Trembling* also treats experience as ambivalent, for the knight of faith's willingness to love and be loved rests on the same experiential grounds as the knight of resignation's refusal of love, change, and temporality. Both responses are possible on the basis of the exact same empirical scenario. Because no empirical scenario stands on its own, however, because no actuality is "bare" but rather constantly shadowed by and implicated with idealities, it's the collision that counts. As George Willis Williams puts it, "There is, in other words, no direct or necessary life lesson that the world imparts to us; our experiences are always filtered through our beliefs, dispositions, characters, worldviews, etc. and could always be appropriated in another—indeed opposite—way."[75] Like the gambler that Haufniensis speaks of in the final chapter of *The Concept of Anxiety*, successive losses by themselves do nothing to deter his commitment to another spin of the roulette wheel.[76] Contrary to the caricature of the faithful person as one who doggedly sticks to her beliefs in the face of overwhelming defeating evidence, it is the fatalist who, according to Kierkegaard, can never be disabused, no matter how many losses she suffers. The fatalist, like the committed gambler, is always ready to play again in the barest hope of a hollow victory.[77]

Because "experience" already is the collision of the ideal and actual, I believe Kierkegaard uses this principle as the basis for a form of communication that seeks to foment this collision so that a new ideal, the ideal of actuality, can become possible for us. Furthermore, the collision of the ideal and actual is not just characteristic of experience or of communication about subjective truth and self-transformation but is also embedded in the structure of consciousness itself, as we see upon returning to *Johannes Climacus*.

Johannes spurns the path of empirical investigation in order to work out what sort of existence it must be that is capable of doubt; he therefore knows that "another route" is required—"*Doubt's ideal possibility in consciousness*."[78] If consciousness itself is the basis of the possibility of doubt, then "whatever produced doubt in the individual could be as different as it pleased"[79]—an important qualification, since we have already seen that the causes of doubt can be myriad and unpredictable, even bringing about this effect when precisely the opposite was intended. At the same time, since doubt must happen to and for a consciousness, then the possibility of it is securely located "in the individual" and this possibility would be "total"—that is, intrinsic to human consciousness, as opposed to the consciousness of a child, which is immediate or unqualified.[80]

Adult consciousness is by definition already implicated in both mediacy and immediacy, and to ask which comes first is "a captious question."[81] Consciousness cannot remain in immediacy as if forever childlike. "What, then, is immediacy? It is reality itself."[82] The child, it would seem, remains in an unmediated straightforward contact with the real until the advent of language: "What is mediacy? It is the word."[83] Now the importance of language and speaking will return in a crucial way when we examine Problema III, but it is worth noting perhaps at this early stage that language is critically important to Haufniensis's account of earnestness and associated phenomena in *The Concept of Anxiety*. According to Haufniensis, language is the hallmark of the birth of spirit in its emergence from nature, a moment he too associates with the innocence of unqualified consciousness: "Innocence can indeed speak, inasmuch as in language it possesses the expression for everything spiritual."[84] As Ronald Hall has observed, language for Kierkegaard exhibits in its structure the basic quality of human transcendence: "I am *in* the world and yet transcend it," Hall writes, "just as meaning is *in* the sounds of my spoken words but constantly transcends those sounds. The structural separation of meaning and sound, their relationship of dependence (sound is the *means* of meaning) and their relationship of exclusion and opposition, is the best parallel for understanding the Incarnational relationship of spirit to sensuousness, of self to world."[85] As in Nathan's parable told to King David, meaning is conveyable by words, but meaning is not reducible to words. As an exercise in language, the retelling of a story involves the interplay of actual and ideal and thus correlates structurally to the very nature of consciousness.

We read in *Johannes Climacus*: "Immediacy is reality; language is ideality; consciousness is contradiction. The moment I make a statement about reality, contradiction is present, for what I say is ideality."[86] To enter into language is to bring ideality into conflicted relationship with reality, and that conflict is definitive of both language itself and the consciousness of the language-user and language-hearer. The awakening of consciousness[87] is coterminous with the acquisition of language, and the intensification of consciousness of the sort toward which all of Kierkegaard's authorship is directed, is achieved in and by the heightened and refined use of language, which is directed toward the communication of a meaning that is dependent upon but transcends the artful and truthful use of words.

That the collision of the ideal and actual is the milieu of both consciousness and language explains how for *Johannes Climacus* doubt is possible:

> The possibility of doubt, then, lies in consciousness, whose nature is a contradiction that is produced by a duplexity and that itself produces a duplexity. A duplexity of this sort inevitably has two manifestations. The duplexity is reality and ideality; consciousness is the relation. I can either bring reality into relation with ideality or bring ideality into relation with reality. In reality by itself there is no possibility of doubt; when I express it in language, contradiction is present, since I do not express it but produce something else. Insofar as what was said is supposed to be an expression of reality, I have brought this into relation with ideality; insofar as what was said is something produced by me, I have brought ideality into relation with reality.[88]

Consciousness is produced by the duplexity of the ideal and actual, as we have seen, and this in turn has two manifestations, which would seem to be either bringing the real into relation with the ideal or bringing the ideal into relation with the real. There is no doubt for either reality alone or ideality alone, because "reality is not consciousness, ideality no more so."[89] Language expresses a contradiction, since what I speak about is not the same as the speaking itself; what is expressed is not the "bare" real (as if such a thing were even possible for adult consciousness) but the expression. Expression is about the real, which is brought into relation with ideality simply by virtue of having been given expression. But since I am the one doing the talking, I have produced the relation of bringing ideality to reality, coloring it with my interpretation, desire, value (again, as if anything else were possible for adult consciousness).

Another way of demonstrating the bedrock indispensability of consciousness is shown by way of contrast to reflection. *Johannes Climacus* defines reflection as "the *possibility of the relation*; consciousness is *the relation, the first form of which is contradiction.* As a result, he also noted, reflection's categories are always *dichotomous.* For example, ideality and reality, soul and body, to know the true, to will the good, to love the beautiful, God and the world, etc. are categories of reflection."[90] Reflection on this definition merely posits we might say the dualities without allowing them to come into genuine collision.[91] For this reason Stokes is surely right to say that "'reflection' is the abstract expression for an activity by which consciousness comes to be."[92] For there to be a definitive collision, a "third" is required, and that third seems to be nothing other than the collision itself. Reflection holds open relations that are required to establish the possibility of truth or untruth, knowledge or error, but it only holds these relations together and does not volatilize them (or sublate them in a higher unity in a Hegelian fashion).[93] "The categories of consciousness, however, are *trichotomous*, as language also demonstrates, for when I say, *I* am conscious of *this sensory impression*, I am expressing a triad."[94]

We should note carefully that the "third" seems to be not so much an addition to the dichotomies but the realization of the dichotomies as dichotomies coming into collision with one another and needing to be related to in a self-conscious manner. As Stokes puts it, "the Kierkegaardian 'third' is not an impersonal mediation to which we are to relate. Rather, it *is* us, standing in a position where we cannot mediate the elements before us but can only bring them into irresolvable collision."[95] In this way the Kierkegaardian "third" is the very holding together in tension of the two. This dynamic is everywhere in evidence in Kierkegaard's writings. It can be discerned in *The Sickness unto Death* in the positing of a self, which is a sort of "third" in relation to the dichotomies of infinite and finite, temporal and eternal, freedom and necessity, yet there too this "third" is not an addition to the two but is the two grasped as such and held problematically together.[96] Similarly, in *The Concept of Anxiety*, the synthetic unity of body and soul is presented by Haufniensis as a kind of third—spirit—but again, spirit as the third seems to be only the conscious grasp of the self as itself body and soul. The third term is, so to speak, less an addition to the synthesis of the two constituents of the human being than the synthesis's own understanding of itself as that very synthesis.[97] The categories of consciousness are now triadic because when the collision is catalyzed, *I* am always involved.[98] Consciousness is always first person; my experience is always for me. This is not true of reflection, which for Kierkegaard is always suspiciously detached. The trichotomous structure of consciousness-in-relation also explains finally why doubt is possible and why, as we know, Kierkegaard perennially argues it cannot be resolved by greater reflective insight. "If there were nothing but dichotomies, doubt would not exist, for the possibility of doubt resides precisely in the third, which places the two in relation to each other."[99]

Reflection, then, is an activity of consciousness but is not identical to it.[100] This is why it is always possible for Kierkegaard to literally lose one's self in reflection; it need not concern me but can be airily entertained, even *per impossibile* indefinitely, without decisively engaging my commitment, assent, or interest. As *Johannes Climacus* puts it pithily: "Reflection is *disinterested*,"[101] and indeed it is to this disinterest that modern philosophy aspired. Hence doubt is not a function of reflection and cannot be resolved by it. As *Johannes Climacus* concludes, "We could not therefore say that reflection produces doubt, unless we would express ourselves in reverse; we must say that doubt *pre*-supposes reflection, without, however, this *prius* being temporary."[102] Doubt is a permanent possibility for consciousness, which operates at a level below the reflective, such that even protracted reflection cannot vanquish it. "Thus it would be a misunderstanding for someone to think that doubt can be overcome by so-called objective thinking. Doubt is a higher form than any objective thinking, for it presupposes the latter but has something more, a third, which is interest or consciousness."[103]

This point brings us to the relevance of this material on consciousness to the argument of *Fear and Trembling*. If I am right that the collision between the aesthetic and ethical is a potentially useful interpretive key for the text, then everything that is established in *Johannes Climacus* about doubt is also relevant to faith. Faith, like doubt, can neither be intensified nor diminished by reflection alone. Faith, like doubt, is fundamentally interested in a way that reflection cannot be. If Stokes is correct that "in doubt the subject relates the elements of ideality and reality, of the concrete and the abstract, by positing a noncorrelation between them, *and* positing itself in relation to the noncorrelation,"[104] then faith can perhaps be construed as another possibility afforded by and emergent from the collision of ideality and reality. For the same reason that doubt cannot be vanquished by further reflection, so it is the case that reflection cannot decisively shore up faith, or to put the matter in Silentio's words, "Faith begins precisely where thought stops."[105] Thought stops not because faith is lunacy, stupidity, or stubborn refusal but because either doubt or faith puts a stop to thought's otherwise interminable speculations.

Faith cannot be just a question of actuality but must be made possible by the collision of actuality and ideality that is determinative of consciousness itself. As we read near the very end of the unfinished *Johannes Climacus*, "If that fallacy discussed above could remain, that ideality and reality in all naiveté communicated with one another, consciousness would never emerge, for consciousness emerges precisely through the collision, just as it presupposes the collision."[106] This collision is tantamount to the arising of repetition, a category of indisputable importance to Kierkegaard's authorship.[107] Like consciousness, repetition does not occur merely in reality nor in ideality. "When ideality and reality touch each other, then repetition occurs."[108] Repetition does not occur in reality alone because even the variety of difference is insufficient to produce it. In reality everything is different, but this does not make anything repeated. Repetition is always contrasted by Kierkegaard with merely mechanical variation, here in *Johannes Climacus* as elsewhere: "If the world, instead of being beauty, were nothing but equally large unvariegated boulders, there would still be no repetition. Throughout all eternity, in every moment, I would see a boulder, but there would be no question as to whether it was the same one I had seen before."[109]

It is telling that the contrast is drawn here between endlessly distinct-but-nevertheless-the-same sensible phenomena and *beauty*. Can we surmise that for Kierkegaard beauty is precisely the nonidentically repeated?[110] This supposition will underpin much of what follows in this book on the recuperation of the aesthetic by faith. For the merely aesthetic, as we have already intimated, there is no actual beauty because there is only the static, timeless ideal. "In ideality alone there is no repetition, for the idea is and remains the same, and as such it cannot be repeated."[111] This book will argue that for the religious life alone there is goodness and beauty, where the ideal construals of these are continually shattered against the rocks of actuality and continually reborn anew.

This is the primary interpretive key by which I seek to understand Silentio's treatment of the Abraham story. Two points about this dynamic should be kept in mind. First, an ideal is something I think for Kierkegaard we cannot live without. We are forever and necessarily, as conscious beings, existing in the interstices of the actual and ideal. We can never avail ourselves of actualities that are unembellished by ideals or decide the question of whether immediacy or mediation "comes first."[112] Second, and this point is inextricably tied to the first, an ideal is bound up with the real (in and for consciousness, interest, repetition), and it is, at this site and for this moment, what defines what *matters* to me.[113] Faith is the difficult holding together of the ideal and real; despair and resignation are the loss of this anguished but creative tension. To illustrate how important these two interrelated points are, I will anticipate one of the key parts of the argument of this book. I will argue in chapter 5 that what is principally resigned by any knight of faith is not so much a person or object *per se* but a form of consciousness that encapsulates the relation of actual to ideal. Abraham is asked to sacrifice a living person, but this is equally a sacrifice of himself as an individual whose whole consciousness is his fatherhood of Isaac. The lad in love with the princess has to refuse to be the one who he thinks he is, the one who loves the princess with an undying love. When we speak of resignation in these cases, what I will argue is that what specifically is resigned is neither Isaac nor the princess alone (since there can never be an "actual" Isaac or princess that is not already touched by the ideal insofar as Isaac and the princess are loved) but a consciousness of the relation of ideal to actual: myself as Isaac's father, myself as the one who loves the princess. Resignation therefore does not just concern the person resigned (as if one could simply detach one's love from the beloved) nor is it simply a matter of changing our perspective on reality (as if reality and our perspective upon it could be neatly separated in the first place). To resign is to resign the world and others and myself in the respects that these realities matter to me.

Faith then restores the ideal conception once it has been resigned, but crucially, it does this by reinterpreting the conscious relation between the broken ideal of who I take myself to be and the actuality of who I am. Abraham does not know *how* he will get Isaac back, but he does, in a way that he could not have expected. The lad does not know *how* he will get the princess back, but he will, in a way that he could never expect. Neither Abraham nor the lad gets exactly what he wants. Isaac cannot be the same on the way down from Moriah as he was on the way up. And the princess that the lad loves will prove to be a different person from the one he thinks he knows. The point is that for both of them the reality proves to be ideal in a fashion that is both good and beautiful, though the goodness and beauty of their lives can only be secured when both are put to the test of the most anguished risk, and in that risk, they resign themselves as well.

Plan of the Work

Much of the exegetical work that follows is focused on discerning these patterns of collision between ideality and actuality and the dynamic of resignation and faith, where both pertain to the ideality-actuality nexus that is Kierkegaardian consciousness. The first chapter deals with the extensive preliminary material in *Fear and Trembling.* It focuses in particular on the position of the text's pseudonymous author, Johannes de Silentio. The case made on this score is that Silentio denies both that he is a philosopher and that he is a poet, despite many commentators' continual reference to Silentio as precisely a poet. But what Kierkegaard means throughout his career by the activity of poeticizing is clear from many journal entries and other published texts, and these descriptions cannot be applied straightforwardly to Silentio. To be a "poet of the religious," according to Kierkegaard, is to be conscious of one's having not attained the ideal, where "the essentially Christian, after all, is itself the ideal."[114] Johannes de Silentio, like a sort of religious poet, negatively presents the ideal of faith by continually contrasting it with what it is *not*, a strategy at which he is particularly adept, being an outsider to faith. As such an outsider, he also lacks a clear conception of sin, which puts him in the same camp as the "poet-existence verging on the religious" psychologically delineated by Anti-Climacus at the very beginning of the second part of *The Sickness unto Death.*[115] The description of such a figure by Anti-Climacus proves to be especially fitting as a way of thinking about Silentio's posture toward the issues he discusses. Anti-Climacus contends that the poet-existence verging toward the religious "has something in common with the despair of resignation, except that the concept of God is present."[116] For Silentio too the thought of God is continually present but kept at arm's length as well, as Silentio frequently asserts that he cannot believe in God's concern for the quotidian in the life of the believer nor can he reconcile the love of God with the particulars of experience, though he is lyrically inspired by the *idea* of the love of God. Such a self-characterization accords well with Anti-Climacus's diagnosis of the poet-existence verging on the religious as having "a profound religious longing" and even love for God that nevertheless remains incommensurate with the poet's insistence on his own anguish, which he will in the end not give up in order to be healed. Such a person Anti-Climacus likens to the poet of happy love, who becomes so as a result of disappointment in love; he cannot open himself to genuine love but clings longingly to its ideal form.[117]

Such a person is Silentio as well, which means that his perspective on faith is limited but not woefully distorted or untrustworthy. Ultimately Silentio's most conspicuous blind spot is that he lacks a clear conception of sin in its relationship to faith, which makes his account negatively illustrative and "poetic" in a new sense that cannot be constrained by classical forms of poeticizing. According to Kierkegaard, classical poetics proceeds by way of idealizing a less-than-ideal actuality, but such an effort is redundant and risible when directed toward an actuality that is already ideal, as Socrates would be an ideal of philosophizing or Abraham an ideal of faith. To the extent that Silentio poeticizes Abraham he does so not by idealizing what is already ideal but again by indirectly shedding light on an ideal that is already actual and thus adopting communicative strategies that he at every turn explicitly contrasts to the tactics of poetry. This understanding of Silentio's character and production likewise explains the significance of his name's reference to "silence," which means not absence of communication but precisely nonverbal communication or wordless intimacy.

Chapters 2, 3, and 4 cover the first preliminary sections of *Fear and Trembling* and argue they should be read as differing methodological approaches to the text's principal subject matter, each one designed to illustrate the limits of philosophical theorizing, straightforward poetic storytelling, and full-blown oratory as communicative strategies for tackling the story of Abraham and its key problems.

The philosophical tenor of the Preface, examined in chapter 2, identifies within the history of ideas exceptional moments wherein something like the faith that Silentio wants to describe (or more precisely, the revealed conjunction between faith and a kind of doubt best understood as sin-consciousness) was anticipated; it is in this section that the first illustration of the central dynamic of resignation and faith is provided through a creative (and unique in the Kierkegaardian authorship) retrieval of Descartes. The Exordium, treated in chapter 3, likewise pursues its task indirectly, this time by telling and retelling the story of Abraham with essential elements of his praiseworthy faith missing or distorted. The point of the section is once again to demonstrate the limits of a certain kind of technical approach to the text, in this case not philosophical but narrative, and thus to shed light indirectly on how Abraham's faith must be discussed. Particular attention is devoted to the much-neglected segments on the weaning mother and her child, which on this analysis vividly drive home the point that what faith involves is a deepening of intimacy in relationship that nevertheless gives the appearance of just the opposite: attenuation of relationship and even imposition of trauma and suffering. The key lesson of the weaning passages is that they demonstrate how continuity in life and relationship is achieved across the disruptions of suffering and pain; the mother *must* wean her child for the good of them both, and the delicate negotiation of loving association amid and beyond the shock of distress is vividly illustrative of a life lived in faith.

The fourth chapter deals with the Eulogy on Abraham, which is arguably yet another indirect effort to negatively limn the contours of the Abraham story and to discount the efficacy of highly rhetorical panegyric as a means of proper access to the essentials of Abraham's faith. Contrary to the prevailing interpretations, I read this section not at face value as a direct contribution to a progressively better understanding of Abraham but as an exposure of the inability of "the poet" to capture the essentials of faith, much less to inspire true faith in her reader.

Chapter 5 treats the Preliminary Expectoration and especially its two highly significant examples of the contemporary knight of faith and the lad in love with the princess. The contemporary knight of faith vignette is indicative of how broadly faith must be construed in its actual outworking in human life; the contemporary knight of faith is not conspicuously religious but allows his faith to radically transform every aspect of his life: his relationship to his world, to other beloved individuals, and to his own self. One detail of this portrait is singled out as particularly lively: the contemporary knight of faith's expectation of a lavish dinner awaiting him at home. Despite the humor that this homely incident has inspired, I read it as the most telling of all the particular descriptions Silentio lavishes upon the contemporary knight of faith and interpret it as an indispensable key to understanding his relationships with other human beings in his life. Notwithstanding the unquestionable importance of this episode, however, in the end I maintain that the example of the lad in love with the princess is even more important to Silentio's purposes than the contemporary knight of faith. This example more than the former highlights the pain of loss and problematizes human relationships and thus strikes closer to home than the contemporary knight of faith. In contrast to other analyses on the relationship of resignation to faith, I argue that resignation must be fully in effect at every moment as an active element of faith (not as an annulled possibility), that it does not entail embracing "selfless care," and that it must in an obviously complicated way affirm both that something crucial must be resigned and will be gained back. The essential element of the argument is to do with *what exactly* is resigned, and the answer to that is neither a desired person or object, nor the desire itself, but an *ideal* that encapsulates the self's desiring relation to a desired other; correlatively, it is also an ideal that is restored in faith.

Chapter 6 provides an analysis of Problema I, which of course is devoted to the question of whether there is a teleological suspension of the ethical. Amid the numerous ways in which this question has been understood, my preferred interpretation argues that what is at stake in the teleological suspension is the religiously revealed critique of all humanly inspired ethical systems and more important, their transformation. To use the language of Haufniensis's introduction, *Fear and Trembling*, principally through the teleological suspension of the ethical, operates at the pivot point between the old and new or second ethics. The teleological suspension is another way of referring to the shipwreck of the ethical ideal on the rock of repentance. What that means in turn is that "the ethical as universal" in *Fear and Trembling* is shorthand for any ethical thinking that remains untransformed by specifically religious revelation, one that has no place for sin or faith. The teleological suspension then has almost nothing to do with an allegedly superior appeal from the divine that would trump the good; it has to do instead with the correction of humanly conceived notions of the good by the revealed God, whose appearance will be decidedly foreign to the good understood according to limited worldly conceptions and perhaps also revolting to humanly constructed standards of beauty.

More than that, however, it ultimately has to do with the birth of the second ethics, an ethics informed by the revealed notions of sin and faith; such revelations do not merely make their appearance and then gleefully demolish the ethical. They give rise to new ethical thinking. It is on this score that *Fear and Trembling* is admittedly less revealing; a fuller account of second ethics has to await later works of Kierkegaard's pen. Nevertheless, the textual evidence is strong that ultimately Silentio is interested in more than merely the cancellation of the ethical but in fact in the ethical's transformation and reinvention.

At this point I engage in a speculative exercise to imagine how the logic that Silentio opens up by postulating the teleological suspension could be more fully fleshed out in view of other Kierkegaardian concerns. To anticipate this coda to the chapter, I present there the forgiveness of sins as a paradigmatic case of the teleological suspension of the ethical. Since the teleological suspension on my view concerns not just the possibility of faith but the possibility of demonic sin and the consciousness of sin that always attends faith, forgiveness combines these twinned concerns in a distinctive way.[118] While it is true that I have a generalized duty to love my neighbor,[119] that duty can be discharged in any number of specific ways. Forgiveness is *sui generis* in a sense, since I can forgive only by forgiving (not even by waiting to be asked for forgiveness, a waiting that itself already in Kierkegaard's view betrays a defect in the lover's forgiveness).[120] Forgiveness is exemplary of the teleological suspension because in forgiveness I "tear up," so to speak, the rules of the ethical as universal and thereby inaugurate second ethics. I do so in such a way as to hold together the consciousness of sin (both of myself and of others)[121] with the faithful and loving remission of that sin.

To apply Silentio's phrase in connection with the faith of Abraham, it seems to me that forgiveness is an act of "purely personal virtue."[122] To forgive a wrong done to me may from the standards of the ethical as universal or the codes of justice look questionable or even offensively wrong. By the canons of humanly constructed visions of the good, whether in their pagan or spiritless forms, such an action has not always been recognized as obviously praiseworthy and to some visions of the good life may even be risible or even contemptible. What the teleological suspension calls readers of *Fear and Trembling* to take stock of is just how demanding the religious imperative is, and furthermore, to envision how the religious imperative scandalizes our human, all-too-human notions of the good with an eye to revising these notions. What would ethics look like if indeed forgiveness was taken seriously as a moral imperative? These are the questions I think that the teleological suspension at least points to, though *Fear and Trembling* itself does not fully answer them.

The seventh chapter concentrates on Problema II, which focuses on the possibility of an absolute duty to God. The most salient point in this section that is not often highlighted with sufficient emphasis is the explicit argument by Silentio that the person of faith does not dispense with the ethical but transforms her relation to it. One of the most important sentences of the entire book is contained in this section: "From this it does not follow that the ethical should be invalidated; rather, the ethical receives a completely different expression, a paradoxical expression, such as, for example, that love to God may bring the knight of faith to give his love to the neighbor—an expression opposite to that which, ethically speaking, is duty."[123]

Here again my argument is that we see a signaling toward the need for second ethics. The point of *Fear and Trembling* is not to argue for a rejection or elimination of ethics but to change it, even into its opposite. Part of this chapter's account of Problema II, then, is to speculate on what is the opposite of duty, and here we continue the meditation begun above on how the ethical would change if religiously motivated imperatives to forgive sins or love enemies were taken seriously and incorporated into an ethical view, a view that would surely be more individualized, more free and spontaneous, and less likely to regard the moral task as one akin to a burden needing to be shouldered but more as a delight with its own rewards. To complement this account I pay special attention to Silentio's exposition of Luke 14:26, wherein Jesus claims that anyone who does not hate his father, his mother, his wife, his children, his brothers, sisters, and even his own life cannot be his disciple. Like the other "hard sayings" of Jesus, this one too, I believe, encapsulates much of what is meant by the appeal to the teleological suspension. In the case of this example, what readers are able to appreciate with special clarity is the nature of an "absolute" command, according to Silentio. As is clear from the meditation on Luke 14:26, the absolute relation to God is not *exhaustive*. On the contrary, the absolute relation to God entails a repudiation of any notion that love is finite and results in a redoubling of intensity of all other relations. When one attends to the absolute duty to God, one is not thereby inhibited from fulfilling other responsibilities; in fact, one is enjoined to *deepen* all other responsibilities and loves in light of an absolute that precisely does not trump all else but propels the lover back to renewed and intensified commitments to all other loves. In one of the most dazzling paradoxes of the entire text, Silentio insists that to "hate" your father and mother is actually to love them *even more*.

Finally, chapter 8 is devoted to the protracted and circuitous argumentation of Problema III, which is for this interpretation an essential portion of the text. Despite being the longest part of *Fear and Trembling* it has long been minimized by otherwise serious engagements with the book. While the first two Problemata obviously focus on the limits of the ethical ideal and its implicit transformation by religious commitment, the final Problema deals principally with the limits of the aesthetic and an implicit transformation in the meaning and character of stories once narratives are informed by the absurd and storytelling conventions are subverted and completed by incorporation of possibilities for living that humanly constructed aesthetics cannot anticipate. In keeping with Silentio's ongoing indictment of unreconstructed poetics, in every narrative featured in Problema III he imposes a change that is explicitly meant to mark a differentiation between his version of the story and that of "the poets."

Picking up on the analogy Silentio draws between his own artistic and communicative practice with the billiard game carambole, this chapter traces out the complex interactions that Silentio stages between the ethical and aesthetic ideals as they are put to the test in a series of memorable vignettes. The first, on the Delphic bridegroom whose impending marriage is threatened by the augurs' promise of doom, is couched in pagan terms of fate and stoic resolve in the face of fate. Here the limits of the aesthetic and ethical are brought into relief, but no religious ideality is realized from the collision. The unresolved outcome of the story is stranded in the ambiguity of fate, which the lovers can either defy or accept, but in either case they face the self-vindicating ambivalence of the terms on which they make their choice: accept fate and be resolved to their separation or defy fate and be resolved to the imminent catastrophe.

The second, on Agnes and the merman, is vitally important to the text as a whole. The merman's lecherous intent is exposed by the unimpeachable innocence of Agnes, and like the Delphic bridegroom he is left with a choice. In his case the limits of the ethical are revealed with shocking starkness, for his ethical self-conception is well and truly shipwrecked on the rock of repentance. Ethics alone cannot decide for the merman whether he will remain in demonic self-recriminating repentance, forever tormenting himself with guilt, or accept the love and trust of Agnes while repentantly conceding that he is unworthy of her devotion. This is why the merman needs faith to return to a transformed ethical form of existence and why Silentio argues he is at once impossibly close to, and at the farthest remove from, Abraham. Essential to my understanding of the text as a whole is Silentio's assertion in connection with the merman that he too is in an absolute relation to the absolute, which is the flipside so to speak of the teleological suspension of the ethical explored in Problema I. That the teleological suspension of the ethical can be accomplished by the demonic as well as the divine reinforces my claim that what is at stake here is not a religiously motivated betrayal of ethics but a matter of coming to ethical terms with the entire apparatus of revelation: both sin and salvation. Equally important to the reading of the whole text is Silentio's admission in connection with this passage that he is *not* addressing the issue of sin, an oversight that has ramifications for how we think of Silentio as a guide in matters of faith. The final ingredient of the merman story is the issue of the continuity in his life, which Silentio maintains cannot be secured by merely aesthetic devices. This is proof positive that the life of faith will not only in the end subvert and fulfill the ethical ideal but will also overcome and satisfy the aesthetic demand for a satisfactory way of thinking about the course of our own lives as a whole. The merman's story, while just as unresolved as the Delphic bridegroom's, nevertheless introduces the possibility of the demonic and thus enlarges the dramatic and moral terms on which the story can be understood to involve a religious component. Again the aesthetic ideal and ethical ideal collide, but again no religious ideal is fully realized.

Finally, the vignette of Sarah and Tobias from the deuterocanonical book of Tobit realizes the religious ideal that arises from the collision of the aesthetic and the ethical. Sarah's doomed marriage to Tobias threatens the happy fruition of her desires and strains the ethical norms of family life. Sarah's heroism, though, consists in her willing acceptance of the love of another, even as her trust and courage seem to spell the death of Tobias. It is their mutual faith that delivers them from danger, securing the happy ending that is the desired ideality of the aesthetic and the marital bond that is the epitome of the required ideality of ethics. I argue that this story captures the full beauty and moral majesty of the life of faith and does so in a way that is intuitively appealing and closer to our own ordinary experience.

In my conclusion I consider Silentio's final return to Abraham and his analysis of the words he speaks—"God himself will provide the lamb for the burnt offering, my son." My contention is that this utterance, which Silentio claims expresses the double movement of resignation and faith, is the model for understanding *all* speech about faith, including the speech of the text of *Fear and Trembling* itself. Abraham's words are true and therefore fulfill the ethical ideal, and they are beautiful and haunting and ironically heighten dramatic suspense and therefore fulfill the aesthetic ideal. To the extent that we can understand Abraham at all[124] we do so through these unpredictable and strange words. This meditation finally returns us to the beginning of the book; in keeping with a distinctly dramatic logic, and indeed the logic of life itself, which must be lived forward but understood backward, *Fear and Trembling* can only be understood at the end, but it must be begun at the beginning. Recapitulating the epigram of the text from Hamann, we see now as we could not at the outset the mystery of Silentio's communication, which essentially consists in being a kind of prophecy or a speaking in tongues. To communicate about faith is ultimately to adopt a form of expression that imitates and intimates the marriage of the beautiful and the just; it is to speak true and beautiful words that the speaker herself cannot fully understand.

1 Titular Matters

It is no secret that the title "Fear and Trembling" comes from the letter of Saint Paul to the Philippians, chapter 2, verse 12. It is clearly meant to capture the pervasive mood of the text, as Kierkegaard himself approvingly noted in the review of it that was penned by Bishop Mynster. In that review, Mynster asked the question, "But why is that work called *Fear and Trembling*? Because its author has vividly comprehended, has deeply felt, has expressed with the full power of language the horror that must grip a person's soul when he is confronted by a task whose demands he dare not evade, and when his understanding is yet unable to disperse the appearance with its demand that seems to call him out from the eternal order to which every human being shall submit."[1] In *The Point of View for My Work as an Author*, Kierkegaard wrote that he had been pleased to find that Mynster's remarks found the proper emphasis.[2] So clearly part of the reason Kierkegaard chose this title was to create an atmospheric effect in the mind of the reader. It is meant to summon a mood of seriousness, of anxiety in the face of being called to an exceptional task, a task that cannot be explained in traditional philosophical terms. An examination of the chapter from Paul reveals other clear associations that also pervade the text. The context of verse 12—which reads, "Wherefore, my beloved, as ye have always obeyed, not as in my presence only, but now much more in my absence, work out your own salvation with fear and trembling"—is immediately following one of the more important passages in Scripture for kenotic theological speculation,[3] which is itself situated before and after exhortations by Paul to the distinctive moral life that the Philippian faithful should be living out. He calls them to have "the same love, being of one accord, of one mind";[4] he instructs them to "let nothing be done through strife or vainglory; but in lowliness of mind let each esteem other better than themselves";[5] and he encourages them to "look not every man on his own things, but every man also on the things of others."[6] These moral directions find their justification in the kenotic passage; the Philippian believers are to act this way in order to model the mind of Christ: "Let this mind be in you, which was also in Christ Jesus: Who, being in the form of God, thought it not robbery to be equal with God: But made himself of no reputation, and took upon him the form of a servant, and was made in the likeness of men: And being found in fashion as a man, he humbled himself, and became obedient unto death, even the death of the cross."[7]

The Philippians, then, are to be as Christ was; they are to imitate his humility, his adoption of a life of service, and his obedience to the Father, even if that obedience means submitting to the worst kind of death. Having done all this, Christ is exalted by God the Father and is given the name that is above all names.[8] Thereafter, in verse 12 Paul instructs his hearers to work out their own salvation in imitation of Christ's kenotic self-emptying and (one presumes) in anticipation of sharing in his rewards. Less often noticed is the subsequent verse, which reads, "For it is God which worketh in you both to will and to do of his good pleasure."[9] The faithful are to work out their salvation in fear and trembling because it is God who is working in them. The reference to Paul can be understood quite straightforwardly as a preliminary intimation of the text's intent to lay the foundation for a "second ethics," to suggest how the ethical ideal can be rejected and rereceived in altered fashion as a component of the life of faith.[10]

The theme of Philippians 2 is one that is forever in the background of *Fear and Trembling*; as Christ emptied himself radically, so must the faithful believer empty herself and adopt a wholly transformed style of life, one inclusive of obedience to the will of the Father, humility, service to others, unity, and the setting aside of all self-interest and rivalry. Without making too much, then, of the connection between the content of *Fear and Trembling* and Philippians 2 we can easily say that they both take as their concern the morally significant ways in which the believer's life ought to be transformed by her faith. The believer is exhorted by both Paul and Kierkegaard to be conscious of the reality that it is God who works in her life to effectuate her conformity to Christ's moral model and that this work is done by God to capacitate her knowledge of, and ability to execute, his will. So not only is the particular verse an appropriate choice with respect to the atmosphere or mood of the text as a whole, so also the chapter's larger theme is one that echoes with the text's content as a whole.

The subtitle to *Fear and Trembling*, "Dialectical Lyric," has posed a challenge for commentators if only because no one knows what to make of it. It seems fairly obvious that Kierkegaard meant to refer to the form of the work, which he was elsewhere perfectly content to call "aesthetic,"[11] so clearly there is no conflict between the designation of "aesthetic" and the designation of "dialectical lyric"; and it seems equally obvious that the form of the work is meant to combine two seemingly incongruous genre descriptors. "Dialectic" suggests the methodical rigor of modernist discursive reason, while "lyric" suggests the stylistic elegance of poetry or song. It is undeniably the case that Kierkegaard intended that the work innovate in terms of its form, that it partake of philosophical rigor and beauty in expression, but much more than that is difficult to say, especially (and this may be the most salient point to note about the subtitle) since Kierkegaard never again had recourse to the term "dialectical lyric" and did not use it again in his published writings.[12]

Certainly the term "lyric" in the subtitle has contributed to a common way of understanding who the text's author, Johannes de Silentio, is—namely, as a poet. Yet I wish to complicate matters because Silentio's status as a poet in a straightforward sense is far from clear, and calling him a poet leads to the dubious implication that his work is of a piece with the project of idealization, which is not his agenda at all but is part and parcel of resignation and the dead-end of unreconstructed aestheticizing. As scholars of this text know, on the original title page drafted for *Fear and Trembling*, Johannes de Silentio was billed as "a poetic person who exists only among poets."[13] And scholars further know that Silentio denies that he is a philosopher.[14] The combination of the two observations, as well as the lengthy meditation on the relationship between the poet and the hero found in the "Eulogy on Abraham," has led many to characterize Silentio as a poet; however, this is a highly problematic attribution for three reasons, in escalating order of importance.

First, Kierkegaard withdrew the original characterization of Silentio as a poetic person existing only among poets and presumably did so for a reason. The deliberate nature of this exclusion is underscored by the one-time presence in the preface of a description of Silentio as a "formerly poetic person."[15] Second, there is no real reason to identify Silentio with the poet spoken of in the "Eulogy"; this has been repeatedly done because one could construe a parallelism between what Silentio says there and what he is currently undertaking in the text before us, but that Silentio thinks of himself as a poet or as "the poet" of the "Eulogy" remains an unwarranted assumption. This is especially so in view of the third reason, which is that every time Silentio introduces an illustrative narrative in the third Problema section he explicitly *dis*sociates his use of the narrative vignette from poetic usage and always distinguishes between his own use of the narrative and the use that would be made of it by "poets."

This final observation will be developed at greater length in the chapter on Problema III, but suffice it say for now that I do not take the view that Silentio can be unproblematically viewed as a poet; in point of fact it is quite clear that he always distances himself from "the poets."[16] This distancing was always part of the original plan for the text, as an outline of *Fear and Trembling* from the journals reveals. There Kierkegaard wrote, "If the present age had a poet he would be able to relate what these two men (Abraham and Isaac) talked about along the way," and again he asks, "Where indeed is the contemporary poet who has intimations of such conflicts? And yet Abraham's conduct was genuinely poetic, noble, more noble than anything I have read in tragedies."[17] So even in germ, *Fear and Trembling* was intended to be "poetic" in a different, more genuine vein. It must first be taken into account that Silentio more often speaks of himself as not a poet than as one, and then, in the course of this work, I will develop a richer account of what sort of poetics Silentio is engaged in. To anticipate, let me point out that a clue is provided by Kierkegaard himself in an 1849 journal entry:

> I understood myself to be what I must call a poet of the religious, not however that my personal life should express the opposite—no, I strive continually, but that I am a "poet" expresses that I do not confuse myself with the ideal.
>
> My task was to cast Christianity into reflection, not poetically to idealize (for the essentially Christian, after all, is itself the ideal) but with poetic fervor to present the total ideality at its most ideal—always ending with: I am not that, but I strive. If the latter does not prove correct and is not true about me, then everything is cast in intellectual form and falls short.[18]

Silentio could arguably be understood as a poet in the same sense that Kierkegaard thought of himself as a poet; in this connection, "poet" signifies principally one who recognizes oneself as not realizing the ideal. For Kierkegaard the man, writing in his journal, to be a poet means to recognize that one is not the ideal but that one strives for it. This part perhaps is not perfectly analogous, inasmuch as Silentio may not be actually striving for faith, but he does respect it and even is sometimes clearly impressed, not to say shattered, by it. But the comparison still holds for two principal reasons.

First, Silentio, like Kierkegaard himself, could be said to "cast Christianity into reflection." This is not the same as pretending to comprehend Christianity philosophically, something Silentio argues cannot be done.[19] It is to "shed light" indirectly or set off the phenomenon in question negatively, by contrast with what it is *not*, and this Silentio does quite frequently. Again in the journal, Kierkegaard says plainly of this pseudonym: "Johannes de Silentio has never claimed to be a believer; just the opposite, he has explained that he is not a believer—in order to illuminate faith negatively."[20] It is quite clear from the text itself that Silentio is not a faithful person, and so from him we get an "outsider's perspective." There is in this some good to be had surely, as outsiders often see more clearly than insiders, but readers of *Fear and Trembling* also should be on guard against potential distortions in the account. It is my view that these are few and far between, and I will remark on them as they come up, but for the most part Silentio reports on faith accurately and sympathetically and only sometimes imperfectly, owing to his inability to know what only the faithful themselves could know.[21] In one of his unpublished replies to Theophilus Nicolaus, Kierkegaard clarified Silentio's strategy as an effort "merely to illuminate Abraham, not to explain Abraham directly, for after all he cannot understand Abraham."[22] Once again, this seems to speak to a distinction in Kierkegaard's mind between explaining the phenomenon at hand directly and indirectly casting light upon it, which seems to have been the aim of both his own authorial project and the small part of it that he attributed to Silentio.

Second, both Kierkegaard himself as an author and Silentio could be said to be at a remove from poetically idealizing; this too is distinguishable from what they are doing as writers and is not the same as casting into reflection. Kierkegaard writes in the entry above that the reason he is not poetically idealizing is because "the essentially Christian, after all, is itself the ideal." This is in fact another reason to question whether Silentio can be called a poet. An extremely important journal entry speaks on the connection between the poet and idealizing in these words: "What does it mean to poetize? It means to contribute ideality. The poet takes an actuality which lacks something of ideality and adds to it, and this is the poem."[23] So if the poet is principally one who takes from actuality and idealizes it in order to create his poem, neither Kierkegaard nor Silentio can be a poet in the conventional sense because for both of them the actuality they take up in their examinations, the actuality they attempt to cast into reflection, is itself already the ideal. Kierkegaard calls himself a poet of the religious and says that he cannot be a straightforward poet, however, because the essentially Christian is already ideal. In the same journal entry, Kierkegaard ridicules Adam Oehlenschläger's attempt to poetize Socrates, because Socrates is already the ideal and cannot be poetized. The very attempt of a poet to idealize what is already actually ideal renders the poet a "laughingstock."[24] In much the same way, Silentio aims to shed light on Abraham, but if Abraham is the true ideal of faith, then Abraham cannot be poetized any more than Socrates could be poetized. This must be kept in mind, particularly when reading the "Eulogy on Abraham" and particularly in order to keep an appropriate separation in place between Silentio's project and that of a conventional poet. It is of course true that like Kierkegaard himself Silentio brings "poetic fervor" to his work, but this does not make him a poet in a straightforward sense.

The obvious reference in the pseudonymous author of this text's name to silence must also be accounted for briefly here.[25] The irony of our author's loquaciousness on faith and its apparent contrast to his own name has been noted, but fortunately there is not much in the way of mystery here with respect to the nature of silence. We have a clear sense of what Kierkegaard intended on this score from two sources: first, his own writing in the journal and *Point of View*, and, second, content internal to the text itself.

First, if we turn to *Point of View*, from the same passage where Kierkegaard hailed with approval Mynster's reaction to *Fear and Trembling*, we find these words: "I had made up my mind that I was a religious author whose concern is with *the single individual*, an idea (*the single individual* versus *the public*) in which a whole life- and worldview is concentrated. From now on, that is, as early as *Fear and Trembling*, the earnest observer who himself has religious presuppositions at his disposal, the earnest observer to whom one can make oneself understood at a distance and to whom one can speak in silence (the pseudonym: *Johannes—de Silentio*), became aware that this surely was a very singular kind of esthetic production."[26]

So, most obviously the name "Silentio" signifies the intimate confidence enjoyed between friends who are able to communicate without words. Even in everyday language we often speak of wordless communication between persons as a mark of the depth of feeling and mutual understanding enjoyed by them, and quite simply, Kierkegaard intended the atmosphere of *Fear and Trembling* to be charged with this communicative ease. While the full case to be made on this score will be developed throughout the pages to come, a few passages from the journals and other writings can swiftly make the main point, which is that silence is not thought of by Kierkegaard or Silentio as incompatible with communication nor construed as an absence of content. In *The Concept of Irony*, for instance, Kierkegaard calls the "nothing" of mystical contemplation not an absence of content but asserts that it "is a nothing with regard to the representation, a nothing that is just as full of content as the silence of the night is full of sounds for someone who has ears to hear."[27]

The clear meaning is that silence is not empty but full for one who can listen to silence properly. Similarly, in the journal Kierkegaard makes it clear that he distinguishes between a silence that is sheer absence of content or communication and a silence that is communicatively efficacious. He wrote in 1849: "'To be silent' means while reflecting to be able to speak, that is, about everything else imaginable, for otherwise it is conspicuous and suspicious for someone to be silent, and then it is not exactly silence, not complete silence."[28] Kierkegaard calls silence "complete" when it is in fact precisely speaking, but speaking in an indirect manner, about everything except what the silence is *about*. By contrast silence is called "conspicuous" and by implication incomplete when it is mute. This description comports quite well with what I have sketched as the basics of Silentio's approach to his subject matter: though his name is "Silence" he speaks about faith only by talking *around* the point, illuminating by contrast, not speaking *to* something he understands directly.

Kierkegaard himself seemed to think of this as his own authorial gift, as we again read in the journal. In 1854 he called himself "the most silent man in the present age" but simultaneously affirmed that his "genius" was a "gift of being able to converse and talk with any man." He went on: "Silence concealed in silence is suspect, arouses suspicion; it is almost as if a person betrayed something, at least he betrays that he is silent. But silence concealed in a most striking talent for conversation—that, now, is real silence."[29] Once again silence as mere muteness is called conspicuous, but silence that communicates is both deflective of suspicion and more genuine. The one who is truly silent, as Kierkegaard thought of himself as being, is one who does communicate and does so unnoticeably and through indirect means.

Finally, in a passage very much worth considering in connection with my interpretation of *Fear and Trembling*, Kierkegaard wrote in his journal that silence is often God's own mode of communication. In a passage from 1846 where Kierkegaard recorded a prayer, he addressed God in these words: "Father in heaven, you speak to a man in many ways; you who alone possess wisdom and understanding, you nevertheless wish to make yourself understandable to him. You speak with him also in your silence." Kierkegaard goes on to name other examples of human cases where silence is communicative. A teacher, he remarks, might examine a student by means of silence. A lover might test his beloved through silence. And one who speaks in silence, he says, may do so in order "that the hour of understanding, when it comes, might be all the more inward." This is precisely the sort of concern that drives *Fear and Trembling* as a whole. My argument is that the silence that communicates throughout this text, the silence that pervades Silentio's discourse with the reader, the silence that haunts God and Abraham, the silence that Abraham in turn casts over those he loves, is motivated principally by a desire that the understanding that results from the communication among parties be more inward than it might otherwise have been. Silence is not a hindrance to this intimacy; it is required for it, even in relation to the divine. Kierkegaard continues his prayer:

> Father in heaven, in the hour of silence, when a man stands alone and abandoned and does not hear your voice, does it not seem to him that the separation will last forever. In the hour of silence when a man is prostrate in the desert where he does not hear your voice, does it not seem to him as if it had disappeared completely. Father in heaven, is it not true that this is merely the moment of silence in the intimacy of conversation. Bless this silence, then, as you bless each and every one of your words to a man. Let him never forget that you also speak when you are silent. Grant him the confidence, if he prays to you, that you are silent out of love, just as you speak out of love, so that whether you are silent or whether you speak, you are still the same father, whether you instruct by word of mouth or educate with your silence, it is still the same fatherliness.[30]

What remains consistent whether it is by silence that God communicates or by "word of mouth" is the Father's fatherliness. Silence is a means of communication, and surely the one that interests Silentio the most, though it is clearly not the only one God uses, and God remains the loving Father across all the means of communication he uses. Certainly silent communication is one that plunges us into fear and trembling, and it requires the hearer's confidence that it is still the father who speaks in that silence, so it is not without its difficult and anguished aspects. Nevertheless, God is still the Father, and his silence is still a mode of his speaking, a mode that will ultimately intensify the relationship between the father and his children.[31]

Indeed, the epigram I submit references the phenomenon of wordless communication, specifically a case of communication between a father and a son, and therefore sets the stage for much of what is to come. Silentio chose as an epigram a passage from Hamann: "What Tarquinius Superbus said in the garden by means of the poppies, the son understood but the messenger did not." The reference is to an episode in Roman history when the son of Tarquin the Proud surreptitiously earned the trust of the citizens of Gabii by pretending to have fallen out of favor with his father and fled into self-imposed exile. Having established trust in this new hostile environment and seeking direction from his father, Tarquin's son sends a messenger back to Rome to ask his father for instruction. Not knowing whether the messenger could be trusted or not, Tarquin *says* nothing to the messenger. Instead he goes into the garden and strikes off the tops of the tallest poppies with his cane. The messenger returns to Tarquin's son and reports to him that his father bears him no message at all; his report is that Tarquin said nothing and merely struck off the poppy heads in the garden. The son, though, understands that this *is* the message. The message from Tarquin is that his son should execute the leading men (the tallest poppies) of the enemy city in order to seize power himself and make the city vulnerable to conquest by the Roman army.

The simplest point of this anecdote is that communication can happen silently. As we will see in the final chapter, Abraham's communication to his son is not strictly wordless but does have an elliptical character that could be seen to parallel Tarquin's gestural communication. Another point worth noticing here is that the communicative act in this case takes place between a father and a son. Father and son relationships will appear again in this text and are worth considering for their special nature, their likeness and unlikeness to other human relationships. The substance of the communication it seems to me in this case is typical of father and son dealings with one another. The son seeks the advice of the father, not knowing what to do or where else to turn, trusting only the father and deferring to his wisdom. The father offers his wisdom, and his advice consists in an encouragement for the son to execute his will. As intimated by its title, *Fear and Trembling* is largely about learning how to do the will of the father and to be conscious that it is the father who is at work within us to empower the knowing and doing of that will.

2 A Philosophical Preface

There are four preliminary sections to *Fear and Trembling*, a fact all the more conspicuous if we take into account the original titles for each section: first there is a *Forord* or "Preface"; then *Stemning* (which Kierkegaard originally intended to call a *proem*),[1] translated by the Hongs as "Exordium"[2] but perhaps more felicitously by Walsh as "Tuning Up"[3] or by Hannay as "Attunement";[4] then there is the *Lovtale over Abraham*, rendered as "Eulogy on Abraham"[5] by the Hongs or as "Speech in Praise of Abraham"[6] by Hannay; finally, the *Problemata* are announced but preceded by a *Foreløbig Expectoration*, perhaps the most improbably titled of all given that the fourth section of any work could hardly be called at that point "Preliminary,"[7] as the Hongs have it, or a "Preamble"[8] as Hannay has it. It has been observed that Silentio has trouble getting started with his book. What has not been accounted for as readily is why there are so many initial "approaches" to the main body of the text.

The best way to understand what role these sections play is to think of them as experiments with different methodologies. The preface, in fairly conventional fashion, introduces our author and outlines some of his preliminary concerns while striking a philosophic or theoretical note, complete with allusions to the contemporary academic scene and to Descartes, and inclusive of remarks on conceptual analysis. The exordium is an exercise in storytelling that appeals directly to the imagination and depends for its effect on richly rendered narrative and character study, very much in the vein of the novelist's art. The eulogy on Abraham exchanges narrative for rhetoric; often overheated, florid, and even bombastic, it is oratorical and exuberant. Finally, the preliminary expectoration (originally designated by Kierkegaard merely as "Introduction")[9] switches back to first person and begins to sketch the themes that will echo throughout the three Problemata sections.[10]

Movements and Doubts

To begin with the preface, which again has a philosophical bent and situates the program of the text in the current intellectual milieu, we read the opening words: "Not only in the business world but also in the world of ideas, our age stages *ein wirklicher Ausverkauf*. Everything can be had at such a bargain price that it becomes a question whether there is finally anyone who will make a bid."[11] Silentio does not elaborate on this image at all as such and moves on to his well-known sarcastic condemnation of those in his day who presume to "go further" than "doubting everything."[12] This latter line of argument certainly is the dominant theme of this section, and it should govern our interpretation of the economic metaphor, which on my reading does not call for an artificial exercise in price manipulation but rather for diligence in pursuit of the "enormous task" of doubt (or faith).[13]

Silentio's preoccupation with "going further" has been rightly explained by many commentators as a satire on the drive of Spirit in Hegelian thought toward a "realized eschatology" that eclipses the significance of faith and ultimately discards it in favor of the full conceptual clarity that only speculative philosophy can provide. Surely when Silentio claims that everyone in his day, every professional and amateur, every student and assistant professor "is unwilling to stop with doubting everything but goes further"[14] he is satirizing the easy, self-congratulatory comfort of the intellectual classes (whether actually in lecture halls or of the armchair variety), who imagine themselves as having accomplished in a trice what obsessed minds as great as Descartes and the ancient Greek skeptics. "Perhaps it would be premature and untimely," he quips, "to ask them where they really are going, but in all politeness and modesty it can probably be taken for granted that they have doubted everything, since otherwise it certainly would be odd to speak of their having gone further. They have all made this preliminary movement and presumably so easily that they find it unnecessary to say a word about how."[15] As already remarked, this series of introductory sections in *Fear and Trembling* can be characterized generally as "preliminary movements," and there may be an implicit contrast here between the sheer number and complexity of the "preliminary movements" provided by the text at hand and the tacit consensus among the learned of Silentio's day that they have in fact performed the requisite "preliminary movement" that must logically precede "going further." The text itself, then, forces its reader to perform a series of preliminary movements, arguably as a corrective to the assumption likely made by Silentio's audience that they have already made these movements.

Movement in general of course is of interest to Kierkegaard, but the precise character of that movement is not always well understood. It is widely recognized that Kierkegaard is a dynamic thinker in the senses both that he is interested in *dynamis*, becoming and change, and that his own conceptuality is self-consciously flexible and responsive to change. *Fear and Trembling* is no exception, as it often discusses movement and change. What I will argue throughout this treatment though is that Kierkegaard is equally interested in *stasis* and that for him thinking about human life is always a matter of not merely insisting upon the rightful place of change but is preeminently about continuity and the marriage of change and stability. This pairing finds itself expressed as a relationship of contradiction between divergent dialectical poles: being and becoming, change and permanence, and most important, the ideal and the actual. Kierkegaard at one time considered naming *Fear and Trembling* "Movements and Positions,"[16] a title that would itself have combined two such dialectically opposed conceptions. The phrase survives in a footnote[17] to the all-important Problema III, in a passage wherein Silentio is introducing his distinctive treatments of the Delphic bridegroom and his bride, Agnes and the merman, Tobias and Sarah, and Faust and Margaret. The placement of the phrase in this key passage would itself suggest its residual importance in Kierkegaard's mind, though a full account of how he seeks to embroider together change and permanence, the ideal and the actual, can be developed only as the interpretation proceeds.

If the preface, then, (as well as perhaps the remaining preliminary sections) is an exercise in encouraging the rehearsal of preliminary movements, then one of its paradoxical tasks is precisely to force a "slowing down" rather than a speeding up. Silentio satirizes the haste with which his audience is moving toward an unclear goal and instead exhorts them (and us) to tarry a while. His purpose in doing so is certainly not to grind to a halt but to link movement and stability in a way that is appropriate to mirroring the structure of the self and the life lived by a self. In *The Sickness unto Death*, Anti-Climacus claims that "to become is a movement away from that place, but to become oneself is a movement in that place."[18] This remark I think also encapsulates Silentio's theory of life lived according to faith: it is not a matter merely of becoming or change but a matter of becoming within, becoming and being at once, or as Walter Lowrie put it somewhat more felicitously in his translation of the same passage, "To become is a movement from the spot, but to become oneself is a movement at the spot."[19] Kierkegaard is interested throughout his authorship with "movement at the spot," and this interpretation of *Fear and Trembling* will flesh out in greater detail what that means.

Suffice it to say for now that the preface too is not merely about movement nor about inhibiting movement but about movement at the spot. The reader learns something of what movement at the spot can look like from the analogy Silentio constructs in the preface between doubt and faith. Just as his contemporaries insist on "going further" than doubt so too they insist on "going further" than faith. The comparison at first seems an odd one, but perhaps it is appropriate to the dialectical approach, which allows opposed figures to play off each other, and it is explicable in terms of the true relationship between doubt and faith as Kierkegaard understands it. A passage from the journal composed somewhere around the time of the writing of *Fear and Trembling* reads: "Doubt is produced EITHER by bringing reality into relation with ideality; this is the act of cognition; insofar as interest is involved, there is at most a third in which I am interested—for example, the truth. OR by bringing ideality into relation with reality. This is the ethical. That in which I am interested is myself. It is really Christianity that has brought this doubt into the world, for in Christianity this self received its meaning.—Doubt is conquered not by the system but by faith, just as it is faith that has brought doubt into the world."[20]

So doubt arises when ideality meets reality; this is one of the major preoccupations of the text on my interpretation, the collision of the ideal and the real. When reality is brought into relation with ideality, doubt can emerge with the involvement of a third term. As another example of this third term, Kierkegaard names beauty as well as truth in another entry of uncertain dating from the same rough period of time. Knowing that is interested in beauty or truth, he writes, is not interested in myself and therefore "has no continuity." "Interested knowing," he continues, which presumably does have continuity, "enters with Christianity."[21] So what could he mean by bringing reality into relation with ideality, where this takes place by reference to a third term and with no existential interest for myself? If cognition is meant to be a leading example, perhaps Kierkegaard means that in the act of cognition, one seeks in the realm of the actual the means to rise to an ideal; I go out in search of the beautiful or the true. And doubt can arise here because one can legitimately wonder whether the actual yields the true or the beautiful. Hence we have a potential description of ancient skepticism, a position that questions whether the true can ultimately be settled upon and what the wise person should do in the absence of certainty about the intelligibility or attainability of the true.

The other way by which he says doubt can arise is by a reversal of that procedure, when the ideal is brought into relation with the real. This, Kierkegaard says in both entries, is brought into the world by Christianity and involves an interest in myself. In the former entry he says this is not to do with cognition but with ethics and goes a bit further than in the latter entry when he states that the meaning of the self so interested is itself established by Christianity. So what could this mean? In the former case we had an attempt to realize an ideal from the basis of reality. In this case an ideal is posited for reality; this ideal has ethical significance and is linked to a specific revelation that has a bearing on how the human being can think of herself at all.

I submit that this revealed ethically relevant conception that concerns the self directly and is made possible by Christianity is sin-consciousness, the awareness that I am not the ideal, the recognition that the reality of who I am ethically is not what I should be. The form of doubt that this occasions, then, is not of the sort that says "Is this the truth?" but the sort that says "Is this who I really am?"[22] This reading would explain why Kierkegaard goes on to claim that "the system"—his well-known term for the intellectually impressive but ultimately abstract and thus in his sense uninteresting achievement of Hegel and his followers—cannot dispense with doubt. The system cannot quell this doubt because this doubt is not an intellectual problem that can be dissolved by increasing knowledge. This doubt is a matter of who I am individually and what I am going to do about the fact that I am not who I would be. Only faith can resolve this doubt, and again I contend this is a predominant concern of *Fear and Trembling*, because only faith can make it possible for me to go on living in the knowledge that I am not who I should be and at the same time that I am becoming who I should be.

Faith and doubt therefore can be likened in the preface because faith and doubt in this special sense can be (and indeed must be) partners, as we have already seen from the introduction above. Normally, when we think of the relationship of doubt and faith we are thinking of doubt as an abstract intellectual problem, an issue that arises in the absence of epistemological certainty. This is true even when we are prepared perhaps to make a place within the life of faith for doubts; some will concede that one can live faithfully while yet entertaining unanswered theoretical questions, and this may indeed be so. But Kierkegaard is not thinking about doubt primarily in this way in these journal passages. Instead he is thinking of a form of moral doubt that, again, Christianity itself both introduces and overcomes, and this doubt can only be sin-consciousness or at least akin to it, for Christianity at once teaches me that I am a sinner and how to be forgiven of my sins. In this sense, faith and doubt go hand in hand and intensify each other for Kierkegaard.[23]

So it is for Kierkegaard. But Silentio is not thinking about doubt in this exact way. As has been argued, Silentio is positioning his preface with respect to the philosophical milieu of his audience. And he is doing so without full access to faith himself. What I suggest, then, is he is clear about the potential for faith and a certain kind of doubt to be at least likened to one another, though he does not fully understand the mode of personal, interested doubt that is akin to sin-consciousness (this is in fact his first and greatest failing as a guide to what faith is, and in this respect first and foremost his testimony about faith must be regarded as incomplete). What he is able to do, though, in the preface is present close philosophical approximations to the relationship of faith and doubt that Christianity teaches. These two approximations are to be found in the work of Descartes and in the ancient Greek skeptics. Neither of these worthy authorities can have the final word on either doubt or faith, and it is probable that neither would receive either Silentio's or Kierkegaard's unqualified endorsement, but both capture a partial truth, and from Silentio's outsider's perspective both are commendable. Kierkegaard himself would see more clearly than Silentio does what it is they are missing in their respective accounts, but again this is a preface by one without faith, and it is a preface intended to make a philosophical—not a lyrical or rhetorical—statement, so it appeals to philosophical sources.

Descartes and the Greek Skeptics

Imagining the defense his contemporaries might put up in the face of his withering satire, Silentio raises the example of Descartes as one who successfully doubted. The example of Descartes is an unusual one for Kierkegaard to invoke, seeing as how we know from other writings that Kierkegaard had serious reservations about Descartes as a thinker and about the method of hyperbolic doubt specifically. Indeed, the unpublished and unfinished work *Johannes Climacus or De omnibus dubitandum* is clearly a wry rejoinder to Descartes. Since Descartes is often critiqued in the pseudonymous writings, it has been defensibly claimed that this passage is in fact the only one in the entire Kierkegaardian corpus wherein Descartes is treated positively.[24] The terms in which he is praised are worth some attention. Silentio imagines his audience's reply: "'But did not Descartes do it?' Descartes, a venerable, humble, honest thinker, whose writings no one can read without being profoundly affected—he did what he said and said what he did."[25] Unlike those in his audience who imagine themselves "going further" and claiming indeed to go further without in fact doing so, Descartes's words match his deeds, he "did what he said and said what he did," a "rarity" Silentio claims, in his own day.

So what did Descartes say and do? In what respect did his deeds match his words? Silentio provides two quotes from Descartes, two sets of words that he claims comported with his deeds. First, from the *Principles of Philosophy*: "Above all we should impress on our memory as an infallible rule that what God has revealed to us is incomparably more certain than anything else; and that we ought to submit to the Divine authority rather than to our own judgment even though the light of reason may seem to us to suggest, with the utmost clearness and evidence, something opposite."[26] Silentio uses this quote to prove that Descartes "did not doubt with respect to faith,"[27] though it might have been more precise to say that this rule from the *Principles of Philosophy* shows that Descartes did not doubt the *content* of the Christian faith; that is to say he laid it down as a rule that the substance of what had been revealed by God was more trustworthy even than what the light of reason made known.

Two observations ought to be made here. First, in both word and deed, then, according to Silentio, Descartes did not think doubt could be employed against the content of faith. Second, he maintained that what has been revealed by God should be accepted even if reason "may *seem* to suggest" otherwise. Both of these themes reecho throughout *Fear and Trembling*, which, consonant with the rest of the Kierkegaardian corpus, argues that doubt cannot be employed against the content of faith mainly because the content of faith is simply not vulnerable to intellectual interrogation of the kind that Descartes deployed or that is commonly deployed by the contemporary apologist for antitheism. Theoretical arguments simply cannot corrode the substance of faith, which must be either believed or regarded as offensive and is not the object of merely intellectual assent or rejection; this is why Kierkegaard repeatedly insisted that doubt is not the "opposite" of faith but that sin is. Furthermore, that a revelation from God must be accepted even when it seems (and I stress "seem" above from the Descartes quote) contrary to reason, is likewise a major theme of *Fear and Trembling*. What faith makes it possible or even necessary to believe it does so without being subordinate to the modern understanding of reason and thus can overrule and (I would argue this is the more important point) ultimately transform reason so understood.

The second quote from Descartes is meant to show that he was a private thinker with a personally motivated project, not the prescriber of a universally obligatory methodology. From the *Discourse on Method*: "Thus my design is not here to teach the Method which everyone should follow in order to promote the good conduct of his Reason, but only to show in what manner I have endeavored to conduct my own."[28] This much seems meant to show that, in Silentio's words, "he did not shout 'Fire! Fire!' and make it obligatory for everyone to doubt, for Descartes was a quiet and solitary thinker, not a shouting street watchman."[29] So the point is that contrary to the way in which Descartes is held up by the doubters of Silentio's day as a model for their own imitation, Descartes himself was not seeking to be a model for anybody but pursued his own answers on terms that seemed proper to him as an individual thinker; he was thus neither the follower of old movements nor the deliberate instigator of a new one. Moreover, he followed his own path for a specific reason, which Silentio illustrates with a quote from the same work but one that is not contiguous textually with the one just given. Why did Descartes devise his personal method? Because he realized that an ideal he had of himself had been disrupted by the reality. Descartes thought of himself as an educated person in possession of certain knowledge, but his experience proved otherwise: "But so soon as I had achieved the entire course of study at the close of which one is usually received into the ranks of the learned, I entirely changed my opinion. For I found myself embarrassed with so many doubts and errors that it seemed to me that the effort to instruct myself had no effect other than the increasing discovery of my own ignorance."[30]

Not only is it the case that Descartes pursued the method of doubt for his own reason, but to be more specific, his reason was to do with the dismantling of his self-understanding by reality. Descartes had wanted to think of himself in terms of an achieved ideal: I am now officially learned. But reality proves that Descartes is not what he takes himself to be; he is instead aware only of his own ignorance. The Socratic tone of this transformation in self-understanding is obvious, as is Kierkegaard's lifelong appreciation for Socrates, so there is again an appreciative undertone in Silentio's attempt to liken Descartes to Socrates. Clearly, Silentio is trying to distinguish between Descartes himself and institutionalized Cartesianism.[31] The latter he seeks to disparage in sarcastic fashion, the former he seeks to rehabilitate. This much is clear also from the double meaning that attaches to Silentio's signoff at the end of the preface. Bidding a facetious adieu to the professional and semiprofessional systematizers of his day, Silentio writes, "This is not the system; it has not the least thing to do with the system. I invoke everything good for the system and for the Danish shareholders in this omnibus, for it will hardly become a tower. I wish them all, each and every one, success and good fortune. Respectfully, Johannes de Silentio."[32] The Hongs[33] have seen a significant connection between Silentio's reference to the omnibus and the new public transportation system of horse-drawn buses in Copenhagen; a letter from Kierkegaard to his friend Rasmus Nielsen, however, establishes the true importance of this reference, which in point of fact further underscores the separation Silentio is trying to make between Descartes himself and the contemporary "Cartesians." In 1849, Kierkegaard wrote to Nielsen: "Dear friend, Your note of Friday of last week duly received. It may perhaps have escaped you that the association of ideas from omnibus to omnibus is evoked in the maxim *de omnibus dubitandum*. All is to be doubted. Hence when Johannes de Silentio calls the system 'an omnibus,' it must be understood as having a double meaning."[34]

The reference to the "omnibus" therefore probably has little to do with an actual bus and more to do with the connection Silentio is forging between the system and its adherents and the maxim *de omnibus dubitandum*, which Silentio is using as shorthand for the method and mania of the amateur doubters who are mocked both by himself and in *Johannes Climacus*. The systematizers and doubters are simply two faces on the same crowd, a crowd mired in merely intellectual dilettantism whose dabbling in going further than both doubt and faith in fact attains neither genuine doubt nor true faith.

But why use Descartes as a foil for the intellectual crowd? Why at this one place in the whole authorship choose to treat Descartes in a complimentary fashion? My assertion is that Silentio is stylizing Descartes as a knight of faith. The miniature portrait he paints of Descartes here is the text's first expression of the central dynamic of *Fear and Trembling*: an ideal has to be resigned when it is shattered by reality and then can be reborn in chastened form through faith in God. Descartes is a philosophical shadow of a knight of faith, one that is meant to provide a point of contrast to the easy self-assurance of the contemporary doubters, a point of contrast that they would find especially galling, seeing as how they invoke Descartes as one of their own. But Silentio is sure Descartes is not one of their own. He is one who felt no need to "go further" than faith but insisted, rather, that belief in the content of faith cannot be undermined by theoretical doubt. He trusted to divine revelation even when that revelation seemed scandalous to reason. Like Socrates, he was chagrined by his own lack of understanding and sought to repair that lack through an individual quest for knowledge. To do that (and here I am glossing the argument of the *Meditations*, a text that is, after all, highly personal, in a manner that Silentio might have done) he discarded his prior ideal of certainty in knowledge in a moment of resignation. Shaken by the degree to which he was not learned but ignorant, Descartes gave up his prior sense of himself as an accomplished expert in the sciences. Ultimately, the blow reality dealt to Descartes's understanding of himself was so sharp that it required

Descartes to give up the world itself. On the far side of this resignation, however, he had the world restored to him and his sense of himself as knowledgeable and resting confidently on sure foundations. Trusting first to his own existence and second to the existence of God, Descartes got the world back and his enlightened self back, both as gifts from God. It is in this sense that we can read the reference to Descartes not merely as an illustrative example but indeed as *Fear and Trembling*'s first (admittedly imperfect) portrait of a knight of faith.[35]

I call it imperfect because of course Descartes himself, neither in word nor deed, attained to the substance of what Silentio has put into his book. But on a certain (and certainly creative) reading of the movement of the *Meditations*, he comes respectably close. The same could be said for the Greek skeptics, for whom Kierkegaard had a well-documented and thoroughly discussed appreciation.[36] Silentio's usage of them in the preface is much more easily explained than his reference to Descartes. The sarcasm returns when Silentio reminds his reader that the "ancient Greeks, who after all did know a little about philosophy," assumed that doubt was "a task for a whole lifetime, because proficiency in doubting is not acquired in days and weeks."[37] It is clear, and other commentators have noticed, that Silentio is appealing to the classical sense of doubt, which was not merely an intellectual posture but was a means of discipline shaping the whole person's life in a spiritual direction. He praises the old skeptic of the past as one who "maintained the equilibrium of doubt throughout all the specious arguments, who had intrepidly denied the certainty of the senses and the certainty of thought, who, uncompromising, had defied the anxiety of self-love and the insinuations of fellow feeling," and sneers that with such hard-won accomplishments "everyone begins in our age."[38]

The terms of Silentio's praise are significant. The old skeptic is no adherent to the slogan *de omnibus dubitandum* and all that it represents. He is one who maintained equilibrium—*ataraxia*—the mental and emotional self-discipline of nonjudgment; his denial of the certainty of sense perception and thought was not specious or flippant but intrepid, made resolutely in the face of the practical consequence of his skepticism; he was motivated by the desire to overcome self-love and the blandishments of sentimentality, proving himself to be concerned with true virtue. These sober and to some extent praiseworthy qualities, which bespeak the passion of the skeptic and not a bloodless scientism, are not to be found among Silentio's contemporaries. It is worth keeping in mind too, with respect to the ancient Greek skeptics, that their virtues were directed toward the aim of happiness. The skeptic cultivates the wisdom of suspending judgment wherever reliable truth cannot be secured, because the life of the sage is the happy life. The aim of being undeceived is pursued not only for abstract epistemological reasons but because it is conducive to human flourishing and to satisfaction with life amid its vagaries and discontents.

But this too is consistent with Kierkegaard's general posture toward his current age, which lacks not only sincere appropriation of Christian faith (readers of *Fear and Trembling* are constantly reminded of Kierkegaard's lifelong conviction on this point and rightly so) but also the qualified excellences of the Greeks (which readers of *Fear and Trembling* do not hear about quite so often). Throughout the authorship the limits of pre-Christian classical culture are compared to the limits of the spiritless modern age, though quite often it is clear that Kierkegaard thinks more highly of the former than the latter. Both, however, suffer from a lack of fully developed self-consciousness, the Greeks because they had not the advantage of Christian revelation, though progressed as far as any thoughtful people could without it (Socrates being the furthest extent of this progress), the modern spiritless because they had the advantage of Christian revelation and abandoned it. Silentio's choice, then, of a classical Greek example and an example from the modern era is by no means accidental. Descartes and the Greek skeptics to him are the most significant instances of something close to the picture of doubt and faith that he seeks to paint in *Fear and Trembling*; they are proof of the extent to which human reasoning can reach on its own, whether unaided by revelation or insufficiently informed by revelation.

As it is with doubt, so too with faith: "Everyone is unwilling to stop with faith but goes further . . . it was different in those ancient days. Faith was then a task for a whole lifetime, because it was assumed that proficiency in believing is not acquired either in days or in weeks."[39] Neither doubt nor faith is an intellectual pose; it is not possible to "go further" than either in short order. Both are tasks for a lifetime because neither can be wholly outgrown. Silentio writes that "no man outgrows [anxiety and trembling]—except to the extent that he succeeds in going further as early as possible."[40] If one is able to "go further" than faith and its attendant anxiety as quickly as possible, then one indeed will no longer be troubled by it. But if one tarries a while with what the sophisticates of the contemporary age believe they can easily mature beyond, then they will find that the task of a whole life is before them.

I said from the beginning that the preface is a work of philosophical tone addressed to a philosophical audience. It uses examples drawn from the history of philosophy to show how the work at hand situates itself with respect to that history and its contemporary discourse. Descartes and the ancient Greeks are the most natural choices Silentio could make for figures representing "the best" within the philosophical tradition—the grand but finally incomplete achievement of Greek culture, and the imperfect but unappreciated achievement of the modern era. Somewhat as Augustine did in *The City of God* with his Roman forebears, so Silentio points out to his contemporary philosophical reader that the best possibilities within their shared tradition have gone ignored, and he argues that the contemporary generation suffers for that ignorance.

So great in fact is the gulf between the contemporary generation and the luminaries of its past that Silentio would prefer not to be associated with it at all. "The present author is by no means a philosopher,"[41] he writes. It is as if Silentio is saying, "If this is what passes for philosophy then count me out." While there is much to appreciate in the Greeks and even in the highlights of the modern age, there is not much to appreciate in the system, and Silentio makes it clear he will have none of it, chiefly because it rashly ventures what neither the Greeks nor Descartes would have had the temerity to assay: it tries to go further than faith, but this is a doomed project from the start, according to Silentio. "Even if someone were able to transpose the whole content of faith into conceptual form, it does not follow that he has comprehended faith, comprehended how he entered into it or how it entered into him."[42] This is the upshot of the preface, philosophically speaking, the primary theoretical point Silentio wants to make. The point is put more pithily in the preliminary expectoration, when Silentio writes, "Philosophy cannot and must not give faith."[43] Philosophy cannot give faith, not even if it could render the content of faith into transparent concepts. And the most important question about faith, it would seem, is not whether it can be clarified by contemporary philosophical concepts but how and whether one comes to faith. The emphasis, as usual, for Kierkegaard is not on the abstract question but the insistence of the existential demand. The issue is not so much "What is faith?" but "Do I have faith?" This is the only means by which the content of faith can be "comprehended"; to comprehend it is to live it. As is often the case with Silentio, the most important point is made indirectly: he, in effect, tells his readers what sort of account they are *not* going to read in *Fear and Trembling*. It will not be an abstract, conceptual discussion of faith, which cannot comprehend its object in any genuine manner.

The conceptually abstract mode of "comprehension" is the mode of modern science, a vain project that seeks, by imposition of the system and insistence on "rules," to clarify that which by definition can only be appropriated in life and not "known" as a theorem is known. But it is this depleted sense of knowing that the philosophical scene prefers. Silentio writes that he "easily envisions his fate in an age that has crossed out passion in order to serve science."[44] The implication of this opposition that Silentio detects between passion and science in the philosophical milieu of his day is that Silentio is by no means opposed to "science" or knowledge, only to the replacement of passion by "science." Indeed it could easily be argued that Descartes and the Greek skeptics are interesting precisely because they had passion *for* science. In Silentio's day these two have been divorced, and as a result, Silentio says he fears he will be ignored by a public averse to being sharply confronted in their complacency. Likewise, he says he fears being criticized savagely (perhaps because in an age without passion, debate and discussion degenerate merely into criticism for the sake of it). Finally, he says the worst fate would be to fall into the hands of an "enterprising abstracter, a gobbler of paragraphs (who, in order to save science, is always willing to . . . cut him up into paragraphs and do so with the same inflexibility as the man who, in order to serve the science of punctuation, divided his discourse by counting out the words, fifty words to a period and thirty-five to a semicolon."[45] Notice what the example indicates about the sort of science Silentio decries. This form of science is nothing but the rigid and thoughtless imposition of an abstract rule—every fifty words there must be a period—a rule enforced without regard for fittingness or beauty. Clearly, this sort of science and the style of thinking that drives it is objectionable to Silentio but not, as has been said, all science or thinking. This is especially important to keep in mind when we confront claims by Silentio that "faith begins precisely where thought stops."[46] The "thought" he has in mind is certainly not any sort of purposeful mental activity but the sort of thinking characteristic of what is precisely thought*less* as well as bloodless science.

As a philosophical preface, this brief section, then, stakes out the theoretical ground that Silentio wishes to occupy. First, he wants his audience to tarry with thinking about and taking up for ourselves in a certain way the questions of doubt and faith and not be in a rush to imagine ourselves as having moved beyond these issues and the manner in which they can transform our lives. Second, he has gestured toward two examples of philosophers who have done this very thing for themselves, and while their answers to how best to live out doubt and faith are perhaps not exactly the answers that Silentio will give, they are proof that philosophy at its best can approach these issues and grasp them at least partially, a lesson that the amateurs of Silentio's day would do well to learn. Third, Silentio has announced, at least implicitly, his interest in a kind of knowing that is impelled by passion; he has not set knowing aside in favor of passion but seeks to bring them together. While here in the preface and in what is to come, philosophy and, perhaps by implication, reason itself have been subjected to some criticism, it is my argument that Silentio will not want to see these discarded but will instead want to see them transformed in the light of what faith reveals.

3 A Narrative Approach

Exordium

The Exordium is probably the most mystifying and most misunderstood (if not completely ignored) portion in the whole of *Fear and Trembling*. It is, as I have suggested, methodologically distinct from the other preliminary sections, drawing its inspiration from storytelling and experiment with narrative. Its opening words, "Once upon a time," obviously call to mind a fairy tale, a genre for which Kierkegaard had considerable affection and from which he will draw again in *Fear and Trembling*. The Exordium identifies "a man who as a child had heard that beautiful story of how God tempted Abraham and of how Abraham withstood the temptation, kept the faith, and, contrary to expectation, got a son a second time."[1] Generally, commentators take it that the anonymous man is Silentio himself. This may be so, but it need not be so for the purpose of the Exordium to be achieved. That purpose, as outlined above, is to guide the reader through a "preliminary movement," in this case one that is performed in a literary mode, and one that communicates negatively by demonstrating how the story of Abraham (who after all is mentioned for the very first time on this page) can*not* be told in order for it to be communicated effectively to the reader. Whether Silentio is or is not the man in question matters little in the end, and interpretive theories that require the assumption that the man is Silentio can rest only precariously on such an assumption.[2]

The man described in the Exordium experiences the separation of science and passion decried by Silentio at the end of the preface. "When he grew older, he read the same story with even greater admiration, for life had fractured what had been united in the pious simplicity of the child. The older he became, the more often his thoughts turned to that story; his enthusiasm for it became greater and greater, and yet he could understand the story less and less."[3] The man experiences a separation between his knowledge or understanding on the one hand and his enthusiasm or desire on the other. Just as Silentio himself seemed to gesture toward the need to unify science and passion, knowledge and desire, at the end of the preface, so now he paints a portrait of a character who experiences the divergence of these and yearns for their reconciliation. The more the man desires to know, the less he seems to understand; the less he understands, the more he wants to know. The man is like a modern-day Socrates (or perhaps like Descartes and the skeptics from the preface), who knows at least that he does not know and wants thereby to know all the more.

This man "was not a thinker. He did not feel any need to go beyond faith."[4] Our man is thus in another obvious sense unlike the contemporary generation. He is in no hurry to "go further" than faith. He does not imagine himself to be a philosopher or an intellectual sophisticate. He is not a reader of Hebrew and not an "exegetical scholar," so he lacks the official professional requirements for understanding Abraham, but he desires more than most perhaps to understand him. It is not the beauty of the story in any conventional sense that inspires his desire; instead it is the "shudder of the idea,"[5] the tremor within the concept, the shock that Abraham delivers to the system.

His manner of appreciating that shock is, as we have said, the mode of storytelling, and he provides four versions of the Abraham story in an apparent effort to draw nearer to its meaning. A convincing critical consensus has formed around the thesis that these four versions of the story are meant to illustrate four possible mistellings—false Abrahams, in effect—or iterations of how the story of Abraham's sacrifice of Isaac could have gone wrong.[6] My interpretation does not challenge this consensus. There is some disagreement, however, as to how precisely to read each vignette individually and as to the meaning of the weaning passages—the paragraphs appended to each of the four versions that meditate on the means by which a mother weans her child—so in this section I will concentrate on how best to interpret these passages with the basic point in the background that they are surely intended to illustrate how Abraham could have failed to be the father of faith. The single most important point perhaps to keep in mind about these four vignettes is that in each, Abraham actually sets out in full readiness to do the deed; in no version does he fail by failing to act on the divine command. What this makes abundantly clear is that the faith of Abraham consists primarily not in his mere obedience to what God asks but has more to do with the attitude that accompanies his obedience, the manner in which he obeys. *That* Abraham obeys is a given; *how* he obeys makes the difference between true faith and something that falls short.

The First False Abraham

After a brief resume of the story of Genesis 22, the first of the four imaginative variations (a felicitous phrase that Evans has used[7]) recapitulates the story straightforwardly enough but is soon derailed by Abraham's intent to break his silence regarding his and Isaac's journey and its purpose. "Abraham said to himself, 'I will not hide from Isaac where this walk is taking him.' He stood still, he laid his hand on Isaac's head in blessing, and Isaac kneeled to receive it. And Abraham's face epitomized fatherliness; his gaze was gentle, his words admonishing."[8] The intent that forms in Abraham's mind to disclose his plan to Isaac is often noticed by commentators as the centerpiece of this first imaginative variation, but the first noteworthy description of Abraham in this vignette, that his expression "epitomized fatherliness," is not as often remarked upon. When Abraham's attempts to explain and console his son fail, perhaps predictably, his fatherliness evaporates. "When Isaac saw Abraham's face again, it had changed: his gaze was wild, his whole being was sheer terror. He seized Isaac by the chest, threw him to the ground, and said, 'Stupid boy, do you think I am your father? No, I am an idolater. Do you think it is God's command? No, it is my desire.'"[9]

A key element of the complete transformation undergone by Abraham in this first version is the reversal of his role as father. The first denial he makes is that he is himself Isaac's father, before he denies that the command to sacrifice Isaac issued from God. The move from an embodiment of fatherhood to the outright denial of fatherhood could not be more dramatic. Something of the peculiar anxiety of fatherhood could be at issue here. In a quite different context, Jean-Luc Marion reminds us that from time immemorial fatherhood has consisted in the willingness to accept fatherhood.[10] Even in an age of DNA testing, no man can be proven to be a father, much less be compelled to be a father. At most, a man could be proven to be a sperm donor, but to be a father, one must consent to accept the responsibility of fatherhood, a responsibility than in the centuries that preceded DNA testing could be easily avoided. The universal experience of fathers is anxiety for the responsibility that has been accepted—I must now care for this dependent creature, who will look to me as an example, who will look to me to provide for his or her needs. To be a father is to initiate, in the many senses of that word, another into life and even eventually into death. And in the years that intervene, the father must temper his care and superintendence over the child by the necessity to allow the child to grow up, to become his or her own person, to someday declare independence from at least the more tangible expressions of the father's love.

Naturally, no child ever outgrows his or her father's love itself and, to some degree, will always desire that love, but children mature to the point that their father's love has to be expressed in a different manner than the father conveys it to an infant or a juvenile. The father's anxiety is one that must always problematically combine care and watchful defense of the child and the recognition that children will not always need care and protection and must be allowed to become their own person on their own terms. The father's role, then, is one that navigates the tension between being present for the child and, when necessary, being absent as well, withdrawing from the child to allow space for the boy to become the man, the girl to become the woman. The aspect of paternity that involves strategic retreat from more tangible or obvious fatherly affection of course runs the risk of alienating, at least temporarily, the child's appreciation for the father. Some lessons the child must learn are hard ones, some trials have to be faced alone, some truths can be learned only through pain. Prudent fathers know this and know when to leave children to their own resources and defenses, but on those occasions, the children do not necessarily understand why they are being left to fend for themselves. The children never stand alone, perhaps, but they must stand with the father at a respectful distance, and this is required for their maturity and development, in a word, for their own good.

At the extremity that we see this false Abraham attain, the rebellion characteristic of the father's violent reaction to his own responsibility exhibits itself, the denial of paternity. A father, having accepted his responsibility as father, may always be tempted to renege on his consent to paternity, which after all was arbitrarily (or so it could seem to one overwhelmed by anxiety) granted in the first place and could be revoked just as gratuitously. When the relationship with the child is especially fraught, the father thinks to himself in his darkest moment, "Why did I ever agree to this in the first place?" and contemplates abandoning the burden he himself has willingly assumed. It may certainly appear easier (and depending on how resourceful the father is when it comes to rationalization, could seem better) if he were not the boy or girl's father at all. The first false Abraham justifies his decision before God himself, addressing him with the words, "Lord God in heaven, I thank you; it is better that he believes me a monster than that he should lose faith in you."[11]

But surely this is simply a rationalization. It is God who ordained Abraham to be a father from the outset; it was his promise to Abraham that he would be a father, which was Abraham and Sarah's dearest wish. The first false Abraham's gesture can only be seen as an illegitimate attempt to "return" the gift that he has been given. His paternal responsibility in this moment is to guide Isaac through his ordeal, and as could be argued about many trying moments in human life, this one should be approached in the mode of tactical withdrawal rather than false consolation. That this temptation for Abraham of turning away from fatherhood was a live one in Kierkegaard's mind is testified to as well by passages he drafted for but never included in *Fear and Trembling* that imagine Abraham refusing his paternal role in Isaac's life. "Perhaps even one more move could be made," he imagined at one point—"let Sarah get to know about it and let her make an objection, at which point Abraham's despair would find expression in this way: Wretched woman, Isaac is in fact not our child; were not both of us old when he was born; did you yourself not laugh when it was announced."[12] And again in a similar passage written in preparation for the final task: "Abraham said this to Sarah. She became terrified and would dissuade him, but Abraham said: Wretched woman, how did you know it is our child; was it not in your old age that you had him; were not both of us decrepit. It is not our child but a phantom."[13] At the extremity of despair, then, the father's desperation takes a dramatic form: denial that the child is his at all. Isaac is for the despairing Abraham not a son but a changeling. This reaction to the trial is apparently worse than even obedience to the divine command, as shocking as that is. Faithfulness requires precisely delicate negotiation of the relation between father and son; to refuse such an enterprise is tantamount to the demonic denial of paternity altogether. Given the repeated emphasis that the text places on Abraham as *father* of faith, this disavowal of fatherhood is at the polar opposite of faithful parenting.

Conciliatory measures would fail for reasons that again need little explanation. No matter how "admonishing" or "gentle" or "full of comfort"[14] the first false Abraham might have tried to appear (and indeed the description here is cloyingly sentimental to the point of darkly comic inappropriateness), it is little wonder that Isaac "could not be uplifted," that "he clasped Abraham's knees, he pleaded at his feet" and "begged for his young life."[15] Even if there were not a larger theoretical point at stake—namely, that Abraham in Silentio's reckoning cannot speak about his trial—on the level of everyday psychological plausibility it is quite clear that paternal tenderness is no effective shield for the trauma that Abraham and Isaac face together. Similarly, with respect to psychological plausibility, many commentators have pointed out that part of what distinguishes the false Abraham narratives from the true Abraham is that the false Abrahams react to the trial before them in ways that are readily and rationally explicable. It is quite believable indeed that a father might attempt to take the blame upon himself, divert the son's shock and horror away from God onto himself, as a way of coping with the shared trauma they confront. A major point of Silentio's discussion, as we will see, is that the true Abraham's actions go beyond what reason can readily explain. But this Abraham and the Abrahams of the following three vignettes act in ways that are quite defensible and even predictable.

Consolation having failed, then, the first false Abraham resorts to relinquishing the fatherly role altogether. It is as if fatherhood for the first false Abraham consists only in immature and sentimental coddling, and if coddling doesn't work, then he cannot be a father at all. Even his eventual effort to convince his son that the latter's death is his own desire and not God's is an abortive attempt at consolation, and this is so for two reasons. First, it's not even true. The first false Abraham would rather lie to his son (and surely that cannot be excused) than ask him to face the difficult truth (which a father must sometimes do). Second, it seems to assume that God needs protecting, that Isaac cannot be expected to face the horrible truth. In short, this Abraham seems to feel that Isaac has to be deceived both about God and about himself. As a result, the boy's faith remains in a sense infantile. He appeals to God to "have mercy on me God of Abraham, have mercy on me; if I have no father on earth, then you be my father!"[16] Thus is Isaac left subject to a falsehood and to appeal to God only out of fear. The final problem perhaps is that this Abraham seems to think there is no hope for Isaac. As the text goes on, we will learn that essential to Abraham's faith is the conviction that he will receive Isaac back in some fashion, and in this first vignette he acts as if he is sure he will not get Isaac back. He therefore instead takes it upon himself to actively mislead Isaac for the sake of his own vision of what is best for the boy.

But of course the alternative left unexplored is the one means that would make for a successful transformation in the relationship between father and son. As I have already argued, it is necessary sometimes for the father to step back from the child. The child learns to walk, to take a mundane example, by holding the father's hand. But if the child never lets go of the father's hand, the child never learns to walk on his own. That the father hold the child's hand at first, when he or she is little, is essential to the child's growth and progress. But it is equally essential to the child's growth and progress that the father someday *let go* of the child's hand. If this first vignette is meant to illustrate a failed Abraham, then by implication a successful Abraham would be one who acted differently from this one. This Abraham's failure undoubtedly consists in having spoken when he should have remained silent, and again, this is a well-known theme in the text as a whole, and this point has been made by other commentators. My interpretation focuses, though, on what this failure means for the ordinary conduct of human life and what faith can teach us about how we guide our lives. Faith is significantly about transformation of relationship, and in this imaginative variation we see a dramatization of how relationship fails when put under stress. If Abraham had faith under this circumstance, several things would have been different. First, he would not have sought to take control of the situation himself. In this vignette, Abraham tries to manage the situation on his own terms. He acts as if he seems to think if he can pull things off his own way then all will be well in the end. Confronting the failure of his own strategy, he then abandons all responsibility for his son and still imagines that, using his own ingenuity, he has managed to make the best of a scenario that he botched himself. Second, he would have trusted that the truth about God can be known, even when it is a disturbing truth. Third, he would have trusted that Isaac could handle the truth without needing direct paternal intervention on behalf of a father who thought he knew best. Fourth, he would have kept hope for Isaac despite the seemingly hopeless situation into which he and Isaac had been thrust.

That this is so is illustrated potently by the elliptical weaning narrative appended to this vignette. These snippets of text have been often ignored in treatments of *Fear and Trembling*; recent commentaries have incorporated them into a more inclusive reading of the text, but even then their meaning remains a subject of debate. Generally, there has been a failure to account for why this image is even the one chosen, and commentators often express surprise that the example of a mother weaning her child was selected by Silentio at all. The explanation for the choice of weaning as a communicative metaphor, however, is not that far afield. In fact, it is in Genesis 21, the chapter immediately preceding the one that tells the story of Abraham's sacrifice of Isaac.[17] We read there:

> And the LORD visited Sarah as he had said, and the LORD did unto Sarah as he had spoken. For Sarah conceived, and bare Abraham a son in his old age, at the set time of which God had spoken to him. And Abraham called the name of his son that was born unto him, whom Sarah bare to him, Isaac. And Abraham circumcised his son Isaac being eight days old, as God had commanded him. And Abraham was an hundred years old, when his son Isaac was born unto him. And Sarah said, God hath made me to laugh, so that all that hear will laugh with me. And she said, Who would have said unto Abraham, that Sarah should have given children suck? [F]or I have born him a son in his old age. And the child grew, and was weaned: and Abraham made a great feast the same day that Isaac was weaned.

So the proximate association between the matter at hand and the image of weaning has a solid Scriptural basis, a basis that concerns familial dysfunction and testing of relationship. In connection with the weaning of Isaac there is also the traumatic casting out of Ishmael and the jealousy of Sarah over the perceived intrusion upon her domestic tranquility that precipitates that casting out. By contrast, the weaning narratives that Silentio deploys I believe are meant to illustrate a successful transformation in relationship. We have seen that the vignette of the first false Abraham indicates a way in which parental relationship in particular can fail in the face of the test put to Abraham and Isaac by God. The weaning narrative furnishes a deliberate counterpoint to this failure; where the paternal relationship goes awry, the maternal relationship succeeds.[18]

The first weaning narrative reads, "When the child is to be weaned, the mother blackens her breast. It would be hard to have the breast look inviting when the child must not have it. So the child believes that the breast has changed, but the mother—she is still the same, her gaze is tender and loving as ever. How fortunate the one who did not need more terrible means to wean the child!"[19] There is a clear parallel here to the deceptive tactic that the first false Abraham employed; as he portrayed himself as an idolater and murderer rather than a genuine father, so the mother portrays herself as in a sense unappealing, rather than a mother who continues to nurse her child. But this tactic succeeds where the first false Abraham's fails.

To begin to explain the reasons for this success it is worthwhile considering what weaning simply is. A mother weans her child when he or she is too old to continue nursing. This is a step that must be taken on the part of the child for the sake of ongoing maturation. The child must be weaned; the child cannot spend his or her entire life depending on the mother in precisely this way. Naturally, there is something intimate and precious about nursing at the breast that powerfully binds a mother to her child during the child's infancy, but this is an intimacy that cannot last forever. For the child's good, the child must at some stage be denied the mother's breast. So the mother has recourse to a procedure that makes her *appear* to be less maternal, less caring and affectionate. She makes the part of her that the child can no longer have seem undesirable. This is in some ways a harsh measure, an apparent alienation of affection that the child is unlikely to understand for what it is.

As the father must at some point let go of the child's hand, so too must the mother withdraw the breast and feed the child solid food. Their relationship is thereby strained. They cannot be mother and child in the same way as they have been. But negotiating this change is absolutely necessary to the child's well-being, whether the child understands this or not. And the trick of the mother's tactic of blackening the breast is that despite this apparent change in who she is in relation to her child, "she is still the same"; that is, her love for her child is unchanged. The love of the mother for the child does not disappear, but it must express itself in a different manner and this for the sake of both mother and child's increasing selfhood: a mother cannot continue to be a mother, cannot assume the new tasks that motherhood requires with respect to her child if she nurses her child forever, and the child cannot grow to independent adulthood if he or she nurses forever.

So the experience of weaning is a difficult one, a traumatic one, one that nevertheless must be negotiated happily. In the story of the first false Abraham, Isaac's attitude toward his father is completely altered. Abraham is not the same. By attempting to maintain the appearance of concern and solicitude, he ceases to be a father at all; the mother who weans her child remains a mother, though her maternal love must find a new expression, one that appears to the child to be distant and lacking in the affection that the child once found so comforting. For their relationship to remain a happy one, the child must be convinced of the ongoing love of the mother within the alteration in the character of their relationship. This first weaning narrative sets the template that the others follow as well. As we shall see directly, each one serves as a model for how relationship is strained in a way that seems as if it is not for the good of the participants, that it involves an apparent breach of what is truly best, but ultimately how the relationship matures and progresses happily as a result of the strain that is put on it.

Faith is the means by which we go forward in life in the face of tragedy, separation, and loss. Faith in God requires us to abandon childish notions of who God is and how he works in our lives, especially how he works within suffering and setback, experiences that are so often cited as evidence against God's goodness and love for his creatures. In a similar manner, the love of a parent for a child might often mirror the apparent silence of God; as I have already pointed out, parental love must sometimes take the guise of separation. This gesture itself already mirrors the means that the divine takes to push human beings to greater intimacy with him. To see a homology, then, between the mother as God and the mother as a loving parent would be unsurprising and entirely justified by the text, and this homology persists in the remaining vignettes of the Exordium.

The Second False Abraham

In the second false Abraham vignette, silence is preserved, but the silence is deadening muteness. Abraham does not try to disclose what is afoot to Isaac. Indeed, Silentio's language emphasizes silence by dint of repetition of this key term.

> They rode along the road in silence, and Abraham stared continuously and fixedly at the ground until the fourth day, when he looked up and saw Mount Moriah far away, but once again he turned his eyes toward the ground. Silently he arranged the firewood and bound Isaac; silently he drew the knife—then he saw the ram that God had selected. This he sacrificed and went home.—From that day henceforth, Abraham was old; he could not forget that God had ordered him to do this. Isaac flourished as before, but Abraham's eyes were darkened, and he saw joy no more.[20]

I have already established that silence is not univocal in *Fear and Trembling*, and here we see a form that is clearly not the silence that God or a parent might employ in order to eventually deepen a relationship. This silence is desolate. It prefigures the discussion of demonic silence in Problema III. It is a sign not of relational strain that will soon be happily resolved but a sign of despair and defeat.

Notice how in this vignette the false Abraham stares "continuously and fixedly at the ground," not at his son. Relationship has already been preemptively fractured *before* father and son even arrive at Mount Moriah. Isaac may as well be already dead, and indeed he may as well be dead to the second false Abraham after they have journeyed home from Moriah. This Abraham is described in mechanical terms, emptied of pathos. His gestures are pro forma, lifeless, unembellished. His obedience is robotic. Even when the sacrificial ram is provided, this deliverance is unheralded and utterly without joy. Where is the relief that should accompany this moment? It has already been forestalled, for the second false Abraham has steeled himself against the loss of his son so completely that he is mirthless when he receives Isaac back. Little wonder, then, that this vignette ends as it does, with Abraham old and embittered against God, unable to forget the trauma to which he was subjected. Once again he robs himself of his own fatherhood in particular, for what kind of father can fail to take joy in a child who flourishes before his now darkened eyes? And once again this is an arguably understandable outcome; it is easy to see that one way this story might have gone wrong would indeed be for Abraham to be permanently scarred and incapable of taking thankful pleasure in the normal blessings that life has to offer.

Once again we must remind ourselves that this is an indirect lesson as to the real nature of faith. Whatever faith is, it must be the means by which we are able to retain our joy at the naturally inspiring and uplifting experiences of life. If this Abraham can no longer be happy at the prospect of his child's lively progress, then faith must secure such a good for us despite the threats to happiness that life poses. If this Abraham remains bitter at God and resentful for the trial he endured, then faith must be such as to provide us with relief at being delivered from trial and gratitude for the gifts that God dispenses in and among life's terrors. A clue to how this can be is once more provided in the weaning narrative: "When the child has grown big and is to be weaned, the mother virginally conceals her breast, and then the child no longer has a mother. How fortunate the child who has not lost his mother in some other way!"[21] When the child must be weaned, the mother withholds something of herself, but the child of course still has a mother. The child has lost the mother only in the sense of losing a certain form of relating to the mother; the mother herself has not been lost, while in the second false Abraham story Isaac has indeed lost his father, for to have a father who cannot take pleasure in the son when the son flourishes is indeed not to have a father at all.

The Third False Abraham

The third Exordium narrative finds this false Abraham trapped by guilt and self-recrimination at his own actions. Silentio dramatically omits any reference to the outcome of the story on Moriah and includes one of only two references in *Fear and Trembling* to Hagar and Ishmael. "It was early in the morning when Abraham arose: he kissed Sarah, the young mother, and Sarah kissed Isaac, her delight, her joy forever. And Abraham rode thoughtfully down the road; he thought of Hagar and the son, whom he drove out into the desert. He climbed Mount Moriah, he drew the knife."[22] In this version of the story, Silentio leaves Abraham suspended at the point of readiness, a storytelling device that keeps the reader frozen with Abraham at the worst possible moment of potential doubt. He deliberately avoids resolving the conflict at this dramatic height by giving no account of the ram or how Abraham got back down from Moriah with his son received anew. The effect is to leave the reader in suspense and to leave the third false Abraham in a state of self-conflict and self-doubt, which would have been dispelled in the fuller narrative of Genesis 22. Likewise, the reference to Hagar and Ishmael intensifies the sense of brooding and questioning, as this Abraham seems already, before arriving at Moriah, plagued by second thoughts about his actions toward his first son and his mother. Yet according to the Scriptural account, there is little reason for such doubt, which proves that the third false Abraham is already in a state of needlessly self-imposed guilt before the traumatic events of Moriah. If we read the verses subsequent to those quoted above from Genesis 21, immediately following the weaning portion of the story, we find an account of the circumstances attending Abraham's expulsion of Hagar and Ishmael during the feast given in celebration of Isaac's weaning.

> And Sarah saw the son of Hagar the Egyptian, which she had born unto Abraham, mocking. Wherefore she said unto Abraham, Cast out this bondwoman and her son: for the son of this bondwoman shall not be heir with my son, even with Isaac. And the thing was very grievous in Abraham's sight because of his son. And God said unto Abraham, Let it not be grievous in thy sight because of the lad, and because of thy bondwoman; in all that Sarah hath said unto thee, hearken unto her voice; for in Isaac shall thy seed be called. And also of the son of the bondwoman will I make a nation, because he is thy seed.

It is possible that Ishmael is mocking Isaac precisely *because* he has been weaned and can no longer be at his mother's breast. Sarah—the one who laughed at God's original promise that she would bear a son and who only a few verses prior to this moment in the story had said, "God hath made me to laugh, so that all that hear will laugh with me"—it would seem, cannot abide having her little boy *laughed at*. If I am right that the weaning narratives in *Fear and Trembling* are meant to illustrate a way by which relationships can be successfully subjected to stress and deepened thereby, then it would seem Silentio may be presenting them as such in a purposeful counterpoint to the Scriptural example of Sarah, who seems not to have navigated the weaning of her son in such a way as to be unthreatened by challenges to the loving integrity of their relationship. I will argue in the chapter dealing with Problema II that a major component of what faith accomplishes is the intensification of our relationships with the ones we love, an intensification that does not and cannot come at the expense of minimizing some loving relationships in favor of others; quite to the contrary, faith calls for all of our relationships to be intensified and for love to be multiplied. So on my reading, Sarah's love for God (presumably) and for Isaac as well should translate to increased love for Ishmael; her love for God ought not to result in a diminution of love for Ishmael.

As is so often the case in scripture (and in Kierkegaard, I would say), God turns the weakness and wickedness of humanity toward the good; he clearly tells Abraham to act as his wife wishes in this matter and that his concern for Hagar and Ishmael, while well placed, should not prevent him from entrusting them both to God's care. Just as Isaac has been promised to be the father of a great nation, so does God extend the same promise to Ishmael, and the end of chapter 21, in fact, tells how God supernaturally cares for them both in their exile in the desert. That the third false Abraham seems to be reproaching himself therefore shows that in this Abraham there is already a mistrust in God, a suspicion that he will not do as he promised; if this Abraham is worried for Hagar and Ishmael, he ought not to be, as God has already assured him that all will be well for them. In this sense the expulsion of Hagar and Ishmael does not stand in tension with the true Abraham's disposition toward Isaac, but it is a prefiguring of the events at Moriah; as Abraham obeyed God in Genesis 21 with respect to his first son, so the test put to him in Genesis 22 will be whether he will obey God with respect to his second, favored son.

Also unique to the account of the third false Abraham is a narrative section that details events placed at a point in time after Moriah, in an unspecified future. Lippitt has pointed out that the second paragraph of the third vignette is actually set temporally not at or before Moriah but at some future moment. It begins, "It was a quiet evening when Abraham rode out alone, and he rode to Mount Moriah; he threw himself down on his face, he prayed God to forgive him his sin, that he had been willing to sacrifice Isaac, that the father had forgotten his duty to his son."[23] Each of these four imaginative variations begins with the words "It was early in the morning,"[24] but this is not the morning of Abraham and Isaac's departure, this is an evening. As a guilty man often does, Abraham is returning to the scene of the crime. He implores forgiveness from God for what should not have been a sin in the first place. Both the expulsion of Hagar and Ishmael and the attempted sacrifice of Isaac had divine sanction, but this false Abraham behaves as if neither was commanded or even permitted.

Afflicted by guilt and self-accusation, this Abraham too relinquishes the privileges and burdens of fatherhood. Silentio writes that "he often rode his lonesome road, but he found no peace."[25] Again, what kind of father "often" leaves his son and wife behind for solitary journeys? This Abraham is not at peace at home, surrounded by his loving family, but is instead immersed in blame and exhibits a blameworthy inability or unwillingness to content himself with the gift of close, loving relationships. Like Odysseus, he seeks a furtive satisfaction that takes him away from the responsibilities with which he has been entrusted. Once more, this is an all-too-comprehensible reaction. Given the events of Moriah, it would not be shocking if Abraham were to blame himself for having done the unthinkable. Silentio writes, "He could not comprehend that it was a sin that he had been willing to sacrifice to God the best that he had, the possession for which he himself would have gladly died many times; and if it was a sin, if he had not loved Isaac in this manner, he could not understand that it could be forgiven, for what more terrible sin was there?"[26]

The third weaning narrative speaks to this Abraham's restlessness and ongoing sorrow: "When the child is to be weaned, the mother, too, is not without sorrow, because she and the child are more and more to be separated, because the child who first lay under her heart and later rested upon her breast will never again be so close. So they grieve together the brief sorrow. How fortunate the one who kept the child so close and did not need to grieve any more!"[27] It is quite natural that a mother grieves upon weaning her child; it is true, after all, that this is a kind of separation, but the one who successfully weans the child keeps the "child so close" even amid that separation, and note that mother and child "together" grieve what proves to be a "brief sorrow." The third false Abraham does not grieve together with his loved ones, his son and wife, but grieves alone, far away from home. And he does not mourn what should be only a brief sorrow, but gives every indication of grieving for an indefinitely long period. Faith, then, if it is to be the means by which we go forward in life in the face of sorrows, must be of such a character as to relieve us of self-accusation and to restore us to loving relationships, even if those relationships have been tried and tested. Even in the midst of what must be admitted to be certain kinds of separation—separations that life invariably imposes upon us—faith must allow us to keep one another close and to find deeper and more significant intimacy in the face of those separations, whatever form they might take.

The Fourth False Abraham

The final, shortest, and possibly most opaque of the four retellings of the Abraham story finds an Abraham who doubts at the crucial moment. The atmosphere leading up to that moment is one of order and calm. "Everything in Abraham's house was ready for the journey," we are told. Abraham and Isaac "rode along in harmony" to Mount Moriah. There, "Abraham made everything ready for the sacrifice, calmly and gently." And though Abraham draws the knife, Isaac sees that "Abraham's left hand was clenched in despair, that a shudder went through his whole body," and as a result, once they return home again to a joyful Sarah, "Isaac had lost the faith. Not a word is ever said of this in the world, and Isaac never talked to anyone about what he had seen, and Abraham did not suspect that anyone had seen it."[28] In this version, then, it seems a surface tranquility belies the shudder of despair lurking beneath. What Abraham gives with his right hand, so to speak, he takes away with his left. This breach of good order is detected by Isaac, but he never lets anyone know he has discerned it, and Abraham never imagines that it has been discerned by any, including Isaac himself. This is yet again a loss of the paternal; father and son cannot be close on these terms, the son keeping a secret from the father, the father unaware he has lost standing in the eyes of the son.

This result too is plainly foreseeable and poses no challenge to the understanding. It is quite possible that Abraham would lose confidence and courage at the decisive moment, that the brave front of resolution and conviction he put on would be undermined by an almost involuntary spasm of despair, that such weakness would be caught out by the animal alertness of his agonized child. Surely too the possibility that Isaac could come away from Moriah with his faith destroyed, while Abraham's remained strong, is one that can easily be countenanced. At the very least, we can infer from this portrayal of how things could have gone wrong that whatever faith means, it must not be capable of robbing another of faith; the faith of both participants in the relationship must be maintained.

Whether this lesson is supported by the weaning narrative is difficult to say, for it probably poses the greatest challenge to commentators. It reads, "When the child is to be weaned, the mother has stronger sustenance at hand so that the child does not perish. How fortunate the one who has this stronger sustenance at hand."[29] What are we to make of this matter of stronger sustenance? My suggestion is what we see dramatized in the fourth vignette is a common human experience: the loss of faith on the part of a child in a parent, and by extension, the loss of faith in God that can be blamed on the weakness of a parent. All children grow up to realize that their father and mother are not the people they imagine. They are not the outsized heroes of juvenile fancy, faultless and never failing in their duties. Every child is on some occasion or occasions disabused of the idealized picture they have of father and mother. In my argument, *Fear and Trembling* is in large part about how life is full of such disappointments and how faith empowers us to go on despite those disappointments. In the case of the fourth false Abraham, it seems to me we have a portrait of just such an ideal being lost, never apparently to be recovered. Isaac finds out his father is not what he thought he was: he is not the father of faith, for he cannot engender faith even in his literal son, not to mention in the promised millions of spiritual inheritors.

The weaning narrative speaks to how this disenchantment can be responded to and a sense of enchantment recovered. Where the false Abraham again fails as a father by subverting his own authority through failing to deal with a demanding situation in faith, the mother succeeds by having stronger sustenance at hand. She remains the child's mother, but the relationship is transformed; she deals the child a disappointment, she seems to be a mother no more, for the child can no longer nurse at her breast. The availability of stronger sustenance suggests the terms on which they can remain mother and child: the mother can continue to feed the child, but she nourishes with solid food, provision fit for a nascent adult, not an infant. Though she has in a sense changed—she is no longer nurse—she has in another sense remained the same—she is provider, and provider of what the child *needs*, not necessarily what the child wants.

The fourth narrative, then, is in my view the most important, for it signals the basic theme of *Fear and Trembling* in a more complete way than the others in the Exordium do. The other three weaning narratives speak of what the mother withholds in order to bring her loving relationship with her child into greater maturity and intimacy. The final one speaks to what she furnishes in order to achieve deeper relationship, and this positive gesture completes the dynamic of loss followed by recovery. By having stronger sustenance at hand, the mother acknowledges that something in the relationship with the child has already changed and cannot be put back again just as it was. The child has been weaned and now needs a new means of support. The ideal is broken, and it must be rebuilt on new terms. Once reality has disabused us of the imaginary ideal, we cannot naively recover that ideal as if it had never been tarnished. Faith rebuilds the ideal on the other side of its ruination. The baby cannot go back to the breast, but the mother can still love the child and meet the child's needs; she can be the mother again. The father will not be the man we thought he was exactly, but he can be the father in his very imperfection.

Each vignette speaks to a dimension of what faith must mean for the believer's life, but this final one is perhaps the most accomplished statement. The fourth false Abraham falters in a way that seems to contemporary readers almost impossible to avoid; how could he *not* waver at the crucial moment? And again, on the level of mere psychological description, what could be more obvious to us than the fact that a child will outgrow the fantastical vision of his or her parents? Is it not inevitable that the child will perceive the parent as a failure, as a hypocrite, or as a tyrant? Does not this disenchantment, maybe more severe than any other, like no other disappointment, taint the child's impression of the goodness of the world, and even the goodness of God? If mother and father are not perfect, then the child predictably concludes that nothing is. And clearly the child is right. But faith is that power by which we come to love and trust each other, God, the world itself as lovable though broken. The fourth Abraham and Isaac have a superficial relationship after what happens on Moriah. There is no reason to think they are not outwardly dutiful and devoted, but a coolness has set in; they are not in communication with one another. Whatever else it may do for us, faith will reconcile us to those we love, though we know they are not worthy of our love. For that purpose, though, the mother's milk of immature thinking, of childish dependence, of rose-colored idealism will have to be replaced with sturdier stuff. If faith is the task of a lifetime, as Silentio said in the preface, it will have to be nourished for a lifetime, and the faithful person cannot petulantly insist on a baby's food but will have to learn to thrive on adult provision.

The Exordium ends with a note that returns to the man for whom the Abraham story held such spellbinding fascination. "Thus and in many similar ways did the man of whom we speak ponder this event. Every time he returned from a pilgrimage to Mount Moriah, he sank down wearily, folded his hands, and said, 'No one was as great as Abraham. Who is able to understand him?'"[30] I argued earlier that the preface was meant to be a philosophical engagement with the contemporary scene and was written in philosophical terms, in large part to demonstrate that philosophy cannot succeed in understanding Abraham in the terms by which it defines comprehension. In a similar fashion, the Exordium is meant to show that literature is just as powerless as philosophy to understand

Abraham. The man spoken of in the Exordium is moved no closer to understanding Abraham as a result of considering these different possible iterations of the tale. And we know from the journal that Kierkegaard (as the passage quoted above elliptically indicates) considered other possible versions of the story that he could have included, so having too few possible retellings is not the problem; the problem is not quantitative but qualitative. The man could presumably go on endlessly rehearsing different imaginative variations of the Abraham tale and still be no closer to understanding Abraham. The design of the Exordium, then, is in large part to keep Abraham opaque to traditional literary or poetical examination.

Fear and Trembling presents itself in the subtitle as a dialectical lyric; the first two sections of the text are meant to show how dialectic on its own, and lyric on its own, cannot succeed in rendering Abraham comprehensible. As necessary preliminary movements, however, both sections cast light indirectly on their object. We do learn something of the opacity of Abraham to a certain kind of modern philosophizing from the preface, and we learn from it that within the philosophical tradition there are approximations to Abraham's faith that are relevant. We also learn something indirectly from the failed Abrahams of the Exordium. Faith does not meddle with God's commandments in the service of its own vision of what is best. Faith does not seek to protect God from others' incomprehension or mistrust of the divine. Faith does not shield others from who God is and from what he expects. All these things it faces resolutely and with a readiness to be made grateful, happy, free of bitterness and hostility, and at peace with those we love. Faith will put us to a test we cannot understand but that we will be the better for having endured cheerfully, bravely, and with thankfulness.

In every failed instance of Abraham's faith, we glimpse something of how consciousness can be "stalled out" when it relies on worldly understanding or the conscious self's own resources to cope with obstacles to human happiness. When Abraham fails, he does so because he holds to ideals of his own fatherhood that are the best that humanly devised conceptions of the good life can articulate: these conceptions, as I have admitted all along, make within the bounds of worldly understanding solid sense, but they are, in the end, doomed to failure when the humanly impossible confronts the self, the prospect of "going on" in the face of situations that from a human perspective would inevitably precipitate despair. The weaning mother in some sense wills what seem to be evils for her child; she at least concedes in the imposition of a kind of suffering on her beloved but does so in confidence that a deeper form of love and ongoing relationship will be realized across and beyond such suffering. In this sense she is like Abraham, for the knife is in her own hand.

Similarly, the power of narrative alone—or storytelling construed along lines uninformed by the prospect of faith's realization of the humanly impossible—is put into question by the Exordium. Imaginative variation, while performing a useful service, is not sufficient on its own if the full range of human possibilities, including those bequeathed by faith, is not taken into the aesthetic practice of narration in the service of edification and transformation. If Abraham's story cannot be told in such a way as to draw out the most profound dimensions of his faith, then it remains *only* a story.

4 A Rhetorical Rehearsal

Eulogy on Abraham

The preface and exordium are intended to situate *Fear and Trembling* with respect to genre and communicative methodology; they inform the attentive reader that the text will be neither straightforwardly philosophical in the modern style, nor will it be an exercise in conventional storytelling. The eulogy on Abraham is, in part, intended to show that neither will *Fear and Trembling* be a formulaic oration in Abraham's praise. Normally this section is interpreted at face value, as an exercise in singing Abraham's praises: a eulogy or "tribute" as Walsh translates it,[1] or a "speech in praise of Abraham" as Hannay renders it[2]; all of these imply a rhetorical work that is designed to highlight only the good things about the person to whom it is devoted. And indeed, the eulogy seems to be just such a piece of writing. My interpretation, however, dictates that this section be understood a bit more indirectly. It has the form of a eulogy, and it does present Abraham as only unfailing in faith (the one place in *Fear and Trembling* where Abraham's lack of faith in taking Hagar to be the mother of his child is mentioned at all is not in the eulogy, and even there Silentio blames Sarah rather than Abraham himself for having vacillated in his reliance on God's promise).[3] The way the eulogy is constructed, though, gives the sensitive interpreter pause; the eulogy is another preliminary movement, one that, like the others, advances its message with considerable subtlety. My argument is that the eulogy is meant to expose the inadequacy of the method of rhetorical devices to communicate the true meaning of Abraham's faith, and more broadly, to expose the inadequacy of poetry to inspire anyone to true faith themselves. The techniques of "the poet" cannot account for how one comes to faith any more than philosophy can; nor can they inspire another to have faith any more than philosophy can; nor can they help us "understand" Abraham any more than literary methods or philosophical arguments can. The general assumption of commentators is that when Silentio in this section begins speaking about the relationship of the poet and hero, that he is finally commencing the main business of the book by positioning himself as the poet to Abraham's hero. Silentio is thus the poet, on the general consensus, Abraham the hero, and now *Fear and Trembling* really gets going as Silentio spends the rest of the eulogy poetizing about Abraham and celebrating his faith.

However, there is no good textual reason to conclude that Silentio is "the poet." Certainly his approach partakes of poetic conventions, but so too does it partake of philosophical argument and literary recounting of narratives. None of these genres is adequate on its own, and *Fear and Trembling* aims past all of them. The eulogy remains purposefully abstract, like the discussion of "the man" in the Exordium. Silentio is content to speak in the first person in the preface and in the preliminary expectoration. If Kierkegaard wanted Silentio's eulogy to be in his voice, he would have made it so. But I submit that this caginess in identifying Silentio with "the poet" in the eulogy is part of an overall strategy to keep the preliminary movements open-ended and on the level of methodological experimentation. In each of them, Silentio toys with different approaches to the problem of Abraham and employs different styles and means of writing. In the eulogy, he experiments with a classical style of rhetoric and adopts the means of a "poet" engaged in panegyric. He does this to show the limits and shortcomings of this approach, as he does with the preface and exordium. While there are themes of recurrent value first introduced in the eulogy that are repeated throughout the rest of *Fear and Trembling*, the form in which they are presented mandates that the reader take into consideration the possibility that these themes, while important, are put forward in a potentially misleading counterfeit form, a form that is very close to the way in which they will be taken up in the Problemata but here given a rhetorical gloss.

I have already given reasons why Silentio himself cannot be immediately assumed to be a "poet" in any traditional sense. The eulogy provides additional justifications for this claim. Contrary to the critical consensus that Silentio is "the poet," in point of fact "the poet" in the traditional sense is almost *satirized* by Silentio in these pages; the principal concern that is put forward by Silentio against the poet is that the poet attains only to "admiration" of his object and can thereby do no more than preserve the hero's memory. But this act of poetic preservation is just that, a kind of pickling of the hero that transforms the hero into an *aesthetic object*. This object has its usefulness to be sure, but it cannot enliven another's faith; it cannot by itself inspire the beholder of the object to *act upon* the object's example.[4] We have seen already from the preface the implication that Silentio's true interest is not in explaining faith but in how one becomes faithful, and we know that Kierkegaard writes in order to awaken in his audience the need to press themselves on this very issue, to ask themselves whether they truly have the faith they profess and if not, why not, and whether they intend ultimately to *do* anything about faith. The "poet" of the eulogy is not able to do this for his readers. Instead he is a Romantic figure, one who imagines that his happiness can consist in serving the hero's memory rather than imitating his example, and who believes that he is the arbiter of the meaning of the hero and by extension that it is through his creative effort that he gives meaning to life at all. This figure is not Silentio, and Kierkegaard himself does not think such a figure is capable of delivering on his promises.

Rhetoric in the *Phaedrus* and the Eulogy

That this is so can be argued by a potentially rewarding comparison with Plato's *Phaedrus*, which is obviously in the background of the eulogy, a connection established by Silentio's reference at the end of the speech to Abraham's priority in having felt and borne witness to "that prodigious passion that disdains the terrifying battle with the raging elements and the forces of creation in order to contend with God . . . that supreme passion, the holy, pure, and humble expression for the divine madness that was admired by the pagans"[5] a phrase that, as the Hongs point out, is almost certainly attributable to the *Phaedrus*.[6] It must first be observed that Silentio does not attribute divine madness of the sort admired by the pagans to Abraham exactly; rather, he attributes to Abraham the holy and purified form of such a madness. Silentio therefore links Abraham's passionate faith to the divine madness admired by the pagans but does not equate it with divine madness. As is so often the case in the authorship and in *Fear and Trembling* specifically, Kierkegaard establishes connections between revealed religion and pagan wisdom, generally with an eye to showing how the former takes up, transforms, and surpasses in beauty and esteem the latter. So Abraham's faith is being praised not as divine madness per se but as the religious version of the *Phaedrus*'s divine madness.[7] Second, it must be acknowledged that the theme of divine madness, which in its highest form, according to the *Phaedrus*, is understood as love, and in particular the philosophical love of Beauty itself as opposed to sensate love of beautiful things, is just the beginning of a thematic and formal comparison between the eulogy and the *Phaedrus*.

If we survey Kierkegaard's journal, we find that the second speech of Socrates from the *Phaedrus*[8] was on his mind prior to the writing of *Fear and Trembling*. In 1841, we read him referring to "the great picture in *Phaedrus* in which the fourth kind of madness—the madness of love—is described, a description which is just as chaste as it is voluptuous, because voluptuousness is at all times conquered by the chasteness; the voluptuousness is the strong coloring. It ends with a prayer. The whole passage must be examined . . . What is expressed here is love's moment of stimulation, which is so incomparably described."[9] Abraham's greatness is praised, as we see from the beginning of the eulogy, in part in terms of his love, so indeed the eulogy as a whole makes covert reference to Plato's account of divine madness. "No one who was great in the world will be forgotten, but everyone was great in his own way, and everyone in proportion to the greatness of that which *he loved*. He who loved himself became great by virtue of himself, and he who loved other men became great by his devotedness, but he who loved God became the greatest of all."[10]

Besides the potential analogy between the different objects of love and the ideals that Silentio is constantly working with in this text—the one who loves himself aims at the aesthetic ideal, the one who loves others aims at the ethical ideal, the one who loves God aims at the religious ideal—there may also be a larger point at work about the limited nature of Plato's treatment of love in the *Phaedrus*, against which Silentio is deliberately crafting his own rhetorical discourse in the most ambitious direction he is capable of moving. In another journal entry from 1841, Kierkegaard noticed, "How abstract Socrates' dialectic was can also be seen in the basic law for the dialectical movement, which is that only two things can be the opposite of each other (*principium exclusi medii inter duo contradictoria*)" and then provided a citation to the *Phaedrus*.[11] Without delving into the extraordinary complexity of the debates in Golden Age Copenhagen among the Danish and German Hegelians over the meaning of the phrase "principium exclusi medii inter duo contradictoria,"[12] I will simply point out that based on this journal entry it would seem that Kierkegaard himself was dissatisfied with the abstract nature of the Socratic dialectic, which recognized only the divergence between insanity or madness as an unqualifiedly bad state of affairs and divine madness.

In the *Phaedrus*, Socrates distinguishes between two principles of dialectics, which he advocates over rhetoric. The first is "the comprehension of scattered particulars in one idea; as in our definition of love, which whether true or false certainly gave clearness and consistency to the discourse, the speaker should define his several notions and so make his meaning clear."[13] The second principle "is that of division into species according to the natural formation, where the joint is, not breaking any part as a bad carver might." This process of division led to a necessary distinction within "unreason" between the "evil or left-handed love which he [the speaker] justly reviled" and "on the right side . . . another love, also having the same name, but divine, which the speaker held up before us and applauded and affirmed to be the author of the greatest benefits."[14] Those who are able to perform both processes Socrates praises: "I am myself a great lover of these processes of division and generalization; they help me to speak and to think. And if I find any man who is able to see 'a One and Many' in nature, him I follow, and 'walk in his footsteps as if he were a god.' And those who have this art, I have hitherto been in the habit of calling dialecticians; but God knows whether the name is right or not."[15]

Leaving aside the question of whether Kierkegaard is insufficiently appreciative of the possibility that Socrates is in fact endorsing a version of dialectical reasoning sufficiently subtle to embrace both divisions and thus end up being more complex than he seems to be aware, we can nevertheless read the eulogy as if it aspires to surpass the arid opposition between generalization and division when it comes to the two forms of madness, the divine form of which not only encompasses love itself but also prophecy, mystical insight, and poetic inspiration.[16] The rhetoric of the eulogy, then, at its best might strive to overcome the traditional failure of all rhetoric when applied to Christian faith. Kierkegaard wrote in his journal, again in reference to the *Phaedrus*, in 1852 that

> all the ancients (Plato—many places in *Phaedrus*, *Gorgias*, etc.; Aristotle in *Rhetoric*; the later ancients after Plato and Aristotle) were unanimous, as were other later ones who thought about the matter, that the potency of eloquence is based upon probability. Christianity is the paradox. When it came into the world there was no eloquence (for the apostles and martyrs were far from being eloquent speakers; their lives were paradoxes and their words paradoxes just as Christianity is) . . . Christianity is now made probable—and so *eo ipso* the rhetoricians flourish. With reasons upon reasons, they are able to depict and depict and bellow and make all Christianity so probable, so probable—that it most likely is no longer Christianity . . . Christianity as probability—and served by rhetoricians—thus Christianity is abolished.[17]

So if rhetoric—the genre that is so clearly on display in the eulogy—is incapable of communicating the paradoxical nature of faith, then this is yet another reason to regard the work of the eulogy as not the first contribution to a full and proper exposition of Abraham's faith but as another indirection, another negative attempt to show what faith is *not*.

That being said, as conceded from the beginning, there are points put forward in the eulogy that return in later parts of the book, so valid considerations can be gleaned from this rich portion of the text. As in the earlier preparatory material, the eulogy cannot be simply discarded as a wholly fruitless venture but must be read as making an indirect contribution to the correct understanding of Abraham. As with all rhetorical exercises, it has its problems, but as a unique Kierkegaardian contribution to the rhetorical tradition, it stretches the genre to its breaking point in the effort to get it to "fit" the subject matter at hand. Again, if we refer to the *Phaedrus*, once Socrates delineates what he means by dialectic, he and Phaedrus agree that the rhetoricians have no skill in that very dialectical reasoning.[18] Their subsequent search, then, for what rhetoric consists in reveals that, according to the teaching manuals on this art, a speech should begin with an exordium[19] and contain as well a "statement of facts, and upon that witnesses; thirdly, proofs; fourthly, probabilities are to come" and finally "confirmation."[20] As we shall see shortly, the eulogy also contains a preamble, a statement of facts or narrative that rehearses the life of the subject of the speech and his great deeds, and an appeal to witnesses, who, in the case of the eulogy, are actually the readers whom Silentio directly addresses. The place of a proof or probability in the eulogy is much harder to nail down, but given what Kierkegaard said about probability in his journal entry on rhetoric and faith, it is obvious that Kierkegaard knew the place of probability in oratory and questioned its suitability for the topic of faith. Thus, in a sense, the whole of the eulogy could consist in probability.

These elements of rhetoric, however, Socrates and Phaedrus agree, supply only the requisite parts of rhetorical practice and do not define the art in itself.[21] To be a true orator, one must know not just techniques but orient his speech by the light of the truth; otherwise "a skillful rhetorician has no need of truth—for that in courts of law men literally care nothing about truth, but only about conviction."[22] Rhetorical strategies are useful for bringing about conviction, but in themselves they are indifferent to the truth and need not be related to it in order to be effective. According to Socrates, conviction "is based on probability, to which he who would be a skilful [*sic*] orator should therefore give his whole attention. And they say also that there are cases in which the actual facts, if they are improbable, ought to be withheld, and only the probabilities should be told either in accusation or defence, and that always in speaking, the orator should keep probability in view, and say good-bye to the truth."[23]

This Socratic point from the *Phaedrus* is doubtless the inspiration for Kierkegaard's complaint in his journal that rhetoric can never be successfully partnered with Christian faith. If the business of rhetoric is probabilities rather than the truth (so much so that inconvenient truths can, according to the demands of oratorical practice, be strategically omitted) and the eulogy is an exercise in rhetoric, then so too the reader of *Fear and Trembling* should be prepared to regard this experiment as having less than a fully straightforward aim. Insofar, however, as rhetoric can be pressed into higher service to the truth or even to God, then it should not be surprising to discover Silentio stretching the conventional rules of the speechmaker in aspiration of the divine. As Socrates concludes with respect to the best use of rhetoric, "Unless a man estimates the various characters of his hearers and is able to divide all things into classes and to comprehend every one under single ideas, he will never be a skilful [*sic*] rhetorician even within the limits of human power. And this skill he will not attain without a great deal of trouble, which a good man ought to undergo, not for the sake of speaking and acting before men, but in order that he may be able to say what is acceptable to God and always to act acceptably to Him as far as in him lies."[24]

This, then, is the key to reading the eulogy properly: as an effort to tell the story of Abraham in accord with the rules of rhetoric—inclusive of a preamble, a recitation of the facts, and an appeal to witnesses—it will be subject to the limitations of any such example of the genre, but insofar as its rhetoric is illumined by something of the truth, it will, at its best, have some positive contribution to make the reader's understanding as well. The eulogy's purpose is thus broadly the same as the other introductory sections: just as the preface identifies the most valuable moments in the history of philosophy—an enterprise that is otherwise unable to make sense of faith—and the exordium negatively limns the proper narrative retelling of Abraham's tale, so the eulogy with its own methods and devices captures something of the way to tell Abraham's tale without conceding that rhetoric as such is able to attain the truth of faith. How this works in the way the eulogy actually plays out is that it subverts itself in the end and frames its valuable insights with unresolved ambiguities, the sorts of ambiguities that are necessarily the result of rhetoric only partially moored by truth.

Consider the text itself. The eulogy begins with a florid, rhetorically overblown passage worth quoting in full:

> If a human being did not have an eternal consciousness, if underlying everything there were only a wild, fermenting power that writhing in dark passions produced everything, be it significant or insignificant, if a vast, never appeased emptiness hid beneath everything, what would life be then but despair? If such were the situation, if there were no sacred bond that knit humankind together, if one generation emerged after another like forest foliage, if one generation succeeded another like the singing of birds in the forest, if a generation passed through the world as a ship through the sea, as wind through the desert, an unthinking and unproductive performance, if an eternal oblivion, perpetually hungry, lurked for its prey and there were no power strong enough to wrench that away from it—how empty and devoid of consolation life would be! But precisely for that reason it is not so, and just as God created man and woman, so he created the hero and the poet or orator.[25]

Kierkegaard engages in this kind of purple prose often enough, especially in his edifying discourses, which he himself said were meant to be performed aloud, in order to secure the rhetorical effect of heaping up clauses and qualifications and perambulations around a central theme. Commentators rarely note, though, how intrusive and surprising an outburst like this is upon what has been heretofore a relatively restrained composition. It is no mistake that at the end of this passage Silentio equates the "poet" with an "orator," for the reader is now all of a sudden listening to a speech indeed. We are abruptly thrust from the comparative austerity of the exordium into a veritable rhetorical hothouse.[26]

As to the content of this opening salvo, it speaks of the possibility that life is void of meaning, that human history could merely be the brute succession of one generation after the next, without significance or intelligibility, that reality is, at bottom, vacant despair. Without benefit of transition or explanation, the listener is assured that "but precisely for that reason it is not so." What "reason" Silentio has in mind he does not say. This is not argumentation or storytelling, it is waxing rhapsodic. The prospect of the meaninglessness of existence is able to be raised only to be rapidly cast aside again because the poet is waiting in the wings to secure life's meaningfulness. The poet and hero, as indispensable to humanity as man and woman, are twinned in a relationship of mutual dependence. "The poet or orator can do nothing that the hero does; he can only admire, love, and delight in him. Yet he, too, is happy—no less than that one is, for the hero is, so to speak, his better nature, with which he is enamored—yet happy that the other is not himself, that his love can be admiration."[27]

At this point, the acute reader's suspicions should be raised. It is perhaps reasonable to portray the poet as incapable of doing heroic things and to say that he can only admire the hero, but why should anyone conclude that the poet is therefore just as happy as the hero? Only by an act of self-congratulation that would itself border on the heroic could the poet elevate himself to equal status with the hero. Is it right for anyone, poet or not, to imagine himself satisfactorily happy if he is only an admirer of the heroic and not a doer of the heroic, if only a doer on his or her own small scale or in his or her own individual way? Can admiration, appreciation of an edifying spectacle without allowing the example thereof to be personally transformative, be sufficient for happiness? This is not to say that the poet has no significant role to play or that the poet's work in service of the hero is of no value, but particularly when the reader is told that the poet is "recollection's genius" we might wonder whether the poet's service is the highest that can be performed, and correlatively, whether the poet as described in the eulogy doesn't overrate his or her own value to the hero and the meaningfulness of human existence. As Silentio will say later in the first Problema, "A poet is not an apostle; he drives out devils only by the power of the devil."[28] The devil of despair will still have to be cast out, but that work will not be done by "the poet."

That the poet is "recollection's genius" suggests that he is something of an idealizer. At the very beginning of *Repetition*, we read the aesthetically sophisticated Constantin Constantius contrasting recollection with repetition in terms of the former's idealization of actuality in contrast to the latter's genuine embrace of actuality amid change. "Recollection," he writes, "is a discarded garment that does not fit, however beautiful it is, for one has outgrown it," while "repetition is an indestructible garment that fits closely and tenderly, neither binds nor sags." Or again, according to another image, "recollection is a beautiful old woman with whom one is never satisfied at the moment," while "repetition is a beloved wife of whom one never wearies." Finally, in the third image that illumines the contrast, "recollection is petty travel money that does not satisfy; but repetition is the daily bread that satisfies with blessing."[29] What these images suggest is that recollection is always "behind" the inexorable forward march of actual existence, always an ideal that has immediately lost its applicability or desirability: a beautiful garment that has already been outgrown, an attractive woman whose presence does not satisfy, the paltry means supplied for a journey that will not take the traveler the entire way. Repetition is ever old and ever new at once, the moment's satisfaction, the pleasant and needful. In this sense repetition is another key word (and this should not be surprising) for the reconciliation of the ethically demanded and the aesthetically satisfying. If the poet is recollection's genius, then, one might again ask if this form of genius is capable of explaining faith, which correlates to repetition, a category that "is and remains" religious and thus out of Constantius's reach.[30] The "genius" of recollection at key moments in the following section does yield significant insights, but more often than that it issues in confusion and irresolvable ambiguity. The "faithful service" of the poet remains *rhetorical.*

That life is not merely the product of "an eternal oblivion" and not "empty and devoid of consolation" is true, both according to Silentio and Kierkegaard himself surely, but the question is whether these opening assertions are *proven* by the orator or simply asserted as part of the requisite preamble to the speech he must make. It seems more likely that the truth-value of these claims is not what is preeminently at stake and instead the formal demand for a speech to grab the audience's attention from the outset with an inspirational sentiment that will set the stage fittingly for the expressions to come.

This is the first such moment in which the eulogy adheres to formulaic demands, a procedure that I maintain Silentio adopts strategically in order to demonstrate the eventual failure of the genre to communicate Abraham's story properly. That strategic failure is exhibited in the ambiguities of the eulogy as a whole, which begins with a piece of florid overbidding, as we have seen, and ends with a deflating sense that the whole exercise has been unnecessary. Proceeding in our reading of the text itself, picking up as the preamble continues, we find Silentio claiming that "if [the poet] remains true to his love in this way, if he contends night and day against the craftiness of oblivion, which wants to trick him out of his hero, then he has fulfilled his task, then he is gathered together with the hero . . . Therefore, no one who was great will be forgotten, and even though it takes time, even though a cloud of misunderstanding takes away the hero, his lover will nevertheless come, and the longer the passage of time, the more faithfully he adheres to him."[31] Just in this short passage, then, we have a confusing tension between the assertion that the craftiness of oblivion seeks to trick the poet out of the hero and the forceful declaration that "therefore" (again with no obvious antecedent to license the "therefore") no one who was great will succumb to oblivion. The tension is only intensified by a parallel declaration near the end of the eulogy to the effect that "Centuries have passed since those days, but you have no need of a late lover to snatch your memory from the power of oblivion,"[32] so here again at both the beginning and end of the eulogy there seems to be some irresolution over whether the hero's being forgotten is really an imminent danger, one the poet or orator is meant to forestall.[33]

The strategic failure of the eulogy is further evidenced by what Lippitt calls "a series of *prima facie* bizarre claims"[34] about the greatness of the hero in proportion to what he loves, expects, and that with which he struggles. It has already been observed that the threefold structure of love can be seen as another version of the triangulation of aesthetic, ethical, and religious ideals; the same structure is evinced with respect to expectancy and struggle. "One became great by expecting the possible [the aesthetic ideal], another by expecting the eternal [the ethical ideal]; but he who expected the impossible became the greatest of all [the religious ideal]."[35] Furthermore, "he who struggled with the world became great by conquering the world [the aesthetic ideal], and he who struggled with himself became great by conquering himself [the ethical ideal], but he who struggled with God became the greatest of all [the religious ideal]."[36] Viewed this way, it might be overstating matters to call these claims "bizarre," inasmuch as they can be read as generalizations about the relationship among the three ideals that form the triangulated nexus of *Fear and Trembling* as a whole.

Lippitt is right, though, that they don't stand up to critical examination. But if I am right that the eulogy is an exercise in rhetoric, they don't have to. They just have to be plausible and sufficiently richly embroidered to persuade the hearer. Lippitt attributes the strangeness of these claims to Silentio's "poetic licence,"[37] but it would be more accurate to attribute the strangeness to his indulgence in oratorical convention. The substance of these claims may be quite correct, but the point of advancing them is not necessarily to inform the reader more deeply but to celebrate in a poetic and somewhat overblown manner the varieties of human greatness, which even here are being distinguished from one another in order to negatively throw light on the religious ideal. That this is happening is easy to miss given the overriding purpose of the eulogy's preamble, which is less to do with rigorous dialectical and logical demonstration and more to do with capturing the audience's attention and directing the reader's mind to an inspirational vision of great men and their great deeds.[38]

The Facts of Abraham's Case

In keeping with the demands of rhetoric, this high-flying and attention-grabbing introduction to the speech is followed by another classic element of oratory: the narrative or statement of facts. In classical rhetoric, an indispensable part of a eulogizing speech is a recitation of the life of the one being lauded, an account of their origins and achievements.[39] Silentio follows this paradigm to the letter, reminding his reader of the history of Abraham's life prior to the crucial test of Moriah.[40] Again, in this section of the eulogy, valuable insights can be identified, but the primary purpose is to adhere to the rules of the genre of eulogy in order to demonstrate the inapplicability of those rules to the Abraham story. "By faith," Silentio reminds us, "Abraham emigrated from the land of his fathers and became an alien in the promised land. He left one thing behind, took one thing along: he left behind his worldly understanding, and he took along his faith."[41] The first of Abraham's great deeds of faith, then, was his responsiveness to God's original call that he forsake his ancestral home and venture into unknown territory. This incident from his life correlates to the point above about love and is contrasted to an unnamed "another" who also loved and lost and found consolation in his lamentation.[42] In defiance of "worldly understanding" or human visions of the good that emphasize the belongingness of the individual to her designated place, Abraham abandoned the comforts of his own place in favor of a place of promise.

The wisdom of the world dictates that one is born naturally to a place where she stands to inherit the benefits of her ancestral culture and its traditions and practices and is meant to contribute to the posterity of her place and people, even unto her descendants. In short, worldly understanding teaches us to accept contentedly (or perhaps, to use a more provocative term that will be fully explained in the next chapter, to resign ourselves to) the ideal vision of ourselves and our place among others that is bequeathed to us by the accident of our birth. Faith contradicts this seemingly natural vision of what the good life entails and imposes upon Abraham the task of living as "an alien in the promised land," where "there was nothing that reminded him of what he cherished, but everything by its newness tempted his soul to sorrowful longing."[43] That Abraham did not give way to sorrowful longing is perhaps an even more important component of his faith than having left behind his worldly understanding.

It is important to notice Silentio's emphasis here on the fact that Abraham lived as a stranger in the land that had allegedly been promised to him, so Abraham is already experienced in the lurking suspicion that his faith is being "mocked." "As a matter of fact," Silentio writes, "if he had been an exile, banished from God's grace, he could have better understood it."[44] But Abraham is not an exile; he is an alien in a land that is his *only by promise*; it is not "his" in any way that worldly understanding would recognize, but it is his by faith. His faithful response to God's call has caused him to resign a place that the world would be happy to call his for another place that is "his" only in a highly qualified way or according to a revised understanding of what constitutes possession or inheritance; what looks to worldly understanding like exile, merely being banished from where you belong, is in fact a new reward, possession, and blessed home. And Abraham's response to this changed, unworldly state of affairs is a joyful one: "There is no dirge by Abraham. It is human to lament, human to weep with one who weeps, but it is greater to have faith, more blessed to contemplate the man of faith."[45] That lamentation and expression of sorrow are inappropriate in Abraham's case is a theme that is repeated frequently in what is to come (as well as being suggested by the exordium) and is therefore another element of the eulogy that stands as a positive contribution to understanding Abraham's faith.

The next incident in the statement of facts is Abraham's faithful reception of the promise that through him all the generations of the world would be blessed, a promise that by the standards of worldly understanding became harder to believe in as time passed. This incident is correlated with the point about expectancy and is also contrasted to a nameless individual who likewise entertained an expectancy but was not related to this expectancy in the same joyfully faithful manner as Abraham was. This individual, Silentio says, "sorrowed, and his sorrow did not disappoint him as life had done."[46] The reference to disappointment recalls one of the primary concerns of the text as a whole, according to this interpretation: the role of faith in ameliorating the disappointing and heartbreaking vicissitudes of life. Sorrow is a potential consolation for life's disappointment, something that Silentio will grant time and again in his discussions of the tragic hero and of resignation, but he takes this occasion to repeat the point that it is not an ingredient of faith. Another distinctive element of faith is mentioned in connection with expectancy that we must add to the issue of sorrow as being merely human, and that is the relation to time, a relation that the term "expectancy" perhaps signals especially effectively.[47]

Four times in this paragraph Silentio uses the phrase "time passed" in connection with Abraham's patient awaiting of the promise of fatherhood; his expectancy thereof seems to be indifferent to the passage of time. Just as it is human to sorrow, it would seem it is equally human to "gloomily count the days" or "stop the course of the sun."[48] And just as it would have been better according to worldly understanding to be an exile, so too it would have been better in human estimation to *not* be God's chosen one. "What does it mean to be God's chosen?" Silentio asks rhetorically. "Is it to be denied in youth one's youthful desire in order to have it fulfilled with great difficulty in one's old age?"[49] As we will see momentarily, the answer to this question seems to be no, to be chosen is not merely to be denied in youth and to await fulfillment in old age. This question is not immediately answered, though. Instead it precipitates another crucially important insight from the eulogy that echoes in later passages.

Recalling the alternate versions of the Abraham story from the exordium, Silentio imagines that Abraham could have simply resigned his desire for an heir and done so without resentment or insincerity. Had Abraham simply concluded that, after all, "maybe it is not your will that this should be," then, "he would not have been forgotten, he would have saved many by his example, but he still would not have become the father of faith, for it is great to give up one's desire, but it is greater to hold fast to it after having given it up; it is great to lay hold of the eternal, but it is greater to hold fast to the temporal after having given it up."[50] Readers of *Fear and Trembling* will see this logic repeated in many ways on many occasions throughout the rest of the book; while this is not the first anticipation of the distinction between resignation and faith that is so vital to the work as a whole, it is perhaps the most complete anticipation yet. There is something memorably great about one who resigns her desire and does so openly and without anger, but this too is not the greatness of faith, which paradoxically holds fast to what it gives up. Explaining how this happens is the task of the next chapter, but we do a get a clue here in the form of the reference to the temporal and the eternal.

We have already seen that the reality of time passing has been a potential obstruction to Abraham's living out of his faith; as "time passed" it became, by human standards, more and more difficult to believe. But for Kierkegaard in general, the passage of time is not decisive for the prospect of faith. Most notably in the final chapter of *Philosophical Fragments*, Climacus maintains that there is no particular advantage to being temporally closer to the life of Christ when it comes to the possibility of believing in Christ's revelation of the truth.[51] The key is to be prepared within temporality for the inbreaking of the eternal, to be ready for "the fullness of time"[52] or the moment,[53] a posture that by no means requires abandoning the temporal, quite the opposite. It is to remain forever young, even as time passes. "Then came the fullness of time. If Abraham had not had faith, then Sarah would surely have died of sorrow, and Abraham, dulled by grief, would not have understood the fulfillment but would have smiled at it as at a youthful dream."[54]

Without faith, even the fulfillment of the promise would have been *unrecognizable*. This is because, as Climacus tells us, "the wonder *is* not immediately but is only for faith, inasmuch as the person who does not believe does not see the wonder."[55] For the wonder even to be cognized as a wonder, the would-be recipient of the wonder must have faith;[56] with respect to the believer's relationship to time then, he lives according not to the passage of the years but according to the overshadowing of the years by the eternal. This is no mere willful optimism or stoical pessimism; quite to the contrary, "he who always hopes for the best grows old and is deceived by life, and he who is always prepared for the worst grows old prematurely, but he who has faith—he preserves an eternal youth."[57] What is therefore wondrous in Abraham's reception of the promise of God is not primarily that the promise is fulfilled outwardly, that as God had promised, Abraham and Sarah conceived in their (measured by the human reckoning of time's passing) old age, but rather that the parents were prepared by faith to receive the gift of God. "Outwardly, the wonder of it is that it happened according to their expectancy; in the more profound sense, the wonder of faith is that Abraham and Sarah were young enough to desire and that faith had preserved their desire and thereby their youth."[58] For this reason Silentio is able to say that Abraham had "fought with time and kept his faith," but even so, "all the frightfulness of the struggle was concentrated in one moment"[59] yet to come.

The course of Abraham's life, then, is not marked out by the passage of time reckoned as one year mechanically proceeding another but by the signposts of the moment, by the fullness of time as it is realized in the holding together of eternity and temporality, never giving up on the temporal but living it through its pervasion by the eternal. By human standards, Abraham's life consists of "seventy years of trusting expectancy, the brief joy over the fulfillment of faith,"[60] but Abraham's true spiritual itinerary is marked by moments whose distance from one another in the passage of time is immaterial to his faithful conduct. Indeed, living moment by moment, with the conviction that the passage of time is not a matter of mute and brute succession but is overshadowed by the eternal and hence charged with significance, invalidates the very idea of "going further." There is no further to go than to inhabit the moment. Hence the irrelevance of Abraham's advanced age and Isaac's youth.

The Knife in Abraham's Hand

The rhetorical force of the eulogy is compounded by the bathetic references to Abraham as a "venerable old man" and to Isaac as "the innocent child."[61] The appeals to sympathy for a sorrowing old man may also recall once again Plato's *Phaedrus*, wherein Socrates sarcastically praises Thrasymachus's oratory in these terms: "For the 'sorrows of a poor old man,' or any other pathetic case, no one is better than the Chalcedonian giant; he can put a whole company of people into a passion and out of one again by his mighty magic, and is first-rate at inventing or disposing of any sort of calumny on any grounds or none."[62] There is again reason to think here that the appeals to the reader's emotions are qualified by the rhetorical strategy of the passage—for the rhetor, the "gray hairs" of Abraham and alleged youth of Isaac are prime material for expatiation, and indeed from this point for about another page, Silentio launches into another series of overwrought apostrophes and pronouncements of woe.

Once again, however, it is important to notice the substantive points that escape attention amid a new outburst of overheated lamentation from Silentio. Amid all the stirring of distress, two issues are easily missed. First, Silentio raises his audience to a fever pitch with the assertion that "Abraham was God's chosen one, and it was the Lord who imposed the ordeal."[63] One of the points that Silentio seems to want to underscore is that there can be no mistaking the fact that God is the instigator of the trial. Not only does this indicate that Kierkegaard has almost no interest in this text in entering into an epistemological debate about religious knowledge, it goes further than this to suggest that he is trying to create a sort of "worst-case scenario" for Abraham, as if actively refusing the potential consolation that would be won by admitting that Abraham has made some kind of mistake. That it is God testing him and not a delusion is a given for the argumentation of *Fear and Trembling*. And surely it is rhetorically interesting to emphasize this aspect of Abraham's drama. If we keep in mind the rhetorical purpose of the eulogy, then few dimensions of the trial are more dramatically compelling than this one. But the final significance of the fact that it is God that imposes the trial upon Abraham may involve nothing more than that epistemological point, that Abraham simply cannot be in error about the source of the ordeal he faces. Interpretations that write off Abraham's act as nothing more than the product of a necessarily delusional fantasy or illusory dilemma are thereby discounted.[64]

The second issue is a more substantive question, and that is whether it makes a serious difference to the logic of *Fear and Trembling* that God is the one who ordains the trial.

On this score Kevin Hoffman is surely the most insightful commentator, and he teases out the senses in which the knife being in Abraham's own hand both does and does not matter. As he observes, and as we will see in the next chapter, some of Silentio's most memorable and important illustrations of the life of faith omit any explicit reference to God.[65] Indeed, this is perhaps the *only* point in the text where such strong emphasis is placed on the fact that it is God who is compelling the sacrifice. Silentio writes, "Many a father has thought himself deprived of every hope for the future when he lost his child, the dearest thing in the world to him; nevertheless, no one was the child of promise in the sense in which Isaac was that to Abraham. Many a father has lost his child, but then it was God, the unchangeable, inscrutable will of the Almighty, it was his hand that took it. Not so with Abraham! A harder test was reserved for him, and Isaac's fate was placed, along with the knife, in Abraham's hand."[66] Again, this is a rhetorically compelling distinction, but it is made only here. Given the isolation of this observation, then, and the communicative context in which it is placed, Hoffman is likely right that divine agency does not make a determinative difference to the overall message of the book. "But what if explicit divine agency drops out of the equation?" Hoffman asks. "That is, if God does not demand this, does life, does fate? The implicit answer seems affirmative. Assuming this, to the degree that earthly felicity depends on a schedule of goods beyond our control, life may present each of us with a test similar to Abraham's. Abraham's ordeal, then, is not dissimilar to facing a terminal illness, or death generally, one's own or that of a beloved."[67]

At the same time, Hoffman seems to discern a sense in which the knife being in Abraham's own hand does matter: "Abraham is so courageously prepared to face threats to his happiness that he makes ready to accept his son's death by his own hand. This is a crucial part of the story because it forces the issue by rendering the possibility of loss especially clear and present. For in going this far, Abraham must believe the threat is particularly real."[68] Partly this is because on Hoffman's account, the outcome of Abraham's decision is uncertain. As I will argue in the next chapter, the outcome both does and does not matter with respect to understanding Abraham's faith. But at the very least the awareness that the knife is in Abraham's own hand militates at this stage against interpretations that seek to "soften" the dilemma. "Here it is difficult," Hoffman writes, "not to be distracted by the knife. It is raised, no question about it; but de Silentio claims that the interior structure of Abraham's dual belief suspends his desire and obligation to love Isaac without thereby canceling that same desire and obligation. That is, he remains emotionally prepared for and invested in receiving

Isaac back."[69] This is a sound description of what is going on at this stage in the argument of *Fear and Trembling*; a full account will have to take in resignation and its relationship to faith, something Hoffman does in his article and that I will delay discussing until the next chapter. For now, though, we can observe that the knife being in Abraham's own hand suggests at the least a kind of preemptive readiness on the knight of faith's part to sacrifice. We can ask, though, with Hoffman, "what positive virtue there could be in being so starkly prepared."[70] In the case of the lad and the princes, which I discuss in the next chapter, there is no reference to God having kept the lovers apart, while it is clearly still possible for the lad to resign the princess and to have faith in her return. Given that both postures are still possible without a direct reference to the divine, without the knife being in the hand of the agent, then it could be the case that "Abraham is heroic in responding ahead of time, by being actively prepared" but that his situation is not fundamentally different from the lad's.[71]

There are several other considerations with which I will conclude on this particular question, while underscoring the fact that a full treatment of this issue must await the discussion of resignation and faith in the next chapter.

First, it is worth remembering that faith is not just the readiness to sacrifice; it is right and important to concede that the knife is in Abraham's own hand, but the mechanism of loss is not the decisive issue in faith. Faith demonstrates itself in the readiness to receive back what is given up, and the exact mechanism by which loss is suffered may therefore not be the most important issue for the knight of faith.

Second, it is essential to the purpose of having written *Fear and Trembling* in the first place that Abraham's ordeal be in some way illuminating for the human condition as such. If Abraham's example is utterly *sui generis* in every way, then there is nothing to learn from him, no point to admiring him (even given the limits of admiration without imitation), and no way in which his story can be usefully applied to my story. If this is so, then the book is inherently hampered from achieving any reasonable aim. Consequently it is preferable on the whole to seek out interpretations that conduce to admiration and application of Abraham's story as told by Silentio to the reader's own experience, and Hoffman's does this. Presumably not many readers in Kierkegaard's day or our own, even deeply religious readers, regard themselves as having the same sort of relationship with God as Abraham did. Nevertheless, even in the absence of what seems to be presented in scripture as direct discourse with God, readers are within their rights to expect that Silentio's discussion of Abraham's faith will inform and inspire them. Lippitt is right certainly to insist that "the Abraham story only makes sense *at all* against an understanding that Abraham is in dialogue with his God,"[72] but neither he nor Hoffman nor I wish to rest too comfortably on the reassurance that this realization might afford.[73]

Third, there may be a way in which we can understand on a more general basis how Abraham's situation is comparable to the trials afforded us by life. One observation not made in the text as such but compatible with it: a father, as Abraham is a father, not only introduces his child to life, but introduces him to death as well. To live is in the end to die. If one cannot bear the thought of a beloved child's death, truly cannot endure the possibility of it, then one ought not to have a child at all. It is a commonplace that there is something especially upsetting about a parent outliving a child, and with good reason. But any parent is well-advised to be prepared for the possibility of their child's premature death. And even if a parent dies before the child, which seems more in accord with the natural order of things, the conviction that the child will herself one day die is no less certain.

Hoffman's analogy between the complex attitude of faith and the complex attitude of courage (which Silentio frequently likens to faith) is highly instructive here. Consider this passage:

> When I go to battle I believe I am under considerable threat, yet I also believe it is possible I will live through it. This takes courage. If I believe my death is a foregone conclusion, I will probably despair, or lose my mind. If I believe that the threat is not real, that living is a foregone conclusion, then my courage remains untested, a trivial thing, easy. Put differently, to love one's life is easy when there is no threat to it. Conversely, if the threat is so great that I simply give up, and just stop caring whether I live or die, and then I make it through, my taste for life may have become permanently drained.[74]

The logic is the same, Hoffman continues, if the case in question is not my own going into battle but someone I love going into battle: "The question becomes, will I continue to love or despair, hold on to or renounce my beloved? The inner structure of courage/despair plausibly remains the same."[75]

I am arguing further that it remains the same in Abraham's case too with specific reference to the fact that the knife is in his own hand. If I am to have a child, I must realize that there will be dangers to her life, her well-being, her moral integrity, her peace and prosperity. If I am genuinely convinced that those threats are so great that they must be eliminated from her life, then I will become maniacally protective and shield her from every conceivable harm. Sheltered from reality, literally padded within the narrow confines of her danger-proofed home, inexperienced in the world and innocent of every temptation, she will perhaps be "safe," but she will have also never really lived in the fullest sense. If I do not take this course of action and allow my child in the due course of her increasing maturity to confront the ills of life on her own, I can still recognize as genuine evils the plights she may be forced to endure, but insofar as I am the cause of her being in the first place, I cannot pretend that I have nothing to do with the fact that she has to endure those evils herself. In fact, as her parent, I am always invested in her fortunes, interested in the sort of character she develops, and responsible to aid her in her travails in whatever way is appropriate.[76] At the root of this awareness, though, is the recognition that I am so bound to my child because I am her parent, and accepting this responsibility from the outset is a decision that cannot in good faith be revoked.

Fourth, we should keep in mind the context of these remarks and the genre that Silentio seems to be working with here in the eulogy. While Silentio does refer to what would seem to be the blindingly obvious fact that Abraham has to kill his son, he is remarkably restrained on this very point, which would seem to be the most opportune subject for rhetorical embroidery and emotional exploitation. The specifics of his language here are worth observing carefully.

> That sad but nevertheless blessed hour when Abraham was to take leave of everything he held dear, when he once more would raise his venerable head, when his face would shine as the Lord's, when he would concentrate all his soul upon a blessing that would be so powerful it would bless Isaac all his days—this hour was not to come! For Abraham would indeed take leave of Isaac, but in such a way that he himself would remain behind; death would separate them, but in such a way that Isaac would become its booty. The old man would not, rejoicing in death, lay his hand in blessing on Isaac, but, weary of life, he would lay a violent hand upon Isaac.[77]

Again we note the especially tragic fact of the parent outliving the child. And again we do see a reference to the prospect that Abraham will have to "lay a violent hand upon Isaac," but this final mention of the imminent violence entailed by the order to sacrifice Isaac is surprisingly muted.

Despite the pathos, not much of it is directed straightforwardly at the violence in its ghastly particulars. Instead, the pathos is chiefly to do with the transformation in Abraham's own self-understanding of his role as a father. He is *supposed* to outlive Isaac, yet he will not. He is *supposed* to lay his hand in blessing upon his son when the time comes, but he will not. He is *supposed* to take his leave of his son in the sense that his own death will mean their separation, but this will not happen. These expectations are the content of the provisional ideal that Abraham holds out for himself and his relationship with Isaac: this is the content of his ideal, an ideal that life (or God) has placed into question. So the real point of the pathos is not the violence of the act itself, the hours of the literal sacrifice, but the change in meaning that attends the father and son bond.

Abraham has, as we all do, an ideal as to how his relationship is meant to play out, and the emotional force of the drama here consists in the shocking blow to that ideal that the command to sacrifice Isaac involves. Things are not going to turn out as he imagined. The reader is meant to be challenged not with the literal prospect of having to offer a child in sacrifice to God but with the challenge of recognizing that their relationship to a beloved individual will in the course of life necessarily be subject to change, even trauma. It may be instructive to recall the weaning narratives from the exordium. These vignettes too speak directly to the changing perception a mother must accommodate in her understanding of her relationship to her beloved child. Not only must the child be weaned, but it is in the child's best interests to be weaned, and indeed the mother must inflict this violence on her child by her own hand. So too Abraham's faith is tested by the destruction of his self-understanding as Isaac's father; to be his father he must now confront an unexpected change in the terms of their relationship. Having accepted the promise of fatherhood, he is now surprised by the development of his fatherhood into a form he could not have imagined possible at the outset. That being Isaac's father may involve accepting his premature death, being robbed of the opportunity to take leave of his son on his own preferred terms, having to forego the opportunity to peaceably bless him and his future life, he would not have anticipated.

Before leaving the eulogy behind entirely, then, and turning to the fuller account provided in the preliminary expectoration, it is with these thoughts in mind that we should read the central claim of the eulogy that "Abraham had faith specifically for this life—faith that he would grow old in this country, be honored among the people, blessed by posterity, and unforgettable in Isaac, the most precious thing in his life, whom he embraced with a love that is inadequately described by saying he faithfully fulfilled the father's duty to love the son."[78] All commentators are agreed on the importance of this assertion, but the preliminary considerations advanced here will perhaps round out the significance of the claim. At least part of what is meant by saying that Abraham's faith is for this life is that even with the involvement of God, nothing about faith extracts the faithful person from the exigencies of her worldly existence. The faithful person does not abandon the temporal for the eternal in an impossible escapist fantasy. In fact, faith reconfirms her in and recommits her to the this-worldly character of her existence.

That God is the source of the command may be important, but even so, this does not mean the faithful person's solution to her apparent impasse can be won by abandoning her life in this world for a mad flight to God. That her self-understanding, her cherished ideals, and her relationships with beloved others will be subject to unpredictable and unpleasant changes does not mean these changes can be evaded but must be worked *through*. It is in and through the temporal scene that faith realizes its new ideal, an ideal that is the reconstitution, indeed the repetition (with a difference) of the ruined ideal. That Abraham's faith is for this life means that he expects the promise to be fulfilled despite the initial challenge it faces, and he expects it to be fulfilled in a way that is sufficiently like his original expectation that he will, with the eyes of faith, recognize it when it arrives. The content of Abraham's faith is substantially the same as the content of the original promise—that he will grow old in the land, be honored by his contemporaries, hailed by his descendants, and remembered forever in his progeny. All this he still affirms as his rightful inheritance, even though the divine order appears to endanger the very possibility of such an inheritance being his portion. His faith therefore consists in embracing the desirability of the impending alteration to his self-understanding, trusting that the relationship between himself and his son will not only survive the ordeal at hand but will be *improved* by it, and accepting that his desires and hopes really will come true despite the fact that they look to be completely unrealistic by human standards.

That this claim really is the central one of the eulogy is supported both by the fact that the essence of it is repeated in various ways throughout the rest of the text and by the fact that from this point forward the eulogy itself unwinds in a sort of retraction of its own importance, confirming the thesis that it is more rhetorical trial than substantive contribution to the argument. What remains of the eulogy is another vignette of how Abraham could have failed at Moriah, an episode strongly reminiscent of the four different versions of Abraham provided in the exordium; a direct appeal to the reader to consider her own likely response to the call of God upon Abraham; and a final disappointing denouement. As to the retread of the exordium, Silentio assures us that "if Abraham had doubted, then he would have done something else, something great and glorious, for how could Abraham do anything else but what is great and glorious!"[79] In the ensuing brief narrative, the "great and glorious" deed of Abraham is his offering of his own life to God in place of his son's.

Now at least one commentator, John Lippitt, has questioned how this suicidal gesture could be enough to guarantee that "he would have been admired in the world, and his name would never be forgotten; but it is one thing to be admired and another to become a guiding star that saves the anguished."[80] After all, Lippitt reasons, it seems in this case Abraham has offered a gift "of equal or lesser value," so to speak, in response to God's demand.[81] Indeed, Silentio imagines Abraham himself under these circumstances admitting that his own sacrifice of himself "is not the best that I have, that I know very well, for what is an old man compared with the child of promise, but it is the best I can give you."[82] The important and telling point here is that this new version of a failed Abraham does not add anything substantive to the discussion, only another profile of Abraham as he could have gone wrong on Moriah, a fifth version of the four iterations presented in the exordium. The remark that Abraham would have done something great and glorious regardless is the significant giveaway, because soon hereafter, Silentio rejects this logic in favor of the more urgent formulation to the effect that if Abraham's deed cannot be in some way justified then he ought to be condemned as a murderer like anybody else.

In the preliminary expectoration, Silentio pointedly repudiates the thesis that "Abraham has gained a prescriptive right to be a great man, so that what he does is great and when another man does the same thing it is a sin, an atrocious sin."[83] If that is so, Silentio argues in the later passage, "I do not wish to participate in such empty praise."[84] What this later claim implies is that the rhetoric of the eulogy at least borders on "empty praise," inasmuch as it hails Abraham as necessarily great and glorious whatever he does, as if by "prescriptive right." This way of reading the passage where Abraham trades his own life for that of his son, as another rhetorical flourish, accounts for the illogical strangeness that Lippitt identifies; this alternate Abraham can be admired only if we have been carried away by rhetoric of the eulogy and not been sufficiently attentive to the "anxiety" that in the next section Silentio will assert is absolutely indispensable to understanding Abraham's act.[85]

In the end, the eulogy itself seems to confirm its own superfluity. Extending the questionable notion that whatever Abraham would have done would have been great and glorious, Silentio contentiously claims that "if Abraham had doubted as he stood there on Mount Moriah . . . then Abraham would not be forgotten, nor would Mount Moriah. Then it would not be mentioned in the way Ararat, where the ark landed, is mentioned, but it would be called a place of terror, for it was here that Abraham doubted."[86] But this seems like an unusual concession to make in view of the fact that the eulogy began with the assertion that "no one who was great will be forgotten, and even though it takes time, even though a cloud of misunderstanding takes away the hero, his lover will nevertheless come, and the longer the passage of time, the more faithfully he adheres to him."[87] Even if we grant that "everyone was great in his own way,"[88] in order to harmonize these two claims we would have to now concede that not only is whatever Abraham does great and glorious and therefore unforgettable and worthy of poetic preservation in memory, but also that even in the event of his *doubt* he is unforgettably great and deservedly remembered, and Moriah too, even though Moriah is the site of doubt and thereby a "place of terror." The same incongruity is intensified by Silentio's closing apostrophe to Abraham: "You did not need a eulogy to comfort you for what was lost, for you gained everything and kept Isaac,"[89] and again, "Centuries have passed since those days, but you have no need of a late lover to snatch your memory from the power of oblivion."[90] In short, there is a strong tension between the initial statements in the eulogy that no great man will be forgotten as long as there is a poet to preserve his memory (itself an improbable contention) and the final statements that Abraham's greatness (a greatness that is intact even in the event that Abraham doubted on Moriah) is not in need of eulogizing and not in need of a lover to celebrate it. It would seem that either the opening claims are true, and all greatness will be remembered through the necessary agency of the poet, who is the created companion to the hero as woman is man's created companion, or the closing claims are true, and Abraham's greatness is not in question under any circumstances and so universally conspicuous ("for every language calls you to mind")[91] as to not require a poet, orator, or eulogy at all.

Alternately, it could be that the eulogy sabotages its own effort, demonstrating in the end the unfeasibility of the founding assumptions of the speech. Setting out on the basis of inflated claims for the power and purpose of the poet or orator, the eulogy attempts to praise Abraham on these same terms, terms that enable a persuasive and persuasively rosy account of Abraham's faith but not a complete, mature, or plausible one. Silentio's appeal to Abraham himself to "forgive the one who aspired to speak your praise if he has not done it properly"[92] suggests that something has been amiss from the very beginning, that the methodological strategy of rhetoric when applied to the person of Abraham is in fact a misapplication. The eulogy's original pretensions unravel one by one, retiring another experiment in indirection and leaving the main argumentative business for the sections to come.

5 Beginning from the Heart

We have seen how each of the preliminary sections anticipates in a negative manner the truth of Abraham's story, by in every case shedding light on how Abraham *cannot* be grasped and concomitantly showing how a number of classical approaches to the problem are inadequate to the task—philosophical speculation, narrative lyricism, oratorical flourishes. It should be noted that the preliminary expectoration (an unfortunate rendering truly; better would be Hannay's "Preamble from the Heart"[1]) is part of the broader section of *Fear and Trembling* entitled "Problemata." Commentators are accustomed to referring to Problemata I, II, and III as a unit, and that is fair enough, but the preliminary expectoration is itself an introduction to the Problemata and forms a unit with them (yet another reason to regard the eulogy not as the first positive contribution to the theory of faith in *Fear and Trembling* but as the final indirect preliminary).[2]

The preliminary expectoration can be usefully divided into five subsections, each of which is a sort of imaginative meditation: first, a meditation on the proverb "Only one who works gets bread"; second, a discussion of a hypothetical pastor who preaches on Abraham's example and heatedly condemns a would-be imitator of that example; third, an autobiographical reflection from Silentio himself on his own limited capacity to imitate Abraham; fourth, the justly famous portrait of an imagined contemporary knight of faith; fifth, a case study in resignation and faith as dramatized by the lad in love with his princess. Each in its own way studies the tension between the ideal and the real and correlating failures to hold the two in relation. Throughout what comes in these five subsections, it is imperative to keep in mind the goal of the text as a whole: to trace out the itinerary of consciousness as it traverses the field of real experience in light of ideals that are challenged by the real and reconstituted on the basis of faith. At no point is it implied that reality must be forsaken for a flight into the ideal; at no point is the real preferred to the ideal or stripped of relation to an ideal. Throughout, the two are held together in the tentative unity of consciousness, a unity that is nothing but the togetherness of the ideal and real in their dialectical interplay, an irreducible dialectic that never reaches resolution but "resolves" itself only inasmuch as it holds the ideal and real together in their very incommensurability.

"Only One Who Works Gets Bread"

What connects all of the otherwise seemingly disparate parts of the preliminary expectoration is the interplay of two themes: first, the contrast between ideal and real and various ways of holding them together or failing to do so; and second, the problem of appropriating an example for one's own life, specifically the example of Abraham as a figure who is presumably not just admired but also imitated. The first three subsections are diagnostic, demonstrating the difficulties inherent in holding together the ideal and real and imitating an instructive exemplar of faith; the last two are curative, enacting first an imagined solution to the problem in an admittedly fictive person, a contemporary knight of faith of Silentio's own devising, and second, an equally imaginative (but I will argue more complete and more informative) solution that more fully renders the difference between resignation and faith, an absolutely key distinction.

The preliminary expectoration begins with Silentio's introduction of a proverb that he says comes from "the external and visible world" though this piece of worldly wisdom (paradoxically perhaps) does not belong to the world from which it comes but belongs only to "the world of spirit." That proverb is "Only one who works gets bread," and "oddly enough," according to Silentio, "the adage does not fit the world in which it is most at home, for imperfection is the fundamental law of the external world, and here it happens again and again that he who does not work does get bread, and he who sleeps gets it even more abundantly than he who works."[3] So straightaway the reader is reintroduced to the fundamental tension between the ideal and the real. In fact, the reader is arguably reintroduced to the text as a whole; this is in truth a new beginning to the entire book, because in this proverb the reader detects an unmistakable echo of the Pauline teaching about "work" that is anticipated by the title of the book. Just as the titular reference to "fear and trembling" calls to mind working out one's own salvation and the task of sanctification as understood according to the Pauline heritage, so also the notion that only one who works gets bread brings to mind Saint Paul's injunction to the Thessalonian church that "if any would not work, neither should he eat."[4] The connection to Saint Paul's teaching is unmistakable, especially since it is explicitly related to the other main axis at play in the early subsections of the preliminary expectoration—namely, the question of imitating an example.

Saint Paul's exhortation that the busybodies who afflict the Thessalonian church should "with quietness" work and "eat their own bread"[5] comes in the immediate context of his own reminder to his readers that he himself set just such an example among them. The reason Saint Paul particularly insists that the busybodies ought to be mandated to work in order to eat their own bread is that this was the example he himself set among them. "For yourselves know how ye ought to follow us: for we behaved not ourselves disorderly among you; neither did we eat any man's bread for nought; but wrought with labor and travail night and day, that we might not be chargeable to any of you; not because we have not power, but to make ourselves an ensample unto you to follow us."[6] So here we have two major themes that concern the preliminary expectoration in the biblical context that is doubtless their at least partial inspiration and that restates in a new way the theme of the whole book. As Saint Paul set an example for the Thessalonians to imitate, so too the preliminary expectoration concerns itself with the appropriate mode of imitating Abraham, and just as Saint Paul insists on the connection between work and its proper reward, so too the opening subsection of the preliminary expectoration concerns an ostensible association between an intimation of an ideal content—only the one who works gets bread—and an awareness of the reality at hand: those who don't work do in fact get bread. Saint Paul's injunction is just that, a statement of what ethically ought to be the case, not a description of what is the case. Indeed, the very fact that the reality is not as it should be is precisely what necessitates an ethical injunction in the first place, a reassertion of the ideal that ought to govern the reality.

Crucially, what is at stake here is a reassignment of the meaning that seems most obviously referenced by the proverb. It is true that only one who works gets bread. But it is not true, Silentio says, of the world to which it most easily seems to belong. It is true only in a reassigned way, in a way we do not expect. The preliminary expectoration is obviously the first section that deals with the distinction between resignation and faith, but in my view it does so rather earlier than most commentators have noticed; it does so right here in the meditation on the proverbial wisdom that opens the section. The point of the meditation is that there is truth to the claim that only one who works gets bread, but *how* the truth of it is realized is surprising. One can already see that it is necessary to resign the obvious explanation for the truth of the proverb in order to regain its truth in a transformed but nonetheless more satisfactory manner: to really *believe* that only one who works gets bread, the mode under which the proverbial truth presents itself has to be reinterpreted. If this is a statement about the operation of the external world, then of course it is naïve at best. But if it is a truth about the world of spirit, then it may yet hold, though clearly not in the way that one might have originally hoped.[7]

Ideally, only one who works gets bread; only one who puts in effort is rewarded; and rewards do not come to those who have not earned them by the sweat of their own brow. But in reality, as we all know, all too often rewards come to those who have not worked for them, and those who work very hard indeed get no reward for their labors. It is otherwise in the world of spirit, where consciousness exercises itself according to a logic other than that of the "law of indifference." "Here it holds true that only the one who works gets bread, that only the one who was in anxiety finds rest, that only the one who descends into the lower world rescues the beloved, that only the one who draws the knife gets Isaac."[8] Conversely, the one who will not work in the realm of spirit gets no rewards but is deceived. "Here it does not help to have Abraham as father or to have seventeen ancestors. The one who will not work fits what is written about the virgins of Israel; he gives birth to wind—but the one who will work gives birth to his own father."[9]

It would be easy here to cast suspicion on this opposition in a similar fashion to the skepticism that might be correctly directed toward the lofty aspirations of the rhetoric of the eulogy; isn't this celebration of the law of the spirit just another bit of overbidding? And yet we should not leap to this conclusion too swiftly, for there are indications already that a different logic is taking hold of the argument, a logic that is consummated in the famous claim of Silentio that what is generally omitted from the story of Abraham is the "anxiety," the anxiety without which the story of Abraham cannot be told properly. Anxiety *lives* in the tension between the ideal and the real; without this tension there can be no anxiety, and without anxiety there can be no victorious faith, no genuine appreciation for the difficulties of existence nor any justly won confidence in the power of faith to overcome those difficulties, an overcoming within time and existence, not outside them.

The scripture passages alluded to suggest this more complex state of affairs, where it is not a matter of preferring the world of spirit and its rules to the external world and its rules or vice versa. When Silentio says that in the world of spirit it is no help to have Abraham as one's father, he is referring to Jesus's angry condemnation of the Pharisees in Matthew 3:6. The point of those words is of course that mere biological descent from Abraham is not a guarantee of salvation: Jesus insists that all "bear fruit worthy of repentance" and not rely on their inherited identity as a substitute for spiritual descent from Abraham. Less likely to be observed, however, is the simple fact that Jesus's audience *does* have Abraham for their father in this more obvious sense. Were his audience to reassure themselves that they do have Abraham for their father, they would not be deluded with respect to the facts; they are descended from Abraham in the external world. Their error is a more profound sort of self-delusion; they are unaware that the true descendant of Abraham is not his biological progeny but his spiritual offspring.

The virgins of Israel spoken of in Isaiah 26 do labor, but they give birth to nothing: "We have not wrought any deliverance in the earth; neither have the inhabitants of the world fallen."[10] What is at stake, then, in both contexts is an alteration in the *meaning* of an apparent commonplace. Jesus exhorts the Pharisees not to rely upon their descent from Abraham not because they are *not* descended from Abraham but because they are not in the only way that really matters. Similarly, the virgins of Israel do labor but being virgins are not pregnant and thus have no one to deliver. Both images of course trade on parenthood and recall the parallel paternal and maternal images of the exordium. The implication here is that fatherhood and motherhood are rendered impossible by reliance on a straightforward understanding of what fatherhood and motherhood consist in. It is not the case that it is unimportant to be a child of Abraham. On the contrary, it is essential that one be a child of Abraham; it is just that what counts as being a child of Abraham is not what seems most obviously to count as literal inheritance. Likewise, it is vital that one who labors brings forth child, but again, what this means exactly is not what we take it naturally to be.

We should recall that the context for the first subsection is proverbial wisdom. How does proverbial wisdom operate? It speaks a commonplace that is not necessarily false but is misleading in its misapplication of the truth. And it does so in such a way as to diffuse anxiety. As we will see, part of what is emphasized about the story of Abraham in this section, and the ability of the hearer of his story to imitate his example, is that ordinarily the anxiety is missing. Surely proverbial wisdom is designed, even in its objective truth-telling, to diffuse subjective anxiety. It issues a claim *that* something is true (which it is) while obfuscating *how* it is true. A proverb like "Only one who works gets bread" passes itself off as a statement about how things are, but its truth could legitimately be cast into suspicion by recourse to counterevidence, to indications from experience of the real world of cases in which those who haven't worked do get bread or in which those who have worked don't get bread. If we rested with the introduction of just such counterevidences, then the conclusion that the proverb is not true would be easy to affirm, but the logic of faith (which at this point we are only dimly foreseeing) pushes past this impasse to see a sense in which the truth of the proverb remains but must be reunderstood in light of the real counterevidences and their contribution to a new ideal, an ideal that affirms *that* the proverb is true in light of a new understanding of *how* it is true. In this sense the proverb is autoreferential: It is true that only one who works gets bread, but it is doubly true that it speaks about itself. Only one who works will get the bread of realizing *that* and *how* it is true that only one who works gets bread. Whoever realizes this task has not only passed through the test of anxiety (a point that will require further comment) but also has, in a striking phrase not often commented upon in philosophical analysis of this text, given birth to his own father. Seeing as how the key interests of this section are in establishing how to hold together the ideal and real as well as how to imitate an exemplar of faith, it is incumbent upon the reader to consider this metaphor in terms of what it might be saying about imitation as the task of holding together the real and ideal.

Care should be exercised here so as not to be carried away by too much speculation. Any interpretation must be tempered by another deployment of the same image, this time from *Philosophical Fragments*. There, Climacus writes of the paradox that "if that fact came into the world as the absolute paradox, all that comes later would be of no help, because this remains for all eternity the consequences of a paradox and thus just as definitively improbable as the paradox, unless it is assumed that the consequences (which, after all, are derived) gained retroactive power to transform the paradox, which would be just as acceptable as the assumption that a son received retroactive power to transform his father."[11] It seems unlikely in view of this remark that Silentio means by giving birth to one's own father something like a retroactive power to *alter* anything about the example of Abraham. At minimum, it is clear that faith means something like the capacity to provide oneself (though not necessarily only by oneself, solipsistically) with the condition for one's own ongoing existence—probably a figure for new or second birth. Certainly this minimal reading is corroborated by the passages immediately following, which emphasize not assimilating Abraham but repeating his example. At the very least, successful imitation of Abraham seems to be akin to giving birth to my own father, a paradoxical repetition that in the same gesture instantiates my sonship and the fatherhood of my father. An even more pedestrian reading is available if we keep in mind the traditional view that fatherhood is assumed only voluntarily. A straightforward way to read this passage would then be that the child, in being accepted by the father, gives birth to the father precisely *as* father. If we keep this idea in mind in connection with the earlier point about how the Pharisees cannot take consolation in being the sons of Abraham as they understand sonship, then the overall point of the passage seems to be that one must give up the notion that being a father or son consists in the mere fact of biological relationship; one must accept that to be a father or son is to accept the responsibility of fatherhood and sonship. This is a process that is not without work.

The nature of the work that is required in Silentio's view is also worth observing, for it is of a specific kind. Having contrasted the law of the external world with that of the world of spirit, Silentio goes on to assert that "there is a knowledge that presumptuously wants to introduce into the world of spirit the same law of indifference under which the external world sighs. It believes that it is enough to know what is great—no other work is needed."[12] Only to know is inadequate. What is called for is individual action, application of the exemplar's lesson to one's personal situation. This is implied by the reference to Themistocles, who alone of "thousands . . . who knew all the triumphs of Miltiades"[13] acted on his example and made ready in his own generation for future conflict. Fortunately, the power of Abraham's story is undiminished even when not so acted upon: "The story about Abraham is remarkable in that it is always glorious no matter how poorly it is understood, but here again it is a matter of whether or not we are willing to work and be burdened."[14] The work is that of appropriation, making Abraham's story illustrative of and action-guiding for my own situation. For appropriation to take place, though, the anxiety of the story must be preserved. It is a bit surprising that most commentators have declined to refer at this point to *The Concept of Anxiety* and have been content to simply point out that for the story to be properly told, Abraham has to be depicted as being seriously challenged by the call to sacrifice Isaac. That he is seriously challenged is missed by the pietistic retellings of the tale that we are about to see subjected to criticism, but that anxiety is key to the story being told properly is a somewhat more sophisticated assertion than simply cautioning against sugarcoating Abraham's situation in the telling of it.

To extend the connections between *Fear and Trembling* and *The Concept of Anxiety*, we should note that anxiety is addressed as educative and conducive to faith in the final chapter of the latter work in a discussion that could be very informative for the association, much less developed, made between the two notions by Silentio.[15] In short, the culmination of *The Concept of Anxiety* is the argument that anxiety in its most constructive function allows one to be, in Haufniensis's words, "educated by possibility."[16] To be educated by possibility is, according to Haufniensis, to mature into thinking of the course of one's life as overshadowed by providence and pervaded by sin-consciousness, ways of thinking and acting that replace and go beyond dependence upon thinking of one's life as a product of fate or directed toward a trivial, self-satisfied sort of happiness. Significantly for readers of *Fear and Trembling*, Haufniensis twice in this final chapter uses the language of "weaning" to describe education by possibility.

First, he likens the educative power of anxiety to draw the anxious sufferer away from being mired in finitude to the care of a mother who "weans the child before finitude begins to bungle him";[17] and on the very next page he condemns dependence on "shrewdness" as a form of dependence from which an individual must be "weaned away" if they are to be properly educated by anxiety.[18] The similar imagery testifies to a similar purpose to both texts: the goal of Silentio's and Haufniensis's authorships is to dramatize the itinerary of a developing religious consciousness, a journey from immature ways of responding to the vagaries of existence, ways that evince very low levels of self-consciousness, to the distinctively religious response of faith, which evinces a maximal degree of self-consciousness and responds to life with an awareness of the self-conscious individual's own capacity to sin and a commensurate conviction that all things work toward the good under the hand of divine providence. What makes anxiety an education in possibility is that it makes the anxious person aware (as Abraham's anxiety makes him aware) that life calls for our response to it, and not just in any determinate matter of concern but in any capacity whatsoever. The possibility that presents itself in anxiety is not merely the opposite of actuality but is the fundamental solicitation of the self's free response to reality; the anxious awareness of possibility makes me aware that I *can* and that I *must* respond to the actual in accord with a basic orientation toward the whole of reality: I can have faith or I can despair, and which one I move toward is *the* question of freedom's possibility, a question posed within the suspended point that is anxiety. So when Silentio insists that we understand Abraham's story without omitting the anxiety that is occasioned by it, he is not merely requiring that the intrinsic difficulties of Abraham's situation not be forgotten, he is emphasizing that what Abraham faces is not a local decision about what to do in this given situation, but he is facing the fundamental issue of how he is to think about and react to the whole of reality: Do I have faith in God and the goodness of all things or do I despair altogether?

Also significant to a reading of *Fear and Trembling* that is guided by *The Concept of Anxiety* are the references in the final chapter to anxiety's power to deprive the anxious one's reliance upon the world and finite circumstances and to rebestow the world to the person who allows their anxiety to conduct them to faith. There is a clear parallel in the language used by Haufniensis to the double movement described by Silentio. Haufniensis claims that anxiety is "absolutely educative"[19] in that only anxiety over possibility as such can nullify the desirability and reliability of any given set of actualities that might present themselves in the course of an individual life. Haufniensis writes, "In actuality, no man ever becomes so unhappy that he did not retain a little remnant, and common sense says quite correctly that if one is cunning, one knows how to make the best of things."[20] What Haufniensis is arguing here is that no matter how dismal the particular circumstances of one's life get, a person always manages to eke out something that they are willing to invest hope in for the prospect of something dimly like happiness; any actuality, no matter how bad, can be coped with or worked around or mystified or explained away. A person may think of themselves as having lost much in life, but the truth is no loss is ever total: we are always able to cling to *something*. But anxiety raises the prospect of total loss, because anxiety teaches that possibility can always be worse than the actuality of my situation, no matter how awful, because the possibility always remains that I could despair. As he writes, "But whoever took possibility's course in misfortune lost all, all, as no one in actuality ever lost it."[21] Haufniensis does not argue something rather banal like that one must learn to take the bad with the good, but something deeper and much more demanding—namely, that one must regard actuality as a gift and find a way to have faith against despair even in the worst circumstances.

If one will have faith in this way, then not only do they lose all, but they also receive everything back: "Now, if he did not defraud the possibility that wanted to teach him and did not wheedle the anxiety that wanted to save him, then he would also receive everything back, as no one in actuality ever did, even though he received all things tenfold, for the disciple of possibility received infinity, and the soul of the other expired in the finite."[22] The parallel to Silentio's analysis of Abraham's situation is striking, and what it teaches us is that the demand that the anxiety of Abraham be preserved in the telling of his story is insisted upon because Abraham's anxiety removes vain hope, wishful thinking, and bargaining with reality, excluding every means of self-consolation. Without anxiety, Abraham could be seen as someone who copes with the prospect of loss in a half-hearted bad faith, by evasion or excuse-making or some form or another of assuring himself "it's not that bad." By keeping his anxiety foremost in mind, such a mistake could not be made. Abraham has nothing to rely upon but the possibility that all things are possible: even the impossible. And that is why he also receives back everything he loses, for he grasps the eternal significance of the temporal and, by not investing his faith in anything worldly, finds the world anew.

The Unselfaware Sermonizer

Silentio thus underscores the anxiety of Abraham first and foremost to anticipate the double movement of faith and to link this with the means by which faith inculcates in the faithful person a more self-conscious and more profound involvement in, and responsiveness to, life itself. The other dimension of anxiety that Silentio is implicitly highlighting is the capacity of narrative to awaken anxiety in the hearer. Where this capacity is not acknowledged, as it is not by the pious pastor who preaches a thoughtless sermon on Abraham to an uncomprehending listener in the second subsection of the preliminary expectoration, tragicomic misunderstanding "is very close at hand."[23] This subsection dramatizes a possible miscommunication, where the anxiety of Abraham is not attended to by the ostensible communicator, and an anxious listener is thereby misled. The pious preacher has an ideal in mind that he presumably wants to relate, but without an account of the anxiety of Abraham, the patriarch is only an ideal that touches upon reality in no comprehensible way. The question of imitation again intrudes, for had the preacher properly included the anxiety of Abraham in his sermon, the listener would have better known how to appropriate Abraham for his own life. Again, a full treatment of a potential parallel between this section and the final chapter of *The Concept of Anxiety* is beyond the present scope, but it should be noted that chapter 5 of the latter text is in large part concerned with the power of story to educate. As is typical of Kierkegaard's writing style, Haufniensis in this chapter both talks thematically about the power of narrative *and* at the same time deploys narrative to work on his reader, to bring about the effect that he is arguing that narrative can have. So he at once speaks *about* narrative and speaks *in* narrative. Specifically, Haufniensis uses narrative vignettes not merely to moralize or illustrate his points but to solicit a self-identification on the part of the reader, a consciousness that the story I am reading is ultimately about me.[24] Indeed, Haufniensis claims the goal of a story that is *about* anxiety is ultimately meant to *bring about* anxiety in the one who sees themselves in the story. Moreover, Haufniensis argues that all a person needs to be properly educated by possibility is one instructive story as long as the hearer is "honest with himself"[25]—that is to say, as long as the hearer allows himself to be "absolutely identified"[26] with the subject.

In chapter 5 he uses the example of an Indian hermit of whom it was said that after living on dew for two years "he once came to the city, tasted wine, and became addicted to drink."[27] Without earnest honesty, we can react tragically by pitying the poor Indian hermit, or comically by ridiculing his folly and weakness—but neither is a sufficient response. To respond tragically or comically is to put ourselves at a distance from the only real moral of the story: *this is about you.* The key to such an absolute identification is shared sin-consciousness. I have to see myself as just as guilty and prone to sin as the Indian hermit in order to properly appropriate his example, to draw the conclusion that I must go and *not* do likewise. If we patronize the hermit by either maudlin sentimentality or cynical derision then we fail to recognize ourselves in his case and fail to imitate—by not imitating—his example. The point of the story is not what happened to the hermit but what is to happen to me.

So again, the reader of *Fear and Trembling* can learn something here from *The Concept of Anxiety.* Part of why it is important for the anxiety of Abraham to be kept in the story is precisely because it is a story and as such has an inherent power that can be either mishandled or misappropriated or both. So long as anxiety is kept in the story, it will achieve its proper purpose of educating and inspiring. A story told without due awareness of anxiety has no regard for the friction between the ideal and the real, the fact that the story inherently speaks to possibility, possibility that might be appropriated and imitated, translated from the ideal to the real in a way that will always be fraught with difficulty. To speak of Abraham, one must speak of him with full consciousness that his example will be one that will draw people to imitate it; to hold up Abraham as an ideal is to invite the real to rise to its level. This is the mistake of the preacher, that in an abstract and abstracted way, he speaks about the trial of Abraham as if it were neither a matter of concern to himself nor could possibly be a matter of concern to anybody else.

Part of the way this lack of concern is demonstrated also touches on the first point made above about anxiety—namely, that it prepares the way for faith by calling for the individual to reorient herself toward life as a whole and demands a transformation in thinking and acting. Those who refuse to work and be rewarded, those who refuse to genuinely confront the anxiety of Abraham "talk and in the process of talking interchange the two terms, Isaac and the best, and everything goes fine."[28] The problem here is not just one of reducing Isaac (to whom "the father has the highest and holiest [obligation]") to the level of money ("to money I have no ethical obligation"[29]); the problem is that, absent anxiety, no transformation is called for. Rather than issuing a demand to discard one ideal for a new, chastened but revivified ideal, a false equivalence is introduced, and what should be a dynamic development is replaced by a stultifying stasis. One could push the point a bit farther and say that it is just such false equivalencies that anxiety as education by possibility enjoins us to refuse—that is, it enjoins refusal of the *very idea* of equivalencies or comparisons among goods. To equate Isaac with "the best" is to remain within the orbit of finite circumstances, the realm of worldly actualities; it merely designates one actual person as preferred among all persons or things. The comparison of available goods as if they were of equal abstract value is altogether dismissed by faith, with the help of anxiety. This is because anxiety strikes *all* actualities as of only relative reliability and deprives the anxious of *all* crutches. The pastor's sermon has not made this point but has in point of fact encouraged only the sort of mealymouthed and halfhearted self-delusion that Haufniensis decries.

Silentio asks his reader to imagine further what would occur if a hearer of such a sermon were afflicted with the "sleeplessness" of his own anxiety and that such a listener "goes home [and] wants to do just as Abraham did, for the son, after all, is the best."[30] Such a misconstrual would not only be unfortunate and criminal but would represent a total failure of communication. In contrast to Haufniensis's praise for the sermon in which "the single individual speaks as the single individual to the single individual,"[31] this sermon does not establish an act of communication—which itself is arguably nothing but transformation of relationship—in such a way that two persons develop their respective singularity in partnership with one another. Haufniensis in the same section asserts that the sermon is the only really proper medium for communication about sin, which suggests that a sermon should do the same work as a narrative is often able to do, to stimulate sin-consciousness. The sermonizer must have a lively sense of his or her own guilt, an awareness of being in no better a position than the congregation; at the same time, the sermonizer must foster in the audience the same conviction that they are no better than the one who is speaking to them.

The pastor of the preliminary expectoration, of course, "had not noticed any heat or perspiration when preaching about Abraham,"[32] and this absence of passion means, according to Silentio, that "he did not know what he was saying,"[33] such that the improper mood of the sermon vitiated its content. The lack of self-awareness and total indifference, ultimately, to what he was actually saying make the pastor unable to anticipate the not-so-incredible possibility that someone hearing him might take it into their head to do as Abraham did. The misunderstanding of the hearer, though, is no less tragicomic in its extremity; his failure is that in wanting to do what Abraham did, he took it that the only way to imitate an example is by exact literal duplication of their deed. The exordium has already proven that this is the wrong way to imitate Abraham, but it is perhaps the easiest way to do so—that is, the way that involves the least anxiety. Had the preacher done his job, the hearer of the sermon would have recognized in Abraham's story a caution to look out for his own sin and an exhortation to imitate the patriarch's faith with the understanding that, as Silentio goes on to baldly state, "it is only by faith that one achieves any resemblance to Abraham, not by murder."[34]

So again, here we have a misfired relation between ideal and real as well as a misperceived imitation. The pastor represents an ideal of Abrahamic faith in his sermon that has no foothold in the rocky terrain of reality, chiefly in that it does not arise from the sinfulness of the sermonizer nor does it recognize the sinfulness of the audience. For Abraham's story to speak to us it must be told by a single individual with a high degree of self-consciousness to an individual who aspires to a higher degree of self-consciousness, who seeks to identify herself with the exemplar of faith, something that can happen only on the grounds of shared sin-consciousness and shared calling to further self-consciousness achieved in faith. This subsection ends with a rhetorical question from Silentio and an emphatic declaration that will set the stage for much of what is to follow.

> How is a contradiction such as that of the speaker to be explained? Is it because Abraham has gained a prescriptive right to be a great man, so that what he does is great and when another man does the same thing it is a sin, an atrocious sin? In that case, I do not wish to participate in such empty praise. If faith cannot make it a holy act to be willing to murder his son, then let the same judgment be passed on Abraham as on everyone else. If a person lacks the courage to think his thought all the way through and say that Abraham was a murderer, then it is certainly better to attain this courage than to waste time on unmerited eulogies.[35]

Entailed in the implicit affirmation that Abraham is great by prescriptive right is an equal conviction that he cannot be meaningfully imitated. If Abraham is great by prescriptive right, then unless I share in that same right, I am not eligible for his greatness. By clearing away unmerited eulogies, Silentio simultaneously reduces Abraham in a way and elevates his would-be followers. The preacher praised Abraham's greatness without acknowledging that his greatness is available to, even incumbent upon, me as well and without acknowledging the challenges that we all share in attaining that greatness, the work that we must do to secure it. Silentio presents Abraham as being imitable though not without difficulty:

> The ethical expression for what Abraham did is that he meant to murder Isaac; the religious expression is that he meant to sacrifice Isaac—but precisely in this contradiction is the anxiety that can make a person sleepless, and yet without this anxiety Abraham is not who he is. Or if Abraham perhaps did not do at all what the story tells, if perhaps because of the local conditions of that day it was something entirely different, then let us forget him, for what is the value of going to the trouble of remembering that past which cannot become a present.[36]

An Autobiographical Sketch from Silentio

If the first subsection addresses the general problem of communicating a spiritual truth, and the second subsection imagines how a spiritless and unreflective pastor might fail to communicate the specific spiritual truth of Abraham, the third subsection features Silentio experimenting with how he personally might go about assaying the same task. In the course of this autobiographical meditation, the reader learns some important particulars about how Silentio sees himself that must inform how the reader in turn sees Silentio. In the end, what we discover about Silentio's self-understanding does not amount to sufficient cause to dismiss his view as warped or deceptive (as some have feared), but it does place in question the comprehensiveness of his account of faith.

Continuing his argument that one must have the courage to think a thought through and embrace the anxiety-inducing friction between an ethical understanding of Abraham's act and the religious interpretation of it, Silentio claims this virtuous consistency for himself. If the preacher of the prior subsection cannot so speak of Abraham, then Silentio will, though he is more conscious than the preacher of the implicit danger of doing so. "Is it possible," Silentio asks, "to speak unreservedly about Abraham without running the risk that some individual will become unbalanced and do the same thing? If I dare not, I will say nothing at all about Abraham, and the last thing I will do is to scale him down in such a way that he thereby becomes a snare for the weak. As a matter of fact, if one makes faith everything—that is, makes it what it is—then I certainly believe that I dare to speak of it without danger in our day, which is scarcely prodigal in faith."[37] So while acknowledging the potential dangers, Silentio proceeds with caution, aware that the very worst thing to do would be to trivialize Abraham.

Here the analogy that Silentio draws to love might be helpful. Love too can set "snares for the weak" if it is misrepresented as a matter of merely fleeting feeling. There is clearly a danger in speaking of love that love will be mistaken for passing emotion, but love itself is ill-served by complete silence or timidity in the face of such a risk. "It is permissible, then," Silentio concludes, "to speak about Abraham, for whatever is great can never do damage when it is understood in its greatness; it is like a two-edged sword that kills and saves."[38] The image of a two-edged sword preserves the sense that there remains a danger in Abraham's story; it should be emphasized that the implicit risk remains. Readers of *Fear and Trembling* can never rest secure that there is *no* danger to Abraham's story or that, to anticipate the language of the first Problema, there is definitely such a thing as a teleological suspension of the ethical. Such a question remains open by necessity, according to the argument of the text. If we proceed, then, with Silentio, we do so as he does, with caution.

So how would Silentio propose to speak about Abraham if the task were his? He says he "would begin by showing what a devout and God-fearing man Abraham was, worthy of being called God's chosen one. Only a person of that kind is put to such a test, but who is such a person?"[39] This initial observation will return in Problemata I and II, but it is worth noticing straightaway that Silentio is already preparing for the later argument that only an ethically advanced person is even eligible for faith in the first place, that faith must come *after* the ethical, not fall before it. "Next," Silentio goes on to imagine aloud, "I would describe how Abraham loved Isaac," and he proceeds to underscore this point at some length, again preparing the ground for a lengthier argument later about the imperative to love. Another way Silentio will discern the difference between a knight of faith and a sinner is on the grounds of love; the knight of faith will love in all things, even those that do not seem ethical, while the sinner is a failure at love in all things. These, then, are the two elements of Silentio's rudimentary sketch of his own intentions, intentions that are in fact fulfilled by the argumentative Problemata that follow.

Yet Silentio immediately feels the need to caution the reader against the assumption that because he feels himself capable of extolling Abraham's faith in persuasive terms, he also thereby feels himself to be in fact faithful. This is not the case. "By no means do I have faith. By nature I am a shrewd fellow, and shrewd people always have great difficulty in making the movement of faith, but I do not attribute per se any *worth to the difficulty that brought the shrewd person further in the overcoming of it than to the point at which the simplest and most unsophisticated person arrives more easily.*"[40]

As for his own efforts, they are dramatized at some length by Silentio. He claims that he finds Hegel hard work but not so hard as understanding Abraham: "Thinking about Abraham is another matter, however; then I am shattered."[41] He is interested in the greatness of heroism, but he admits that "I cannot think myself into Abraham; when I reach that eminence, I sink down, for what is offered me is a paradox."[42] And much as he says that there is no additional worth to the difficulty expended by the shrewd in attaining faith, a difficulty not needed by the unsophisticated, so too he does not upon the recognition of the paradoxical quality of faith "conclude that faith is something inferior but rather that it is the highest, also that it is dishonest of philosophy to give something else in its place and to disparage faith."[43] Finally, he claims for himself familiarity with "the hardships and dangers of life" but concedes that "my courage is still not the courage of faith and is not something to be compared with it."[44]

These admissions concern intellectual humility: Silentio does not overrate the exertions of the clever at the expense of the faith of the simple; he does not have limitless confidence in the power of the intellect; he does not dismiss what does not give itself to be understood easily. Most important of all, though, are a series of admissions that disclose an even deeper dimension of Silentio's character. Over the next two pages he makes a series of telling remarks: "I am convinced that God is love; for me this thought has a primal lyrical validity";[45] and "I do not trouble God with my little troubles, details do not concern me; I gaze only at my love and keep its virgin flame pure and clear. Faith is convinced that God is concerned about the smallest things. I am satisfied with a left-handed marriage in this life; faith is humble enough to insist on the right hand";[46] and "God is love and continues to be that for me, for in the world of time God and I cannot talk with each other, we have no language in common";[47] and finally, "What was the easiest for Abraham would have been difficult for me—once again to be happy in Isaac!"[48]

What these remarks intimate is that Silentio has an abstract, intellectual appreciation for what faith entails, though as he repeatedly declares, he does not have faith himself. The love of God has for him "a primal lyrical validity"; it is a reassuring thought, but it is not a lived reality for him. The faithful person pesters God with the details of her life; Silentio's standoffishness with respect to God means that he preserves the ideal of a "pure and clear" love but that such a love is one that is undisturbed and is never inflected by change or development. These remarks serve as additional reasons why we might actually liken Silentio to the "poet-existence verging on the religious" described by Anti-Climacus at the beginning of Part Two of *The Sickness unto Death*.[49]

Given that Anti-Climacus's discussion of this character type occurs at the very beginning of the major part of the text that concerns itself with despair before God, we could presume that the sort of individual described in these pages occupies a pivotal place between generic despair and the "aggravated" despair that besieges the despairer when she is conscious of her selfhood before God.[50] The poet-existence verging on the religious, Anti-Climacus tells us, "has something in common with the despair of resignation, except that the concept of God is present." Since Silentio is about to embark on a detailed discussion of the difference between resignation and faith, and he has just confessed that what was essential to Abraham's faith, that he be happy upon receiving Isaac back, is missing in his own detached perspective upon that faith, we know that Silentio himself is in resignation, but clearly the concept of God is present to him as well, but only the concept, only the thought of God, not a lived relationship with God. In Anti-Climacus's more advanced religious judgment, such a person is "in sin, the sin of poetizing instead of being, of relating to the good and the true through the imagination instead of being that—that is, existentially striving to be that."[51]

We have already seen that Silentio cannot be straightforwardly classified as a "poet," but it might be fair to say that he has substituted an imagined relation to God for a genuinely lived one. For Silentio too the thought of God is continually present but kept at arm's length, as Silentio frequently asserts that he cannot believe in God's concern for the quotidian in the life of the believer, nor can he reconcile the love of God with the particulars of experience, though he is lyrically inspired by the *idea* of the love of God. Anti-Climacus admits that such an imagined relation can be full of yearning and even positive "content," so to speak—intellectual conviction that God is love—but a poet-existence keeps something of himself in reserve: "A poet like that can have a very profound religious longing, and the conception of God is taken up into his despair. He loves God above all, God who is his only consolation in his secret anguish, and yet he loves the anguish and will not give it up."[52] Something about his own suffering—perhaps the fanciful notion that it is the source of his poetic gift—cannot be relinquished, cannot be turned over to God in faith and humility.[53] Such a person could never get on without God, though he will never fully surrender to the divine either. Silentio's self-characterization accords well with Anti-Climacus's diagnosis of the poet-existence verging on the religious as having "a profound religious longing" and even love for God that nevertheless remains incommensurate with the poet's insistence on his own anguish, which he will in the end not give up in order to be healed.[54]

When he considers the story of Abraham directly, there are a few key observations to keep in mind. First, as has already been shown, a crucial ingredient in the Abraham story is his happiness, the happiness that was easy for him but hard for Silentio. The joy of Abraham and its vital connection to finitude, to the stuff of lived experience, is repeatedly emphasized by Silentio: "He climbed the mountain, and even in the moment when the knife gleamed he had faith—that God would not require Isaac. No doubt he was surprised by the outcome, but through a double-movement he had attained his first condition, and therefore he received Isaac more joyfully than the first time. Let us go further. We let Isaac actually be sacrificed. Abraham had faith. He did not have faith that he would be blessed in a further life but that he would be blessed here in the world."[55] So Abraham's faith, we learn in this crucial passage, is not wholly contingent on the outcome of the test of Moriah. "Abraham I cannot understand; in a certain sense I can learn nothing from him except to be amazed. If someone deludes himself into thinking he may be moved to have faith by pondering the outcome of that story, he cheats himself and cheats God out of the first movement of faith—he wants to suck worldly wisdom out of the paradox."[56]

The "outcome" may have been a surprise to Abraham, but it is his faith that has equipped him to receive Isaac more joyfully than the first time; this phrase too might arrest our attention, since the first time Abraham received Isaac was certainly joyful enough, seeing as how it was a genuinely miraculous event. How can Abraham be said to be more joyful the second time? On a pedestrian level, one might simply observe that when we fear a beloved person is lost to us—for whatever reason—and it eventuates that they are restored to us after danger has passed, then it could be reasonably said that their return is more joyful than the original meeting. The challenge and promise of faith is that it makes possible not just ongoing joy over the course of our lives but that it might even magnify that joy, even in the face of potential loss. This joy seems to be intact even when loss is apparently more definitive and irrevocable: "Let us go further. We let Isaac actually be sacrificed." So if the outcome is as dreadful as we fear, if the worst does come to pass after all, faith remains what it is: a source of renewed joy and joy in fact over this life, not joy from an expectation of blessedness in the next life but in and for this one. Even if it involves seriously entertaining the possibility that "God could give him a new Isaac, could restore to life the one sacrificed,"[57] Abraham's faith insists upon divine faithfulness to the promise here and now. The exact means by which God delivers upon his promise are unknowable to Abraham and cannot be specified in advance. It is in this respect that the "outcome" is a matter of indifference: whether Abraham has to go through with the sacrifice or not does not determine the capacity of faith to affirm the goodness of this life and the availability of joy in and for this life. Abraham's faith concerns itself with the details, troubles God with its petty cares, insists on the right-handed marriage.

Again, the relevance of faith to this world is precisely what keeps it from being a sort of escapist fantasy or despairing resignation.

> Indeed, if Abraham, the moment he swung his leg over the ass's back, had said to himself: Now Isaac is lost, I could just as well sacrifice him here at home as ride the long way to Moriah—then I do not need Abraham, whereas now I bow seven times to his name and seventy times to his deed. This he did not do, as I can prove by his really fervent joy on receiving Isaac and by his needing no preparation and no time to rally to finitude and its joy. If it had been otherwise with Abraham, he perhaps would have loved God but would not have had faith, for he who loves God without faith reflects upon himself; he who loves God in faith reflects upon God.[58]

So it's Abraham's joy that is the proof of his faith, not even the biblical witness; one might think if one wanted to "prove" that he did not decide to sacrifice Isaac right there at home, all one would need to do is point to the scripture that says otherwise, but Silentio argues that the most secure assurance that Abraham did not give way to resignation is that he exhibited joy and rallied to finitude rather than abandoning it in favor of a flight from reality into abstract detachment. Had he failed to rally to finitude and joy Abraham still could very well have loved God, but this love in the end would have been only self-focused (and probably self-flattering); here we cannot help but think back to Silentio as the poet-existence verging on the religious. One like Silentio, or like a failed Abraham, can love God and remain in resignation, though this love would be alienated from, and unreconciled to, reality. The movements of genuine faith "must continually be made by virtue of the absurd, but yet in such a way, please note, that one does not lose the finite but gains it whole and intact."[59] The faithful person's adherence to the finite must not only be preserved, but like the redoubling of Abraham's joy in Isaac, strengthened. And note too that this adherence is to the finite "whole and intact" not even just to one element of it, to one beloved person or cherished thing; faith saves the finite as such and redelivers it to the faithful person as the fit correlate of her even greater joy and gratitude.

Finally, it should be observed that there is an artfulness to this movement of faith. Silentio observes, almost in passing, that "it is commonly supposed that what faith produces is no work of art, that it is a coarse and boorish piece of work, only for the more uncouth natures, but it is far from being that."[60] His observation is as applicable to our own time as his own, surely, for faith is generally thought of, it would seem, as clumsy, artless, and suitable only to the unsophisticated. Silentio, however, places this comment right before his claim that he would not need Abraham if all Abraham had done was to resign himself to sacrificing Isaac and had saved himself the trouble of journeying to Moriah. So there is something not only dramatic and admirable about Abraham's faith and the joy it brings; it is also an artful accomplishment. The dialectic of faith, he says, is the "finest and the most extraordinary of all" of which he can "form a conception" but which he cannot imitate despite, he says, his own ability to "make the mighty trampoline leap," his expertise as a "tightrope dancer," and his skill at walking "upside down in existence."[61] The gymnastic or choreographic metaphors serve to underline the grace of faith, the refinement and elevation of its movements. In our study of Problema III, we will return to this point, but it is worth mentioning here that part of what captivates Silentio about faith, part of what amazes him, is surely not just its shocking, ethically outrageous dimensions but also its beauty.[62]

The Contemporary Knight of Faith

Beauty is in evidence here, for sure, in the justly celebrated portrait of the contemporary knight of faith painted by Silentio after his imagined discussion of how he would react to the challenge that was put to Abraham. Confessing that he could himself get no further than the tragic hero, Silentio allows that "I presumably can describe the movements of faith, but I cannot make them."[63] And describe them he does, again with an emphasis on the fact that the movements of faith are "the movements of finitude" and thus are "likely to disappoint" with respect to externals. Though Silentio asserts that he has sought such a person for many years, he cannot say whether he has never found "a single authentic instance"[64] of a contemporary knight of faith or if every other person is one, given that such an individual would not conspicuously give herself away. From the beginning, then, we know that the picture Silentio gives us of a knight of faith completely at home in the world of nineteenth-century Copenhagen is not a synthesis of his own experience, not a composite character of real people whom Silentio has actually encountered but someone that Silentio says "I may very well imagine."[65]

That the unforgettable dramatization that follows is avowedly a work of Silentio's imagination is not a basis for questioning its legitimacy. It should also be clear that we are not dealing with a poetization of the actual, which, as we have seen, runs the danger of risible redundancy, according to Kierkegaard. The poet adds ideality to actuality, but this portrait is not based on any actuality.

Instead, what I would suggest is that it is an attempt to picture the ideal of actuality, the religious ideal. It is avowedly an imagined rendering, and it certainly seems to serve as a sort of paradigm. Silentio never suggests that the portrait is for imitation exactly, but it may be read as an attempt to render faith more intuitive; the story of Abraham is remote, and the external details difficult to appropriate, but the contemporary knight of faith is striking for his ordinariness and approachability.

Indeed, commentators generally remark on the inconspicuous character of the contemporary knight of faith. He seems for all the world like an ordinary man on the street. His movements do not reveal "a bit of heterogeneous optical telegraphy from the infinite," his bearing "belongs entirely to finitude."[66] Again, Silentio emphasizes throughout the reconciliation of this man to the world, his being at home in finite circumstances, the fact that his faith does not lead him out of the world of his experience but puts him even more deeply at home within it, so much so that "he finds pleasure in everything,"[67] even the most trivial details of his everyday experience: the sights of "a rat scurrying under a plank across the gutter, children playing"; smoking his pipe, conversing with a stranger on the street.[68] He is neither a poet[69] nor a genius.[70] He applies himself to his job, and he goes to church,[71] though, interestingly, this is the only overtly religious detail that finds its way into Silentio's characterization. Apart from going to church, where he sings the hymns loudly,[72] there is nothing else about this man that suggests conventional religious belief and behavior. His faith is not on display in the customary venues; it is instead transformative of his entire life. His faith informs his attitude toward the world of his experience, and, as the key anecdote up for discussion here reveals, his relationships with others.

Admittedly, it takes some work to discern how the contemporary knight of faith allows his faith to permeate and deepen his relationships with others, but one memorable detail serves as a helpful starting point. The anecdote in question is as follows:

> Toward evening, he goes home, and his gait is as steady as a postman's. On the way, he thinks that his wife surely will have a special hot meal for him when he comes home—for example, roast lamb's head with vegetables. If he meets a kindred soul, he would go on talking all the way to Østerport about this delicacy with a passion befitting a restaurant operator. It so happens that he does not have four shillings to his name, and yet he firmly believes that his wife has this delectable meal waiting for him. If she has, to see him eat would be the envy of the elite and an inspiration to the common man, for his appetite is keener than Esau's. His wife does not have it—curiously enough, he is just the same.[73]

Much can be learned from this one seemingly insignificant, lightly humorous passage. Of all the brief descriptors of the contemporary knight of faith's character, this is probably the one that alludes most extensively to his relationships with others, and this one in particular of course refers to a privileged relationship. The contemporary knight of faith is convinced that his wife will have a "special hot meal" ready and waiting; despite the fact that he has no money to afford anything as luxurious as roast lamb's head, he nevertheless is certain that "this delectable meal" is waiting for him. If he is correct, then he feasts heartily, and if not, "curiously enough, he is just the same." So how can he be just the same? It depends on what he is actually expecting. This short vignette is the dynamic of resignation and faith (which we will see expounded further directly) in miniature.

The point of the contemporary knight of faith's expectation is not the specific item on the plate, the roast lamb's head; if he were fastened to a literal lamb's head, then he could not be "just the same" when confronted with something that is not roast lamb's head. The only way he could be "just the same" is that if the crucial element of his expectation is unaffected by the identifiable alterations in what is actually on the table when he arrives home; regardless of whether it is lamb's head or tinned meat that is for dinner, the knight of faith is "just the same." What I suggest is that the knight of faith is engaged in a dramatization of the interplay of real and ideal that is characteristic of the religious ideal, the ideal of actuality. What the knight of faith actually expects, what he hopes for, is not exactly any given actuality, be it lamb's head or tinned meat, but an intensification of relationship that is betokened by the availability of the dinnertime meal, regardless of what that meal actually turns out to be. What he expects is ongoing intimacy with his wife, which is both indicated and fostered by the proffering of the meal. He believes, Silentio says, that "his wife has this delectable meal waiting for him," so he does not we could in fairness say, believe *in* the meal; he believes *in his wife*. He has an ideal situation in mind on the way home—she will serve roast lamb's head—and in an important sense this expectation is disappointed, but more important is the fact that the knight of faith is *not disappointed*. The thwarting of one ideal scenario is not sufficient to thwart the knight of faith's happiness or to undermine his relationship with his wife. It would not be accurate to say that the knight of faith is indifferent to what is actually for dinner, that he is equally prepared to eat lamb's head or tinned meat because he just doesn't have an actual preference or has come to regard all dinners as equally satisfactory in every way. The knight of faith is not grudgingly content because he is a Stoic or because he is an ascetic.

Another misreading would be to attribute to the knight of faith a false belief. His faith does not consist in proving "correct" about the outcome of his expectations in every case. Faith is not clairvoyance. Sheridan Hough, for one, seems to say that the knight of faith does entertain "a false belief,"[74] but she is on surer ground when she points out that "the knight's intentional state—whatever it is—must be distinguished from merely *wanting* or *hoping* for stew."[75] She helpfully points out that Silentio does provide a contrasting example, of a young girl who "in the face of every difficulty . . . remains convinced that her desire will be fulfilled."[76] Faith is also not the young girl's pig-headed optimism or willful and immature insistence on the eventuation of the improbable. As Hough points out, the difference here is that the girl is bound to be frustrated when her wish is not granted, but the knight of faith is never frustrated, even when things don't turn out as he hopes. What the example proves is that faith means accepting whatever you are served for dinner *as* roast head of lamb with vegetables, even if what you are served is not roast head of lamb with vegetables. The point is not that this involves some kind of epistemological contradiction but that the knight of faith has resolved out of love for his wife that whatever she serves him he will greet with enthusiasm and delight not because he is "actually" disappointed by the meal on the table but because whatever his beloved bestows on him he finds an occasion for joy.

What would motivate such a way of proceeding? Why should the knight of faith adopt such an attitude, a disposition (one could even say perhaps an acquired and cultivated disposition) to receive a gift from a beloved person as the fulfillment of his highest hope? Some clarity can be had if we imagine the reverse scenario: suppose the knight of faith comes home to find that, indeed, there is no roast head of lamb. A less savory reaction can be readily imagined: he could become bitter, resentful, critical, irate, and even hostile. Such reactions would be anything but loving, and the knight of faith is certainly a lover. Determined to love his beloved, he resolves to hail everything she does as the occasion for further rejoicing. A crucial reminder: the faith of our contemporary knight is less to do with what he does or what happens to him and more to do with how he does what he does, how he reacts to the stuff of his life.

There need not be anything false about this faith: we need not think that the knight just disguises his revulsion of tinned meat simply in order to ensure that no one's feelings are hurt. The knight of faith could still be a judicious and frank critic, could speak the truth in love should the occasion call for it. His faith is driven by a determination to regard the giver before the gift, to allow the character of the gift to be configured by the love of the giver rather than to question or malign the giver on the grounds of some aspect of the gift that he happens to find distasteful. He is grateful, celebratory, and pleased not because he is a willful optimist or is insistent on maniacally seeing the good in everything but because if he were ungrateful, sour, and resentful, that would do harm to someone he loves and who loves him. The contrary response, a peevish insistence that there actually be roast head of lamb with vegetables on the table even if there is not, would be indicative of the so-called knight of faith's contempt for his wife and for her efforts to please him even if on some "objective" measure—she serves tinned meat instead of roast head of lamb and vegetables—her effort does not seem as grandiose as it might have been. It is more important to him to promote the intimacy he shares with a beloved human being than it is to have exactly what he wants, as he wants it, whenever and wherever he wants it. If dinner is perfect for him, that's because his wife is perfect for him.

There is an obviously ethical component to this stance: the knight has made a moral commitment that motivates him to practice an attitude of loving receptivity and joyful responsiveness. This is not, as we will see in later chapters, a matter of duty or compulsion. The knight's moral being is not simply a matter of rigid adherence to principle or programmatic execution of duty. At the same time, there is an aesthetic component to the knight. Part of the reason readers have traditionally responded so warmly to the contemporary knight of faith is that there is an artfulness both to Silentio's rendering of him and to his character itself; there is an unmistakable beauty and grace about his bearing toward the world and especially toward his beloved. It is not hard for a reader to appreciate the possibility of being *like* the contemporary knight of faith. It is perhaps even easier to appreciate the possibility of being *liked* by the contemporary knight of faith. Such a person would not only be good to be loved by but would be attractive and pleasant to be around. To the extent that Silentio can imagine what faith is like (and again there is an important limit to his imagining), his imagined contemporary knight of faith is both good and beautiful: "To change the leap into life into walking, absolutely to express the sublime in the pedestrian—only that knight can do it, and this is the one and only marvel."[77] The marvel, or miracle, of the contemporary knight of faith's life is that it expresses the sublime in the pedestrian; his faith is transformative for the whole of his existence, and while outwardly it makes him indistinguishable from his ordinary peers, inwardly the whole of his existence is transformed. Kierkegaard of course never used the phrase "leap of faith," but the leap is a common figure for the sort of movement that faith requires—a leap involves commitment, passion, risk, and resolute courage. But the knight of faith's most impressive feat is not the leap itself but the ability to leap with every step, to make his walking a series of leaps, in such a way that nobody notices he is leaping at all, and for him the movement, though learned, practiced, and disciplined, is now as natural as putting one foot ahead of the other.

The Lad and the Princess

The principal points of importance taught by the contemporary knight of faith are reinforced by the example of the lad and the princess. Kierkegaard loved fairy tales, and in the last major vignette of the preliminary expectoration he has Silentio provide his reader with another one that is arguably even more significant—though not more attended to—than the portrait of the contemporary knight of faith. The tale of the lad and the princess, being a fairy tale, also intimates that marriage of the good and the beautiful that is at the heart of *Fear and Trembling*: a fairy tale always has a moral message, an ethical lesson to impart, but it is also a story and must be an artful one to achieve its communicative purpose. The lad and the princess are introduced in a surprising way, immediately after the concluding words of the contemporary knight of faith episode. Having given us his impressive picture, Silentio somewhat strangely says, "Nevertheless, this marvel can so easily deceive that I shall describe the movements in a specific case that can illuminate their relation to actuality, for this is the central issue."[78] So the first question we might ask is in what way could the marvel or miracle of the knight of faith's expression of the sublime in the pedestrian deceive? The reason it might be deceptive is to do, I would argue, with the phrase "relation to actuality." Silentio himself admits that the sketch he has provided of the contemporary knight of faith is a figment drawn from his own imagination; he is imputing the qualities he admires in Abraham preeminently to an ordinary figure at home in the world of nineteenth-century Copenhagen. The portrait of the contemporary knight of faith is arguably an idealized one, wholly the product of Silentio's appreciative imagination: there is no question about the validity of the contemporary knight of faith for the points that Silentio wants to make, and no interpretation of *Fear and Trembling* can fail to take seriously the portrait Silentio renders for us, but the knight of faith in his account is idealized in two ways that the example of the lad and the princess is meant to correct.

First, quite simply, the contemporary knight of faith doesn't really have any problems. While Silentio tells us "He drains the deep sadness of life in infinite resignation . . . he has felt the pain of renouncing everything, the most precious thing in the world,"[79] nevertheless there is nothing in the portrait of the contemporary knight of faith that would bring that aspect of his character vividly to life, and at this point in the text even an attentive reader barely has any inkling of what "resignation" even means. His resignation is surely as incognito as his faith, that may be so, but in terms of the effort Silentio is making to communicate with his readers, and especially to do so in such a way as to shock them from their lazy pseudo-Christian mindset and refresh them with the particulars of the faith in all their urgency, the portrait of the knight of faith simply does not provide the necessary shock nor does it dramatize for the reader the power of faith to really overcome the worst that life has to offer. This is why Silentio says that the "relation to actuality" is the crucial component: it is well and good to ponder an ideal, and, as I have said, I genuinely think there is much to be learned from the portrait of the contemporary knight of faith, but the relation to actuality is what puts an ideal to the test.

Second, we have just seen that the reference to the knight of faith's wife is both sincere and highly illustrative; at the same time, it is only one mention in an otherwise seemingly solitary life. The contemporary knight of faith is in an important sense alone; of course it is the case that the knight of faith wherever we find him or her is in an important sense alone, but the solitude of the contemporary knight of faith is in fact in sharp contrast to nearly every other significant example that Silentio draws upon in the rest of the book. The stories of Agamemnon, Jephthah, Brutus, the Delphic bridegroom, Agnes and the merman, Tobias and Sarah, Faust and Margaret, and indeed Abraham himself all involve at their very heart a relationship between the knight of faith or the analogue thereunto and a significant other, we might say. The most important stories that approach a description of the knight of faith—the Delphic bridegroom, Agnes and the merman, Tobias and Sarah, Faust and Margaret—in fact all at least gesture toward marriage, the paradigmatic relationship with a significant other, and for Kierkegaard certainly also the paradigmatic ethical relationship.[80] The contemporary knight of faith is only sketchily described in terms of his relationship with another, even his wife, but this is perhaps a drawback by Silentio's own admission, an example that can easily deceive; it is not the case, then, that faith excludes relationship with others, and *Fear and Trembling* when read as a whole bears precisely this point out, but it is the case that the contemporary knight of faith does not in fact support this point very readily (it is perhaps an unfortunate consequence of the fame of this passage that Kierkegaardian faith has continued to be construed as perniciously solipsistic).

So on these two scores, the example of the lad in love with the princess is an improvement upon the contemporary knight of faith. The lad in love with the princess, as we will see, has in fact received a shock and a setback that strikes the reader as more plausibly sufficient to cause him to feel the pain of renouncing everything. His love cannot be, and so actuality delivers a not inconsequential blow to his equanimity, to his ability to express the sublime in the pedestrian; he has a problem in a way that the contemporary knight of faith does not and in a way that is much closer to the actuality of the human situation, which is fraught with such problems. And his difficulty in life is directly tied to his relationship with another beloved human being; the meaning of his life is bound up with another's, and this too is much closer to the actuality of life as Silentio conceives it. As we have seen, some very important inferences can be made about the contemporary knight of faith's relationship to others, but all in all his example seems to have less compelling force for the reader, less capacity to shock and console, to the degree that it does not address itself directly to the actual state of human affairs, which is to be in constant association with and desire for others. Before turning to the example itself, let's also remind ourselves of the phrase Silentio uses here—this is the central issue—these words surely mark out a point worthy of the most serious consideration. The central issue is the relationship to actuality, and this relationship is dramatized more effectively by the lad in love with the princess than by the contemporary knight of faith. What this means more specifically is something like the question of how are we to respond to the ways in which the actual circumstances and vicissitudes of our lives put challenges in our way, how are we to react when our relationships with others seem to have been endangered to such a degree as to render our happiness impossible. That this is the central issue is another reminder that *Fear and Trembling* has a largely therapeutic purpose: to help the reader move forward with her life after she has received a serious setback to her own hopes, ambitions, and plans for happiness.

The story of the lad and the princess is at first told quite schematically: "A young lad falls in love with a princess, and this love is the entire substance of his life, and yet the relation is such that it cannot possibly be realized, cannot possibly be translated from ideality into reality."[81] The young lad's love is the whole substance of his life; this is not a passing fancy but a meaningful devotion to his beloved. That this example involves a relation, then, as Silentio says, is painfully obvious and may in this way be an improvement over the prior example of the contemporary knight of faith. Observe the terms Silentio uses to describe the young lad's predicament. His love cannot be translated from ideality to reality. The young lad is in possession of an ideal, a vision for what he wants his life to be: "I am the one who loves the princess." This is his ideal, his cherished vision of himself and how he relates to others, how he hopes others (especially his beloved) will view him in turn. This ideal cannot be made real. The central issue is, then, how he relates to actuality. The actuality of his situation is that the ideal he has in mind—I am the one who loves the princess, I am the one destined to marry the princess—cannot be made real. The question, then, the question of *Fear and Trembling* as a whole, is what does he do now? How does one relate to the actuality of one's situation?

One possible scenario is discounted by Silentio right away as being unworthy of a person whose love was serious and wholehearted. He could simply forget the whole matter and "settle" for somebody else. This is out of the question. "Having totally absorbed this love and immersed himself in it, he does not lack the courage to attempt and to risk everything."[82] The young lad is far too committed to merely slough off his love as if it could easily be exchanged for that of the "rich brewer's widow."[83] Instead Silentio says of the young lad, "He examines the conditions of his life, he convenes the swift thoughts that obey his every hint, like well-trained doves, he flourishes his staff, and they scatter in all directions. But now when they all come back, all of them like messengers of grief, and explain that it is an impossibility, he becomes very quiet, he dismisses them, he becomes solitary, and then he undertakes the movement."[84] The young lad undertakes a comprehensive survey of his situation and concludes that his love cannot be. He will not merely forget this love, but instead he will "concentrate the whole substance of his life and the meaning of actuality into one single desire."[85] Lacking such an ability to concentrate oneself on a single desire makes the self like a shrewd investor, Silentio says, one who diversifies his portfolio in such a way as to protect himself from loss.[86] But this is not the strategy of the young lad, who is pictured as aiming for resignation at least, if not faith, and as such does not cope with loss by simply abandoning his desire.

So how can resignation, which sounds like a passive gesture, be distinguished from abandonment? In a footnote, Silentio says, "*This requires passion*."[87] Resignation is an impassioned gesture, not a letting slip of either desire or the object desired. It is an "act of consciousness,"[88] we are told on the very next page, not a passive stance of relinquishment but a determined renunciation. So if resignation is a conscious act that is actively performed, what does it involve? "Will he forget it all," Silentio asks, "for this, too, constitutes a kind of concentration? No, for the knight does not contradict himself, and it is a contradiction to forget the whole substance of his life and yet remain the same . . . Only the lower natures forget themselves and become something new. The butterfly, for example, completely forgets that it was a caterpillar . . . The deeper natures never forget themselves and never become anything other than what they were."[89]

The example of the butterfly might be instructive here and may help us to realize the essential point of the comparison. The butterfly can become something completely different without remembering what it was before; it does not now know what it is and did not then know what it was either. The lad in love with the princess has a sufficient degree of self-awareness to have concentrated "the whole substance of his life and the meaning of actuality into one single desire." To then forget this desire would be tantamount to forgetting himself, to being untrue to himself in a fundamental way. As one of the deeper natures, he cannot forget himself and he cannot become anything other than what he is, another puzzling phrase that recalls Pindar's famous panegyric injunction, and one that could invite a Nietzschean interpretation but is best read as a statement about the continuity of selfhood for Kierkegaard. How can the lad not become anything other than what he is? Does not the self admit of change? For Kierkegaard assuredly so; his entire conception of selfhood is meant to be sufficiently flexible to admit of change as one of its constitutive features. He cannot become anything other than what he is because he remains what he is—himself—though of course his self is changing, it is that changing self that he remains. The question, then, is how does he continue to be the self he is, consequent to the disruption of the self he aspired to be, after the shock that has been dealt to him by actuality?

One strategy is infinite resignation. Silentio tells us, "The knight, then, will recollect everything, but this recollection is precisely the pain, and yet in infinite resignation he is reconciled with existence."[90] The knight of resignation does not abandon his desire but holds to it in recollection and as such also holds to his own pain, but within his pain there is a kind of reconciliation and indeed we will be told there is "peace and rest"[91] as well. This peace and rest is won at the price of the pain of unfulfilled desire but a desire that, while not lost, does undergo a significant transformation: "His love for that princess would become for him the expression of an eternal love . . . in an eternal form that no actuality can take away from him."[92] The lad in infinite resignation does not give up his desire; he remakes it, and he does so in such a way that he is at some kind of peace with existence. If his love for the princess can be eternalized, can be made into a static ideal, then no actuality will be able to take his love away from him: if his love cannot be realized, then it must be idealized.

The only way his love can now be of such a form that no actuality can take it away is if it has been immured from reality altogether. Consider the way Silentio describes this new idealization of the lad's love for the princess. We are told, "He keeps this love young, and it grows along with him in years and in beauty. But he needs no finite occasion for its growth."[93] Again from the same page, "He is no longer finitely concerned about what the princess does" and, "What the princess does cannot disturb him."[94] Finally, we get the surprising declaration that "he has grasped the deep secret that even in loving another person one ought to be sufficient to oneself."[95] If we were not suspicious yet, now we would have to be, for certainly this seems patently false, that in loving another person one ought to be sufficient to oneself. It seems clear that what we are dealing with here is the supplanting of a real relationship with a beloved individual—a real relationship that would entail precisely not being sufficient to oneself, that would need finite occasions for growth, that would concern itself with what the beloved is doing, that would potentially be disturbed by the beloved—with a relationship with an object, not a real flesh-and-blood princess but an image of her, an inert fantasy that never grows old, never proves bothersome, never needs tending to, that indeed, no actuality could ever take away. And this explains how there can be peace and rest and comfort in infinite resignation: the lad is now safe, immune from risk, never to be harmed by anything his beloved could do or not do. Both the lad and the princess have been removed from the vicissitudes of life; he has excepted himself by remaining with his love to the exclusion of any other or new possible relationship in the future, and he has made her an unchanging perfection, not an existing person.

The lad can be understood in terms of the ideal he had for himself, the understanding he had of himself as the one in love with the princess. That ideal is put to the test by actuality—he cannot be the one to have the princess—and it is this ideal that is the primary object of resignation. What the lad gives up is not his desire, per se, that he holds to. Silentio says, "The desire that would lead him out into actuality but has been stranded on impossibility is now turned inward, but it is not therefore lost, nor is it forgotten."[96] And he does not give up even his beloved; he keeps her too in the strange way I have described. In fact, in a parenthetical note Silentio even concedes the following: "For it is also conceivable that the knight of resignation could get the princess, but his soul had full insight into the impossibility of their future happiness."[97] This is not often remarked upon, but it is a striking admission, that the knight of resignation could even get the princess and still be the knight of resignation. That, it seems, is possible only if the manner in which he has resigned her itself makes it impossible for him to be happy with her even if she were to be his. And this is consistent with the emphasis Silentio puts on the finality and wholeheartedness of his resignation. If he has truly given up on the vision he had of himself as happy with the princess, truly given that up, then if the princess were to actually be available, the worst sort of awkwardness would result. The point is that it's the surrender of the ideal he has of his own happiness with her that he resigns, not his desire nor her exactly. What he gives up is the ideal he had in mind for himself, the vision of what he reckoned would bring him happiness, the ideal he had hoped to translate into reality. And in giving up this ideal through infinite resignation, he in fact embraces a sort of ideal to the second power, so to speak, an ideal that he neither expects, nor even intends, to be actualized.

So let's turn, by contrast, to the lad imagined as if he were not a knight of resignation but of faith. Despite the fact that Silentio says things like "Infinite resignation is the last stage before faith, so that anyone who has not made this movement does not have faith,"[98] and "resignation is antecedent,"[99] it is best to try to understand the double movement of faith as not composed of two separate moments, one of which (resignation) temporally precedes the other (faith). The double movement involves instead a simultaneity of two gestures, the one (resignation) going hand in hand with the other (faith). Keeping in mind that the central issue is how the lad relates to actuality, let's examine how his faithful response to actuality differs from that of the resigned lad. "Now let us meet the knight of faith on the occasion previously mentioned. He does exactly the same as the other knight did: he infinitely renounces the love that is the substance of his life; he is reconciled in pain. But then the marvel happens; he makes one more movement even more wonderful than all the others, for he says: Nevertheless I have faith that I will get her—that is, by virtue of the absurd, by virtue of the fact that for God all things are possible."[100]

Again, it's a bit misleading to make this sound like two gestures that succeed each other in time, but Silentio does need to distinguish these moments in some fashion, for the first is exactly the same for the knight of faith as it was for the knight of resignation. The knight of faith in his relationship to actuality adds something to what the knight of resignation has already accomplished. Both the lad in resignation and the lad in faith are convinced that their love cannot be made actual as a result of human effort, presumably chiefly they are interested in what their own individual efforts can bring about, not even human possibility in the abstract. The ideal that the lad in resignation once depended upon was an ideal of himself as the princess's lover and beloved. This was an ideal that he himself devised and that he sought to actualize on his own power. He resigned that ideal when he realized it was not within his own power to achieve the realization of that ideal. What that original ideal has in common with the ideal to the second power—the ideal of the princess that is no longer really about the living, breathing princess at all but an objectification of her—is that both are the products of his own ingenuity.

Silentio tells us repeatedly in these pages that while it takes strength and determination to be a knight of resignation, it is possible on our own heroic efforts, and indeed we can easily fashion idealizations of our own unfulfilled desires. In fact, it is probable that most everyone has done this very thing, translated a hurt-filled memory or an unrequited desire into an ideal object. Looking back to a lost love it is easy to idealistically imagine that if only things had worked out differently, then happiness would have been possible, whereas of course there is no guarantee at all that an alteration in either partner's behavior—a more judicious word here, a more courageous resolve there—would have made the difference between love lost or love gained, or even any guarantee that love gained would have proved happier than the current situation, untouched by nostalgic longing, really is. Such retrospective idealization is also, as Silentio repeatedly tells us, an understandable strategy, not at all absurd, but indeed a reasonable way to inure ourselves from pain and regret.

The reasonableness of idealization is itself a negative indicator of the fact that, for Silentio, the absurd is not a logical impossibility but what he calls a human impossibility, a human impossibility thrown into relief by the difficult but achievable work of resigned idealization. The lad does not believe in something that is inherently self-contradictory, like a square circle; he believes in a possibility that is not humanly achievable, and this is where he parts ways with the knight of resignation. "The moment the knight executed the act of resignation, he was convinced of the impossibility, humanly speaking; that was the conclusion of the understanding, and he had sufficient energy to think it."[101] So when Silentio says that the lad in faith believes by virtue of the absurd, by virtue of the fact that for God all things are possible, he will get the princess, he is saying that the faithful lad believes in a prospect for himself that is not a self-contradictory one, he does not believe the patently impossible, but he believes in a prospect for himself that he cannot devise for himself on his own power; he believes in a possibility beyond merely human imagining or understanding. That prospect is that he will nevertheless get his beloved. If he is not convinced in the first place, however, of the futility of his own efforts to do so and the vanity of his own desire for her, then he has not even got as far as resignation, and his so-called faith—Silentio is plain on this point—is nothing more than "childlike naiveté and innocence"[102] that, while capable of exhibiting a girlish "assurance [that] is most captivating,"[103] in the absence of any real confrontation with the harsher realities of disappointment and distress boils down to an irritating Pollyannaism.

Faith must pass through the conviction of resignation, and it is this element that distinguishes it from willful optimism; Silentio writes, "After having made the movement of resignation, then by virtue of the absurd to get everything, to get one's desire totally and completely—that is over and beyond human powers, that is a marvel. But this I can perceive: that the young girl's assurance is nothing but rashness compared with the unshakability of faith in the full recognition of the impossibility."[104] What is characteristic of faith is the expectation that what I resign I will receive back, the second moment of faith that takes courage, "a paradoxical and humble courage to grasp the whole temporal realm now by virtue of the absurd, and this is the courage of faith."[105] Invoking the example of the rich young man commanded by Christ to sell all he had and give the proceeds to the poor, Silentio argues, "By virtue of resignation, that rich young man should have given away everything, but if he had done so, then the knight of faith would have said to him: By virtue of the absurd, you will get every penny back again—believe it!"[106] It is the return of the finite, or even better, the recapitulation of the finite, of what is resigned, that is the hallmark of faith. Silentio says pithily, "Temporality, finitude—that is what it is all about."[107] The knight of faith reinhabits the world of the finite while the knight of resignation, as we have seen, removes himself from this world, distances himself from the course of worldly experience that has proved so disappointing. "It must be wonderful," Silentio writes, "to get the princess, and the knight of faith is the only happy man, the heir to the finite, while the knight of resignation is a stranger and an alien."[108]

Resignation abandons something temporal and worldly and is thereby no longer at home in the world; the knight of resignation does not open himself to new possibilities to come or expect that life will furnish for him unanticipated blessings. Faith gets the abandoned back and is happy to live in the world of the finite and time-bound, despite the recognition that the world is fraught with perils, perils that the knight of faith is prepared to accept, to endure, and within which she is prepared to find even a reward. Silentio writes, "To live happily every moment this way by virtue of the absurd, every moment to see the sword hanging over the beloved's head, and yet not to find rest in the pain of resignation but to find joy by virtue of the absurd—this is wonderful."[109] This passage lends further support for a reading of the two movements as being simultaneous. The wonder of faith is that it sees the sword hanging over the beloved's head *at every moment* and yet does not find rest in the pain of resignation, something that would be possible at any moment but instead at every moment lives happily by virtue of the absurd. This is another way of saying that the knight of faith expresses the sublime in the pedestrian; as he walks, he is leaping, step-by-step. He has become the butterfly that does not forget it was once a caterpillar but is grateful for the change and is ready for further change when it comes.

The image of the butterfly reminds us of another key point: the happiness of the knight of faith dwelling in the world comes from receiving again what he has resigned in transformed condition. Repetition for Kierkegaard is never mere identical reiteration of the same but the same born anew, nonidentical recapitulation. If it is right that what the knight of resignation principally gives up is not so much his desire or the object thereof but an ideal relationship to the actuality he loves, then this is also what the knight of faith gets back: a new ideal, but unlike the ideal to the second power that the knight of resignation constructs, an ideal that is in fact actual too. But this ideal is not one of his own devising. It is one that he is prepared to receive from the hand of God, one that is made real for him in a way that he cannot have expected. This way of thinking clarifies a potential misunderstanding that would render Silentio's claim wildly implausible. Silentio claims that the lad in love with the princess believes he will get the princess and that it is humanly impossible for him to get the princess, which seems to bring us back into the terrain of the grossly contradictory, as if the lad's faith entails believing two different contradictory propositions at the same time, a problem akin to the dangerous interpretation that faith enjoins belief in the logically contradictory. But there is no need to affirm this intolerable conclusion.[110] If what the lad resigns is his beloved, this particular princess in this particular castle, then it would seem to follow that his faith can be vindicated only if he gets back the very same princess, the one in the same castle, which we have been told is humanly impossible. Faith so understood would seem to demand that God give the lad that particular princess by the most intrusive sort of divine intervention.

But this is not what Silentio is claiming. The essential element of the argument is to do with what exactly is resigned, and the answer to that is neither a desired person or object, nor the desire itself, but a form of consciousness, an ideality-actuality nexus that encapsulates the self's desiring relation to a desired other; correlatively, it is also an ideal-actual relation that is restored in faith. The lad has to be firm in his resignation of his prior ideal, and with the renunciation of that ideal comes his abandonment of any prospect for happiness on his own terms as well as the loss of a major part of his own self, insofar as the ideal he has created for himself is also inclusive of his sense of self; it is his very consciousness that is at stake. If he has faith, he expects to get this ideal back, to have his relationship to actuality restored, and with it a renewed appreciation for happiness and a transformed self. If this is right, then he does not have to get that exact princess in that exact castle. The lad's assurance is not so much that having given up this princess he will nevertheless against all hope get the same princess back. His assurance is that his princess is still there—not this particular princess in this particular castle but one he has not yet met perhaps. Or one he has met perhaps but does not yet recognize as a princess. In short, he believes that the one for him is the princess, more so in fact than the princess with whom he cannot be, the one he thought he loved. His faith is that a greater love is available.

Of course it is possible that he will get the exact same princess back (this interpretation does not rule that out[111]), but the logic would still be the same—namely, it would still be a matter of getting what he wanted under conditions that he could not have expected. And even if he does get the exact same princess back, she cannot be the exact same princess simply because time has passed, circumstances are different—in short, no one, whether princess or lad, is ever the same person twice. The point is that whoever his beloved turns out to be, the one whom he loves and who loves him in return, *is* the princess. On this reading, the lad's faith is plainly not a matter of believing two different, opposing propositional truths at the same time; it is a matter of simultaneously accepting that I must resign my ideal princess at the same time that I am convinced that the truly ideal princess is the one that I have not formed an ideal of.

I think this interpretation picks up some of the valuable components of other commentators' viewpoints and is ultimately more satisfying than other possible ways of understanding. John Lippitt sketches a number of these positions quite expertly and offers his own in the *Routledge Philosophy Guidebook to Kierkegaard and "Fear and Trembling."* I do not wish to recapitulate his arguments in full here, of course, but I do find his itinerary a useful one to follow.

Edward F. Mooney reads the relationship of resignation and faith as a matter of the lad's ability to remain invested in his care for the princess in a way that is not proprietary or possessive. He is right to say that "the capacity of faith is neither the capacity to believe God capable of two mutually exclusive actions, nor the capacity to believe two incompatible propositions," but there is some question in my mind whether it is wholly adequate to say, as Mooney does, that faith "concerns a capacity for care."[112] What the lad and Abraham on this reading renounce is a "proprietary claim, the sense that one has ultimate dispositionary rights over the object of one's deepest devotion."[113] Mooney calls this forgoing of proprietary claim a "selfless concern" or care.[114] On my reading, the giving up of a proprietary claim over the beloved would be *entailed* by resignation, but it would not *define* resignation. Kevin Hoffman is right when he writes that "Mooney is correct that we must somehow adjust ourselves to what is significantly beyond our control, and in such a way that real care is nevertheless a component of this process."[115] I think my interpretation does this as well without raising some of the questions that Mooney's does.

For one thing, my interpretation is consistent with Hoffman's observation that "we can associate virtues *and* vices with *both* movements internal to faith. Infinite resignation can result in stoic self-inclsoure; but it is also the precondition of a mature moral outlook."[116] The lad does indeed give up any sense of ownership or entitlement vis-à-vis the princess, but such renunciation can still take the form of what I have called idealization to the second power, which is a kind of perverse reassertion of ownership that claims a rigid idealization of the beloved as the knight of resignation's perpetual possession. On another front, I am able to avoid the pitfall of calling the lad's investment "selfless," which does seem to run counter to the fact that the lad is vitally concerned about his own happiness. As Silentio observes of Abraham, he expects to get the promised blessings in this life[117] and acts "for his own sake,"[118] which does not seem to comport well with an unqualified selflessness (though clearly it excludes pernicious egotism).[119]

Lippitt takes from Ronald Hall an understanding of the relationship of resignation to faith along the lines of an "annulled possibility." Hall is completely right that faith calls for the deepening of personal obligations and commitments to others—I will argue this throughout the rest of what follows. But Hall needlessly complicates matters when he argues that resignation is an ever-present possibility for the knight of faith, one that the knight moment by moment resists. In order to explain the relation of resignation to faith then, he denies that resignation is constructively twinned with faith but asserts instead that it is an "annulled possibility" within faith, that faith is operative when resignation is suppressed, not activated. Hall draws on the relationship of despair to faith in *The Sickness unto Death*, where Anti-Climacus says that "not to be in despair must signify the destroyed possibility of being able to be in despair; if a person is truly not to be in despair, he must at every moment destroy the possibility."[120] Detecting a similar logic in *Fear and Trembling*'s relating resignation to faith, Hall construes the latter as requiring the former to be a "live option" that the knight of faith "at every moment, destroys, negates, annuls, as a possibility."[121] Resignation is therefore required for faith only in the sense that faith needs resignation to be available in order to assert itself against it; the knight of faith can be who she is only if she always could prefer resignation but chooses not to.

The trouble with importing this conceptuality into *Fear and Trembling* is that the point that Anti-Climacus is making in the passage that Hall favors is that despair is like a sickness that never "clears up" on its own. The person in despair cannot wait until she feels better; every moment she is in despair she is making herself sick, and the only way to be healed is if she actively vanquishes despair at every turn. This is not a statement, then, about how despair is negatively ingredient in faith.[122] An "annulled possibility" is in fact a suppressed ingredient in something actual, but that is not how Anti-Climacus thinks despair relates to faith. Furthermore, the association of despair with resignation downgrades the obvious importance of the latter. Consistent with Hoffman's observation above, we can acknowledge that resignation on its own amounts to a stoical escapism (which would put it in the company of despair), but when accompanying faith it is not this at all. Hall's interpretation mandates that resignation be exclusively negative, a conclusion that the text of *Fear and Trembling* can hardly support, seeing as how Silentio is quite clear about the admirable aspects of resignation. The faithful person does not fight against resignation as a temptation (though they could be said on Anti-Climacus's account to so battle against despair); the knight of faith makes use of resignation as an element of her overall posture toward reality. My interpretation, by contrast, indicates how resignation can be active at the same time as faith and how the knight of faith can fully resign a form of consciousness arising from one conjoining of the ideal and actual with the expectation that in faith another conjoining, a new form of consciousness, will be received back.[123]

Lippitt's own view emerges in conversation with Andrew Cross; indeed, Lippitt argues that Cross "gets this matter the wrong way round"[124] and so reverses his position. Cross argues that Abraham's conviction is that Isaac will die, while Lippitt argues that Abraham's conviction is that Isaac will not.[125] "Both readings," Lippitt asserts, "have a significant advantage over a common traditional interpretation, which has Abraham believing two incompatible things: first, that he will have to sacrifice Isaac (and so Isaac will die), and second, that somehow he will not have to sacrifice Isaac (and so Isaac will not die)."[126] I agree that the "contradictory propositions" reading should be rejected, and given a choice between Cross and Lippitt I would prefer Lippitt, but I think my interpretation captures some important things Lippitt observes while still holding together resignation and faith in their complex association, something that both Cross and Lippitt, in divergent directions, oversimplify.

To avoid ascribing to Abraham a mental state that embraces the nakedly contradictory, Cross opts to divorce Abraham's cognitive grasp of his situation from his practical orientation. Attending to Silentio's insistence in Problema III that Abraham "has to know in the crucial moment what he himself will do, and consequently, he has to know that Isaac is going to be sacrificed. If he has not known this for sure, he would not have made the infinite movement of resignation."[127] Cross seeks to eliminate any factor that might mitigate Abraham's alleged certainty about what he must do, up to and including his belief in God.[128] In terms, then, of his theoretical grasp of the matter, Abraham is intellectually convinced by all available evidence that he is going to have to go through with it, but this information has no decisive role in shaping Abraham's action; he proceeds on the basis of his resolve and commitment to his son. One problem with this account is that it seems to posit a dangerous disjunction in the character of a supposedly heroic individual. Can it be right that Abraham has "sequestered" so completely the facts of his situation from his course of action? Don't we normally expect that a person's choices will at least be informed by what they take to be true?[129] We would probably hope that a knight of faith would find the truth as they grasp it to be motivating to a high degree, but this desideratum is excluded on Cross's account.[130] Another problem is that Cross insists throughout that if Abraham in any way dallies with the possibility that a miraculous intervention could relieve him of his burden, he fails to be fully resigned and thus fails to be a genuine knight of faith as well. For this reason, Cross claims that Abraham's theism is actually an obstacle to his faith, since it affords the temptation to a false consolation, a potential "escape hatch."[131]

By contrast, I endorse with Lippitt "an Abraham who trusts in God, who believes in the possibility of divine grace even in this, the most terrible of situations."[132] Lippitt rightly argues that there is no textual evidence for Cross's overly narrow view of Abraham and that Silentio leaves the door open for Abraham to believe in a miracle without that making Abraham a cowardly "vacillator."[133] In fact, the text concedes plainly that Abraham "had faith that God would not demand Isaac of him, and yet he was willing to sacrifice him if it was demanded,"[134] and that Abraham believed "God could give him a new Isaac, could restore to life the one sacrificed."[135] Lippitt correctly points out that "an Abraham who believes in divine grace—in the providence of a trustworthy God—cannot be ruled out (at least, not without further argument) simply on the grounds of being a self-deceived 'dissembler.'"[136]

However, when confronting the apparently challenging passage from Problema III above, Lippitt comes dangerously close to hedging his bet. He claims "there *is* a sense in which Abraham has made the movement of resignation. He has 'resigned' in the sense that he has steeled himself for the eventuality that *if* his faith is misplaced then he will sacrifice Isaac. But—insofar as he has faith—he does *not* believe that this trust in God is misplaced."[137] There are two potential problems with this defense. One is that the sense of resignation here seems rather thin and questionably hypothetical: Abraham "resigns" in scare quotes it would seem, since he does so only if he has to and only in a limited sense. The other problem is that this seems to put Abraham back in the circumstance of having his knowing and his acting dangerously divorced, just in the other direction from Cross. Where Cross thinks Abraham acts as if he won't have to go through with it, while knowing all the while that he will, Lippitt here seems to come close to saying that Abraham acts as if he will have to go through with it, while knowing all the while that he won't.

Both Cross and Lippitt comfortably speak of an Abraham who acts in the face of "all available evidence,"[138] "in the face of overwhelming counterevidence,"[139] "despite the overwhelming evidence to the contrary,"[140] and "against overwhelming evidence."[141] I don't think we can rest easy with this kind of talk, since it comes too close to the stereotypical view of faith as willful insistence on something that can't be proven or is even manifestly nonsensical. Despite Silentio's use of the term "absurd," no responsible commentator regards him as thereby mandating that the knight of faith foolishly adhere to whatever point of view seems least evidentially supported. If I am right about Silentio's discussion of doubt and faith with respect to the insufficiency of experience, then the "evidence" one way or the other is simply not finally decisive. Indeed, doubt and faith as global orientations to reality will even dictate to some extent what can appear or not as "evidence" in the first place. That does not mean that we should tolerate a complete lack of correlation between thinking and acting, as I have already said, and both Lippitt and Cross court this understanding of Abraham. My interpretation holds that Abraham does not act in the face of evidence or a lack thereof because the weighing up of evidence is simply not decisive for whether one will have faith or not. The same might be said about a decision to marry someone: I could of course draw up a ledger of "pros" and "cons" to marrying, but crude bean-counting calculus would hardly settle the issue.

By simply reversing Cross's priorities, one wonders how much Lippitt has improved the basic framework. I have questioned his reliance on the "annulled possibility" reading, and I worry about the possibility that he, like Cross, has imposed a deep division in Abraham between cognition and practical orientation. What I want to hold to is an understanding of the lad and Abraham that keeps together resignation and faith and keeps the knight of faith clear-eyed about his situation but resolved on the possibility of eternal happiness, even in the face of the worst ordeals. I can do that, I think, by arguing that resignation concerns an interplay of the ideal and real that the knight genuinely resigns. To resign the princess is not to be rid of a person or a love for her but to resign a particular construal of her. To expect to receive back the princess is not to anticipate the improbable return of a specific human being but to be ready for the princess who really can be my princess. We can now give an answer to Hoffman's question about what the virtue in being so starkly prepared to resign might consist in. The lad has to be ready to resign his ideal-actual consciousness almost preemptively, reminding himself at all times that the princess is not solely who he thinks she is, not just a function of his love for her, not exhausted by his relationship with her. If he is really to love her, he must be constantly readjusting his expectations, making himself vulnerable to what she does or does not do, opening himself to the unimagined rewards and challenges of ongoing relationship.

A potential objection to my interpretation could be lodged here: if the lad has faith he will get the princess back, but his desire is sufficiently malleable that it need not be satisfied by the exact person in question, in what meaningful sense can he get back what he wanted in the first place? Aren't we getting close to circling back to the territory of settling for the rich brewer's widow? There is an interesting remark in *Repetition* (which, keep in mind, was published on the exact same day as *Fear and Trembling*) to the effect that in the case of erotic love, to serve an ideal and to love an actual woman is *not* to serve two masters. The saying of Jesus to which Constantin Constantius is alluding asserts that no one can serve two masters, God and money, but that everyone has to choose.[142] Constantius subverts this sentiment to say that one does not have to choose between an ideal and a living, breathing person.[143] So how can we have both?

The lad in resignation finds actuality wanting and so evades it in favor of a static ideal to the second power. That is how he relates to actuality. The knight of faith relates to actuality as itself already ideal. He does not choose between them but serves both. How does this work? The possibility of serving both might be more commonplace than it might seem. Consider a typical profession of love: "You are the most beautiful woman in the world," or "I think you're the most desirable man who ever lived." When lovers say things like this, they are clearly not giving voice to an objective truth. Indeed, they would not even *want* the rest of the world to agree with them, otherwise their beloved would be the object of constant harassment, and undisturbed peace between lover and beloved would be practically impossible. At the same time, when we profess love in terms like this, we are not uttering a falsehood either. A lover would find someone who put such an utterance to the test in objective or overly literal terms—"Are you really insisting that your wife is more attractive than Helen of Troy? Is that what you are saying?"—intolerably pedantic and soulless. The point of such a profession is not that we offer it up for evaluative critique or comparison to generally acknowledged standards of attractiveness but that we wish to heap enthusiastic and devoted praise on our beloved. In effect, what such a lover is saying is "You are perfect *for me*. You are *my* ideal." The lover thereby concedes that while there may be something appealing about the prospect of loving and being loved by a Hollywood actor or a Swedish supermodel, such a relationship truly is only a fantastical ideal and not the flesh-and-blood ideal that the lover actually lives with. The lover is saying that he or she would not trade away the beloved for an imagined ideal and is committed to continuing to explore together the further revelations of just how ideal the beloved really is for the lover. The faithful lover has resigned all false hypothetical ideals, all self-flattering pretenses, all expectations that the beloved will be only and exactly who the lover wants him or to be; the faithful lover receives a beloved who will always be a surprise, always a reproof of the lover's selfish demands, but also always a companion and consolation.

Crucial to this reading is the awareness of faithful life as a constant interchange of treasured self-wrought ideals for new living ideals. Yes, the believer is definitely going to have to resign something, but that something is not the desired thing or individual per se, nor is it the desire per se; it is the ideal that the desirer has of herself in conjunction (as it necessarily must be) with the complex of the desire itself and the desired object, the collision of the ideal and real. And yes, the believer will get something back, but that something is the desired thing in a form that the desirer cannot anticipate or imagine (she or he is not the one the desirer thinks) and that something may very well change the character of the original desire (she or he thought they wanted something in particular but find that an unimagined someone is better, more desirable than what they had originally expected). If we apply this logic back to the case of Abraham, we can see that the real issue is not figuring out whether Abraham thinks he is really going to have to sacrifice Isaac or he thinks he is really not going to have to sacrifice Isaac. The issue is that he is going to have to sacrifice the *ideal* he had of his relationship to his son—he will genuinely have to place that on the altar—*and* he is not going to have to sacrifice his son inasmuch as he is going to receive back his son in accordance with a new ideal that will be different from, and better than, the ideal formulation he originally imagined. Will Abraham have to sacrifice Isaac? Yes, in exactly the same sense that the weaning mother will have to sacrifice her baby. Will Abraham *not* have to sacrifice Isaac? Yes, in exactly the same sense that the weaning mother will get her baby back. But she will not be a baby then. Will I have to sacrifice my narrow idea of happiness and my cramped, petty expectations of what life with my beloved will be like? Yes, again and again and again. But I will receive back an expansive happiness that I could not have imagined for myself and will learn that recognizing my beloved as more than whom I want is itself what I in fact want.

A consequence of this view is that there must be substantial latitude for change and for transformation of expectation. Even in a relationship between the same two people stretched out over years, there will still be this dynamic interplay of resignation and faith: a committed relationship simply *is* this open-ended revision of expectation and surprising satisfaction of previously inarticulate expectation. To commit is to recommit, to have steeled oneself for heartbreak, for betrayal, for loss while resolutely welcoming happiness and new, changing life together. This way of reading the lad and the princess would account for why Silentio says the central issue is how we relate to actuality: the choice is between being reconciled to actuality in pain in such a way as to perversely end up alienating ourselves from it or to be fully and more deeply integrated into actuality. Put another way, the choice is between loving this person or loving your idea of this person. The wager of faith is that we will get what we want from life, in a form that is sufficiently akin to our original desire that we recognize it as such but sufficiently different to take us wholly by surprise. And this will happen in such a way that we do not regret the loss of what we willingly gave up and are grateful for what we have gained.

6 Teleological Suspensions

When Silentio poses the question of Problema I—"Is there a Teleological Suspension of the Ethical?"[1]—we must keep in mind that Silentio himself does not explicitly answer this question, probably because it is a question that can be answered only by the reader herself, a question for which the reader must take personal responsibility. A natural way to approach such an answer would be to clarify what is at stake in the disjunction. It's easier, perhaps, to frame the issue in terms of what is at stake if the answer to this question is no. If the answer is no, then the faith of Abraham, given expression in his joyful willingness to sacrifice his son at God's command, is jeopardized to the point of being rendered void, indistinguishable from murder. "If faith cannot make it a holy act to be willing to murder his son," Silentio writes, "then let the same judgment be passed on Abraham as on everyone else . . . In other words, if faith is taken away by becoming *Nul* and *Nichts*, all that remains is the brutal fact that Abraham meant to murder Isaac."[2]

Not much more need be added to what has been said time and again about the teleological suspension and the point that its possible nonexistence would have fatal consequences for faith. I would like to advance a more developed reading. I intend to show that while Silentio's critique takes as its proximate target Hegel's conception of *Sittlichkeit*, the implications of his critique have comparably challenging results for a much broader range of ethical positions that exclude the phenomena of faith and sin. The first part of this demonstration consists in the argument that exclusion of sin is definitive of the limits of the ethical as universal, whether in its Hegelian form or considered more expansively. That the teleological suspension has wider implications than those that directly concern Hegel we can anticipate by pointing out Silentio's observation that "no categories are needed other than what Greek philosophy had"[3] if *Sittlichkeit* is ultimately exhaustive of the ethical as a whole. Kierkegaard had an abiding love of the Greeks, but he also consistently contrasted their insights with those that can be provided only by religious categories. More specifically, recall that the horizon for this interpretation is provided by Haufniensis's contrast between "immanental" or "ethnical" "first ethics" and "second ethics."[4] As Silentio lacks these categories, he perhaps cannot see the full sweep of his own critique with the same clarity as, say, Anti-Climacus does.

The next part of this chapter consists in a consideration of what Hegel actually has to say in the works that Silentio explicitly cites, which I place in conversation with a more nuanced discussion of the relationship of the universal to the exception provided by Constantin Constantius. The reading of Constantius shows that Kierkegaard's logic of the exception is bivalent, extending in the opposed directions of demonic sin and faith, and that this logic demolishes worldly wisdom about justice, fairness, and other canons of "first ethics."

The third section of the chapter deals with some Scriptural examples of how the teleological suspension of the ethical entails a kind of "mismatch" between deserts and reward. Concentrating primarily on the Virgin Mary, I show how her life exhibits the abovementioned overcoming of the canons of fairness. It is, from the point of view of the ethical as universal, unfair that Mary should be favored among women, and it is further unfair that she should suffer as she does for being so favored. Her greatness therefore as a mother of faith (and thus a maternal analogue to Abraham's paternal figure) consists in her acceptance of her own suffering, which seems ethically undeserved. This logic is also reflected in the parable of the prodigal son and in the bafflement of Jesus's disciples at his many "hard sayings." Indeed, I argue that the hard sayings of Jesus—with their disturbing insistence on sacrificing all and loving even your enemies—are excellent examples of what Silentio means by the teleological suspension.

I end the chapter with a coda on how the teleological suspension of the ethical might be helpfully fleshed out by availing ourselves of the resources of sin-consciousness and faith, which are conjoined in an illustrative way by the forgiveness of sins, a doctrine dear to Kierkegaard's heart.

Two Ways to Teleologically Suspend the Ethical

It is well established that without the possibility of a teleological suspension of the ethical, then Abrahamic faith is untenable. What has not been recognized quite so often, however, is that there is more than one way to teleologically suspend the ethical: This formula is not equivalent to having faith. It is equivalent to relating absolutely to the absolute,[5] which can be done not only in faith but also in its dialectically opposite expression: the demonic. The teleological suspension of the ethical is accomplished not only in faith (or better, as an element of the movement of faith) but also in the most extreme form of sin. What is at stake, then, is not just the danger to faith but in fact the entire apparatus of the revealed doctrines of both sin and faith. Normally, the presumption is that if Abraham is not justified in his action by faith, if there is no teleological suspension of the ethical, then he is reduced to the court of the ethical and stands judged thereby. The contention here, however, is that if there is no teleological suspension of the ethical, then Abraham in fact cannot be understood to be either a knight of faith or a sinner. In short, the ethical, the meaning of which likewise needs to be reappraised in light of this expanded conception of the teleological suspension thereof, cannot deal with Abraham *at all*: the ethical is competent neither to judge the knight of faith nor the demonic sinner, whichever Abraham might prove to be. To be either requires that there be a teleological suspension of the ethical at the basis of both. Failing that, sin can appear only as crime or pathology or be subjected to some other misunderstanding of concept and mood of the kind identified by Vigilius Haufniensis. Indeed, recall that Haufniensis puts us on our guard against first ethics's misdiagnosis of sin: "Whenever sin is spoken of as a disease, an abnormality, a poison, or a disharmony, the concept is falsified."[6]

Insofar as a teleological suspension necessarily marks a limit to the ethical, it does so either by surmounting it in faith or in demonic defiance; both are modes of the absolute relation to the absolute and are expressly designated as such in those very words by Silentio. That the teleological suspension implicated in faith is called an absolute relation to the absolute is well known;[7] on only one occasion does Silentio unambiguously relate the absolute relation to the absolute to the demonic, and that is in connection with the tale of Agnes and the merman. It is thus important at this point to break with the procedure pursued heretofore of following through the text in sequential order and anticipate some of the remarks Silentio makes in connection with this incident from Problema III; a full account of that section and the story of Agnes and the merman will be supplied in chapter 8, but for now I will quote from that passage only as much as needed in order to establish the fact that demonic sin is just as much at stake in the teleological suspension of the ethical as faith is.

In Problema III, Silentio declares that "in sin, the single individual is already higher (in the direction of the demonic paradox) than the universal, because it is a contradiction on the part of the universal to want to demand itself from a person who lacks the *conditio sine qua non*."[8] Recall that Haufniensis claimed that pagan ethics assumed the condition that virtue can be realized.[9] The demoniac proves that he lacks this condition: Virtue cannot be realized, at least not on our own power. It is for this reason that demonic defiance is as foreign to paganism as faith is.[10]

So the resolute sinner, the demonic individual, is like the knight of faith outside the universal; here there is indeed a teleological suspension of the ethical, and for reasons that are not hard to appreciate. The ordinary sinner, so to speak, is one who merely misses the mark; the demonic sinner has stopped trying to hit the mark. They are higher in that they have simply abandoned the ethical project altogether. The merman lacks the condition of participation in ethical life because he has chucked the whole of ethical life away. That is why, according to Silentio, the merman would have to resort to the paradox in order to return to the ethical at all. If the merman is to be genuinely saved by repentance with Agnes, "he must, however, take refuge in the paradox. In other words, when the single individual by his guilt has come outside the universal, he can return only by virtue of having come as the single individual into an absolute relation to the absolute."[11] The reason the merman would have to resort to the paradox is that only faith, the reversal of the demonic moment, can restore him to normal human relations in ethical life; only faith can bring back what he has thrust away in defiance.[12] The merman cannot simply undo what he has done but must receive back the ethical in a new way.

If he did so, his action would evince the double movement of resignation and restoration. In order to be with Agnes in marriage (the paradigmatic ethical commitment), the merman has to resign his original vision of her as merely an object of predatory lust, but if he does so then he can receive her back again as a loving partner. It is in this way that faith makes possible an actuality that is greater than the merman can envision for himself. His own sinfulness stands in the way of the attainment of the good he imagined for himself, the desire he thought he had: possession of Agnes. He can, in defiance of course, stay there with the self-pitying realization of his own sin. Or he can accept Agnes's love in repentance, cease being the merman he was, and become a higher self than he was eligible for before, the self that loves truly and is truly loved in return. Of course this means the end of his old self and the end of the desire he had in its original form, but it means also the continuity (through a transcendence, as Haufniensis said) of his new self with the old and the renewal of his desire, now realized on terms he never imagined possible. The great dissimilarity between the demonic merman and Abraham is that the latter teleologically suspends the ethical in the movement of faith, not the demonic, and thus relates absolutely to the absolute in a positive mode, no less transformative of all other commitments and relationships but moving now in the direction of love, courage, and humility, not defiant self-will.

It is because of this breakdown in the analogy that Silentio, for the one and only time in *Fear and Trembling*, therefore raises the question of sin explicitly, which seems to be the wedge that separates the merman—who needs repentance to move him out of the demonic, his mode of negatively relating absolutely to the absolute—from Abraham, who has already entered into the divine absolute relation to the absolute. "I would like," Silentio declares, "to make a comment that says more than has been said at any point previously. Sin is not the first immediacy; sin is a later immediacy . . . An ethics that ignores sin is a completely futile discipline, but if it affirms sin, then it has *eo ipso* exceeded itself."[13]

So if we take the prefatory comment seriously, that Silentio is now saying, at nearly the end of the book, something that goes beyond all else that has been said previously, whether we take that "previously" to mean either the whole of Problema III or the whole of *Fear and Trembling*, either way it makes this passage rather worth our attention. The reason these remarks take us farther than where we have gone heretofore is that here we witness simultaneously the worst and best analogy to Abraham. As outside the ethical by defiance, the merman is at the extremity of one possible movement, "at a dialectical apex."[14] This is also what Haufniensis thinks is most important about *Fear and Trembling*—namely, the collision of idealities that yields the new religious ideality, the breakdown of one conception of ethics and the birth of a second ethics. This possibility is glimpsed in one possible version of the story of Agnes and the merman, though even here the birth of a new religious ideal is only partially limned. This is so if only because Silentio keeps us in suspense as to the outcome. What will the merman do? We are not told. As Haufniensis puts it, "Either all of [his] existence comes to an end in the demand of ethics, or the condition is provided and the whole of life and of existence begins anew."[15]

The implication of positioning the merman at this extremity is that ethics breaks down completely, not only when put to the test by faith (which is commonly acknowledged) but also when tested by demonic sin (which is not commonly acknowledged). If this really is the revelation that Silentio seems to intend, we have to rethink the ethical altogether. While much ink has been spilled on this topic, in brief we can say that the ethical in *Fear and Trembling* is any humanly constructed ethics that is uninformed by revelation.[16] The ethical is limited in *Fear and Trembling* not just by its incapacity to accommodate faith but also by its inability to comprehend sin in the most virulent form. The ethical would thus be any vision of the good life constructed along pagan lines or in the form of modern spiritlessness, first ethics as Haufniensis describes it. As Anti-Climacus reminds us, the deepest insight into the nature of wrongdoing achieved by paganism in the person of Socrates was that "sin is ignorance."[17] But by this limited conception the Greek mind betrays its almost darling simplicity and naivety, in its failure to recognize that one could knowingly do what is wrong. This willfulness, this "defiance," is precisely what is lacking in the Socratic understanding of sin according to Anti-Climacus, and it is likewise what is lacking in the ethical as understood by *Fear and Trembling*. It is for this reason that what is at stake in a "no" answer to the question of whether there is a teleological suspension of the ethical at all is not just the possibility of faith but also the possibility of sin. If there is no teleological suspension of the ethical, then there is no sin any more than there really was any sin for Socrates. *Fear and Trembling* is therefore not just about faith but about sin, even though that topic is barely broached explicitly by the text. It is about whether within the ethical, conceived as the natural man's way of thinking about the good life, there is any room either for sin or for faith. In this sense, the text seeks to refresh its reader as to the essentials of revealed religion (and perhaps—to the extent that this is possible for Silentio—gestures even toward the specific idea of forgiveness of sin), where those essentials include, first and foremost, not faith but sin in the robust sense: defiant, clear-eyed, militant opposition to the good.

Climacus too takes this view of the enterprise in *Fear and Trembling*. In his "A Glance at Danish Literature" he asserts that "Just as *Either/Or* had ensured that the teleological suspension would not be confused with esthetic hiddenness,[18] so now the three pseudonymous books [*Repetition*, *Fear and Trembling*, and *The Concept of Anxiety*] ensured that sin, when it is brought up, would not be confused with this and that, with weakness and imperfection, that sorrow over it would not be confused with all sorts of things, sighing and crying as well as sniveling over ourselves and this vale of tears, that the suffering in it would not be confused with a *quodlibet*."[19] In Climacus's mind, then, there is a parallelism between Haufniensis's effort to clarify the appropriate mood and concept for sin and Silentio's strategy of delineating the teleological suspension as the appropriate conceptual discrimination for distinguishing sin from misunderstood and inapt ethical characterizations. For Climacus too there are both ethical and aesthetic concerns at stake: sin can neither be conceptually confused nor aesthetically bewailed.

We can turn as well to Anti-Climacus, who of course makes this point more clearly than Silentio does: "It is specifically the concept of sin, the teaching about sin, that most decisively differentiates Christianity qualitatively from paganism, and this is also why Christianity very consistently assumes that neither paganism nor the natural man knows what sin is; in fact, it assumes that there has to be a revelation from God to show what sin is. The qualitative distinction between paganism and Christianity is not, as a superficial consideration assumes, the doctrine of the Atonement. No, the beginning must start far deeper, with sin, with the doctrine of sin—as Christianity in fact does."[20] We can read *Fear and Trembling* in light of this principle, even if Silentio does not express it as plainly as Anti-Climacus, who is of course hyper-Christian in his outlook; in fact, this is Silentio's great shortcoming as a commentator on faith: he is unable to give a full account of sin. As we will see in chapter 8, the pagan story of the Delphic bridegroom certainly does not shed light on sin, and the story of Agnes and the merman alludes to it but does not fully explore the implications of it.

In the end, the ethical for *Fear and Trembling* can practically be defined by omission of a serious definition of sin. At one point in the text Silentio writes, "But if the ethical is teleologically suspended in this manner, how does the single individual in whom it is suspended exist? He exists as the single individual in contrast to the universal. Does he sin, then, for from the point of view of the idea, this is the form of sin."[21] Note the crucial qualification: "from the point of view of the idea," the one who has teleologically suspended the ethical sins. But in truth, the ethical does not know what sin is.[22] Sin from its point of view can only appear to be a lapse, a failure, a missing of the mark, a making of oneself an exception to the rule. As it is blind to faith, so it is blind to its opposite.[23]

Additional support for the thesis that the teleological suspension of the ethical pertains to the scandalous introduction of the religious logic (inclusive of both sin and faith) into the unregenerate world of the humanly conceivable can be gleaned from the Scripture references that Kierkegaard associates with the teleological suspension, both in *Fear and Trembling* and the one other place in the pseudonymous corpus where the phrase appears, *Concluding Unscientific Postscript*. In the course of the "Glance at Danish Literature," Climacus has the opportunity to offer his perspective on the teleological suspension, which he explicitly relates to the category of the ordeal as developed by the Young Man in *Repetition*: "An ordeal," he writes, "is a passing through; the person tested comes back again to exist in the ethical, even though he retains an everlasting impression of the terror, a more inward impression than when the gray hairs remind the tried and tested person of the moment of horror and mortal danger when he became gray-haired."[24] Climacus thus identifies a crucial point: the ordeal is a "passing through," a moment that is meant to be lived through but in such a way that it is never forgotten but that the passing through itself has a transformative effect on all else. The ordeal or suspension is not a permanent state of affairs but serves to disrupt the self-enclosed nature of the ethical as universal: to both depart from it and return to it anew.

In order to have a more inward significance than the proverbial gray hair of one confronted with a shock, the "teleological suspension of the ethical must have an even more definite religious expression. The ethical is then present at every moment with its infinite requirement, but the individual is not capable of fulfilling it. This powerlessness of the individual must not be seen as an imperfection in the continued endeavor to attain an ideal, for in that case the suspension is no more postulated than the man who administers his office in an ordinary way is suspended."[25] To recognize the incapacity of the individual to attain an ideal state of moral perfection is a commonplace: that no one is perfect is a given. The point of the suspension is much sharper: the one in ordeal or on trial is qualitatively incapable of achieving the ideal, is excluded from quantitative proximity to or distance from its attainment, for these relative measures have lost their meaning in the face of the suspension. "The suspension consists in the individual's finding himself in a state exactly opposite to what the ethical requires. Therefore, far from being able to begin, every moment he continues in this state he is more and more prevented from being able to begin: he relates himself to actuality not as possibility but as impossibility."[26] Such a state of affairs, Climacus explicitly asserts, is sin, "a crucial expression for the religious existence" and indeed "the beginning of the religious order of things."[27] Without acknowledging sin as the reality of the suspension, "the suspension becomes a transient factor that in turn vanishes or remains outside life as the totally irregular."[28]

At the same time, the logic of the teleological suspension opens the door not just to sin—understood as a qualitatively distinct state of existence that obstructs the possibility of properly beginning the project of attaining the ethical as universal—but also to faith. Climacus does not expand upon this point much here, but there are a few observations that can be made from his brief treatment of Abraham.

> In temptation [*Fristelsen*] (when *God* tempts [*friste*] a person, as is said of Abraham in Genesis), Abraham was not heterogeneous with the ethical. He was well able to fulfill it but was prevented from it by something higher, which by *absolutely* accentuating itself transformed the voice of duty into a temptation [*Anfaegtelse*]. As soon as that something higher sets the tempted one [*fristede*] free, everything is in order again, even though the terror, that this could happen even for one-tenth of a second, remains forever. How long the suspension lasts is of minor importance; that it is, is the crucial point.[29]

Abraham, according to Climacus, is "well able" to fulfill the ethical inasmuch as he is in fact a loving father, a point that Silentio concedes happily as well. Indeed, this could explain Silentio's comment on the unlikeness of Abraham to the merman: "Abraham did not become the single individual by way of sin—on the contrary, he was a righteous man, God's chosen one. The analogy to Abraham will not become apparent until after the single individual has been brought to a position where he is capable of fulfilling the universal, and now the paradox repeats itself."[30] The analogy to Abraham surfaces only when the individual is capable of fulfilling the universal and yet the paradox insists upon itself all the more strongly—Abraham is able to fulfill the ethical (in a way that the merman, who has already failed, is not), but he is placed in the outrageous position of being demanded to exceed the ethical as universal, a summons to excess that would make contentment with the ethical as universal itself a temptation.

In a word, Abraham is confronting not temptation per se but spiritual trial. It is unfortunate that the Hongs have translated *Anfaegtelse* in the passage from *Concluding Unscientific Postscript* above as "temptation" instead of "spiritual trial," for these are two distinguishable notions in Kierkegaard's authorship, indeed in the *Postscript* especially, which gives one of the clearer and more extensive accounts of the difference. Spiritual trial, as Brian Gregor has noticed, works against our inclinations, while temptation works with them.[31] I am tempted to do the sorts of things that appeal to me or that I personally have a particular proclivity toward, but Abraham is not tempted to kill his son specifically nor tempted to be unethical generally. That the ethical could appear as a "temptation" is a function of the fact that he is subjected to spiritual trial. This subjection comes from God, and again, as Gregor argues, serves the purpose of purging the self of any illicit self-congratulatory assurance of her own strength or autonomous resourcefulness. God "tempts" a person not out of fickle cruelty but in order to purge the false self-assurance that one is doing pretty well ethically all on her own, or that one is quite capable of being good on her own power.[32] Similarly, spiritual trial besets us not when we are ethically at our weakest but when we are strongest (hence its relevance to Abraham's situation: Abraham is righteous, God's chosen).[33] It arises not within the ethical as an occasional temptation but from without, as a divinely ordained means of correcting the pretensions of the ethical itself, hence the possibility that the ethical can appear tempting. Spiritual trial therefore pertains only to a religious set of categories: a humanly conceived moral system has no conceivable place for spiritual trial, for spiritual trial places into question the integrity of any system *qua* system.

Once spiritual trial is over, "everything is in order again, even though the terror . . . remains forever." The teleological suspension ultimately issues in the return of the individual to the ethical, but this return is not without revision, for the shock remains with and within the ethical. Nevertheless, there are two ways for the ethical to be teleologically suspended, and both are possible only in strict connection with the religious life: first, when an individual is subjected to spiritual trial by God and invited thereby to faith and freedom by grace; second, when an individual is in sin and "exempted" in a way that parodies freedom from the law by grace. As Climacus puts it, "Just as 'fear and trembling' is the state [*Tilstand*] of the teleologically suspended person when God tempts him, so also is anxiety the teleologically suspended person's state of mind [*Sjels-Tilstand*] in that desperate exemption from fulfilling the ethical."[34] The point is that the teleological suspension of the ethical includes two conjoined possibilities—faith and sin—that together are essential to religious life and neither of which can be accommodated in a natural ethical system.

This is part of the reason why we must keep in mind the essential togetherness of the exceptional and the universal; oftentimes commentators read the exceptional status of Abraham as being the heart of the scandal of faith: the scandal is that Abraham is an exception to the rule, an exception that no universality could acceptably tolerate. But as has been shown, the exceptional is necessarily dual, inasmuch as the exception does not simply establish the possibility of an "outside," so to speak, that would problematically be unrecoverable by the "inside"; the exceptional establishes a completely independent logic that relativizes universality as such by linking up the two possibilities of sin and faith, possibilities that are necessarily coinstantiated and yet are conjoined only as mutually exclusive. That Abraham is an exception is quite right, but the larger issue is the very idea of the exempt—whether exceptional by reason of faith or by reason of sin—and the relationship that the exempt bears back to the universal from which it is the exception. This larger point is intimated in two places: Silentio's distancing of himself from Hegel in the beginning of Problema I, and Constantin Constantius's claims about the exceptional in *Repetition*.

Hegel and Constantius

When considering Problema I, it is wise to pay close attention to exactly how the problem is set up:

> Every time the single individual, after having entered the universal, feels an impulse to assert himself as the single individual, he is in a spiritual trial [*Anfaegtelse*], from which he can work himself only by repentantly surrendering as the single individual in the universal. If this is the highest that can be said of man and his existence, then the ethical is of the same nature as a person's eternal salvation, which is his telos forevermore and at all times, since it would be a contradiction for this to be capable of being surrendered (that is, teleologically suspended), because as soon as this is suspended it is relinquished, whereas that which is suspended is not relinquished but is preserved in the higher, which is its telos.[35]

Silentio stipulates that if the individual is already in the universal, a key provision, as we have seen, and then is drawn to self-assertion as the single individual in terms not otherwise specified, then she can only be in spiritual trial, and the only way to resolve spiritual trial is to return to the universal. If this is right, then what follows is that the ethical has the same character as eternal salvation—and again this seems to be something Silentio is stipulating—but a person's eternal salvation is her "unsuspendible," so to speak, telos. If one surrenders her eternal salvation then she forfeits it altogether; she does not preserve it in "the higher," for there is nothing higher than it in the first place. Teleological suspension assumes the availability of a higher telos for the sake of which the lower is suspendible. This would be another way of phrasing Silentio's claim at the very beginning of Problema I that "the ethical as such is the universal, and as the universal it applies to everyone, which from another angle means that it applies at all times. It rests immanent in itself, has nothing outside itself that is its telos but is itself the telos for everything outside itself."[36]

Silentio's way of setting up the dilemma posits eternal salvation as being the highest aspiration any person could have; the question from his point of view, then, in the engagement with Hegel is whether such an aspiration can be fulfilled by identification with the ethical as universal: is full involvement with the ethical ultimate in the same way that full commitment to one's eternal salvation is ultimate? If so, "then Hegel is right in 'The Good and Conscience,' where he qualifies man only as the individual and considers this qualification as a 'moral form of evil' (see especially *The Philosophy of Right*), which must be annulled in the teleology of the moral in such a way that the single individual who remains in that stage either sins or is immersed in spiritual trial."[37] A clue to what Silentio is driving at can be had from paying attention to what Hegel actually says on this point in "The Good and Conscience." Consider the following:

> With this facet of evil, its necessity, there is inevitably combined the fact that this same evil is determined as that which of necessity *ought not to be*, i.e. the fact that evil ought to be annulled. It is not that there ought never to be a diremption of any sort in the will—on the contrary, it is just this level of

> diremption which distinguishes the human being from the unreasoning animal. The point is that the will should not rest at that level and cling to the particular as if that and not the universal were the essential thing; it should overcome the diremption as a nullity. Further, as to this necessity of evil, [one should note that] it is *subjectivity*, as infinite self-reflection, which is confronted by and present in this opposition of universal and particular. If it rests in this opposition, i.e. if it is evil, then it is *eo ipso for itself*, retains its separate individuality, and is itself this arbitrary will. Therefore if the individual subject as such does evil, the evil is purely and simply his own responsibility.[38]

So indeed the diremption of the universal and particular is a moment in full moral development, according to Hegel, and a necessary one at that, one that is indicative of the human being's self-consciousness and elevation above the condition of the unreasoning animal. Staying with this moment, however, is the real problem, according to Hegel, and it is a problem for a subjectivity that remains "for itself" insofar as it does not resolve the diremption and thus "retains its separate individuality" as an "arbitrary will." So reasoning in reverse from this way of seeing things, we can infer that what Silentio is interested in is dignifying the diremption as itself the final stage on the itinerary of consciousness, not a point beyond which one might conceivably "go further," and what is more, dignifying the subjectivity that retains its individuality in a way that would presumably not be easily condemned as merely "arbitrary."

That it might not be simply arbitrary would be a function of the fact that such a subject would have successfully identified with the universal already. This is why it is so important for Silentio that "faith is namely this paradox that the single individual is higher than the universal—yet, please note, in such a way that the movement repeats itself, so that after having been in the universal he as the single individual isolates himself as higher than the universal."[39] The form of subjectivity envisaged by Silentio is one that is not merely arbitrary or abstract, as Hegel might say, because it has already realized the attainment of moral life as the mutual coconstitution of the good and conscience. *Sittlichkeit* for Hegel is not just about the issue of moral authority but about the capacity of the subject to recognize herself in the life of the community. The very title of this section of *The Philosophy of Right* suggests that the point of *Sittlichkeit* is the concretization of the good and conscience, a concretization that overcomes the abstraction of their alienation from each other.

> For the *good* as the substantial universal of freedom, but as something still *abstract*, therefore, determinations of some sort and the principle for determining them are required (though a principle identical with the good itself). For *conscience* similarly, as the purely abstract principle of determination, it is required that its determinations shall be universal and objective. If good and conscience are each elevated to independent totalities, then both become the

> indeterminate which *ought* to be determined.—But the integration of these two relative totalities into an absolute identity has already been implicitly [*an sich*] achieved in that this very subjectivity of pure self-certainty, aware in its vacuity of its gradual evaporation, is identical with the abstract universality of the good. The *concrete* identity of the good with the subjective will, an identity which is therefore the truth of them, is *ethical life* [*Sittlichkeit*].[40]

If Silentio's question, then, about the ultimacy of *Sittlichkeit*—whether it can have the same unsuspendible quality as the subject's investment in its own eternal salvation—is to make sense, then it may very well keep in place the concrete identity of the good with the subjective will as at least a stage in the itinerary of consciousness's full development of itself: *Sittlichkeit* may indeed be the determination of the good (which is otherwise abstract and unhelpful for moral guidance) and the determination of conscience (which is otherwise abstract and lacking universally valid guidelines). The question is whether both the good and the subjective conscience might be further developed than what is afforded by *Sittlichkeit*, which posits a final identity between the good and conscience, subjectivity's recognition of itself as fully realized not just in submission to the laws and customs of the people but in its discovery of itself as one with the laws and customs of the people.

If faith is the paradox that the single individual is higher than the universal, this does not just mean that the individual regards herself as not ultimately bound by the laws and customs of her people but that the individual does not finally recognize herself in those laws and customs. Similarly, if faith puts the single individual higher than the universal, this implies that there is more to the good itself than the order of moral life can disclose, which again means not only that the laws and customs of the people are not the final authority over the individual but that *Sittlichkeit* simply does not exhaust all there is of the good. That the Hegelian way of configuring the good and conscience is not an advance over the Greek pagan picture of the humanly conceivable good life is indicated when Silentio says, "If the ethical—that is, social morality [i.e., *Sittlichkeit*]—is the highest and if there is in a person no residual incommensurability in some way such that this incommensurability is not evil (i.e., the single individual, who is to be expressed in the universal), then no categories are needed other than what Greek philosophy had or what can be deduced from them by consistent thought."[41] Once again, the target is not just Hegel but any natural notion of the good life. The teleological suspension is shorthand for an alteration in the relationship of good to conscience that is mandated by a serious reckoning with revelation. It is not merely about the elevation of the individual as an exception but about reconfiguring the relationship of the good and conscience, disclosing an aspect of the good that is incommensurable with the generic determinations of the ethical as universal and affording an advance of the subject beyond the ability she has to recognize herself in the laws and customs of her community.

For Hegel, any opposition between the exception and the universal is merely abstract; any interpretation of *Fear and Trembling* that sees the problem only in terms of a tension between the exceptional and the universal leaves unquestioned the Hegelian cadre, which cannot be truly tested simply by asserting the privilege of the exceptional against the universal, an effort that dooms itself to being written off as remaining at the level of the abstract. Merely elevating the individual as construed by the Hegelian system, above the universal, again only posited as Hegel posited it, fails to truly elude Hegel; it only inverts the privileges of both rather than truly altering them.[42] This is why Constantin Constantius speaks in *Repetition* not just of an exception but the ability of the exception precisely to disclose the true character of the universal. What is at issue is the constitutive relinking of the good and conscience, a relinking that is coupled outside the parameters of *Sittlichkeit*. Anything less than a reinscription of the relation itself between good and conscience fails to present a defensible critique of Hegel and remains susceptible to Hegel's claim that concretion is attained only at the point of the dialectic that he takes to be ultimate. The point of pushing the dialectic to another level is to achieve a genuine opposition to Hegel.

If we turn to the *Repetition* passage, we find implied there two companion points that are entailed by the very idea of the teleological suspension of the ethical: one is to do with the necessity of reinterpreting the capacity of the individual for a higher level of developed subjectivity; the other is to do with the necessity of reinterpreting the priority and character of the ethical as universal as a stage—though clearly not the ultimate one—on the itinerary of consciousness's progress unto itself.[43] The passage is worth quoting at length:

> Above all, it is asking too much of an ordinary reviewer to be interested in the dialectical battle in which the exception arises in the midst of the universal, the protracted and very complicated procedure in which the exception battles his way through and affirms himself as justified, for the unjustified exception is recognized precisely by his wanting to bypass the universal. This battle is very dialectical and infinitely nuanced; it presupposes as a condition an absolute promptitude in the dialectic of the universal, demands speed in imitating the movements—in a word, it is just as difficult as to kill a man and let him live. On the one side stands the exception, on the other the universal, and the struggle itself is a strange conflict between the rage and impatience of the universal over the disturbance the exception causes and its infatuated partiality for the exception, for after all is said and done, just as heaven rejoices more over a sinner who repents than over ninety-nine righteous, so does the universal rejoice over an exception. On the other side battles the insubordination and defiance of the exception, his weakness and infirmity. The whole thing is a wrestling match in which the universal breaks with the exception, wrestles with him in conflict, and strengthens him through this wrestling. If the exception cannot endure the distress, the universal does not help him any more

> than heaven helps a sinner who cannot endure the pain of repentance. The vigorous and determined exception, who although he is in conflict with the universal still is an offshoot of it, sustains himself. The relation is as follows. The exception also thinks the universal in that he thinks himself through; he works for the universal in that he works himself through; he explains the universal in that he explains himself. Consequently, the exception explains the universal and himself, and if one really wants to study the universal, one only needs to look around for a legitimate exception; he discloses everything far more clearly than the universal itself. The legitimate exception is reconciled in the universal; basically, the universal is polemical toward the exception, and it will not betray its partiality before the exception forces it, as it were, to acknowledge it. If the exception does not have this power, he is not legitimized, and for that reason it is very sagacious of the universal not to allow anything to be noticed prematurely. If heaven loves one sinner more than ninety-nine who are righteous, the sinner, of course, does not know this from the beginning; on the contrary, he is aware only of heaven's wrath until he finally, as it were, forces heaven to speak out. Eventually one grows weary of the incessant chatter about the universal and the universal repeated to the point of the most boring insipidity. There are exceptions. If they cannot be explained, then the universal cannot be explained, either. Generally, the difficulty is not noticed because one thinks the universal not with passion but with a comfortable superficiality. The exception, however, thinks the universal with intense passion. When one does this, a new order of rank results, and the poor exception, if he has any competence at all, once again, like the girl spurned by the stepmother in the fairy tale, enjoys favor and honor.[44]

There is throughout this passage a clear emphasis on the respect in which the teleological suspension is a struggle, a "battle," a "wrestling match," a "conflict." This battle emerges from within the universal, as the exception asserts itself, stretching in "distress" and "pain" toward a possibility for itself that is uncontainable by the universal. This corroborates Silentio's insistence that the knight of faith has already committed to the universal and lived it out. As such, the universal has a grudging respect for the exception, an odd affection for the one who cannot be conformable to its own ideal. This grudging admiration is likened to the rejoicing of heaven over the one lost and found than over the ninety-nine righteous, a moral elucidated from Jesus's parable of the shepherd who goes in search of the lost sheep.[45] Readers probably do not often regard this passage as akin to the "hard sayings" of Jesus, sayings that are, in my view, excellent examples of what the teleological suspension enjoins, but there is something obviously *unfair* about the declaration that heaven rejoices more over one lost and found than ninety-nine never lost. Why should heaven rejoice more over such a one than over the great many who do not need to repent? The universal demands of justice humanly conceived would seem to insist that the privileges of the righteous majority be accorded greater weight than the repentance of just one. The same outrage is given voice by the prodigal son's older brother in the very same chapter from Luke: "Lo, these many years do I serve thee, neither transgressed I at any time thy commandment: and yet thou never gavest me a kid, that I might make merry with my friends: But as soon as this thy son was come, which hath devoured thy living with harlots, thou hast killed for him the fatted calf."[46]

Once more, from the standards of universally applicable notions of justice, the older brother seems to be in the right. Nothing in the canons of fairness would seem to justify the father's excessive celebration at the return of a son who had scorned him in apparent preference to the one who never left his side. The biblical reference points unmistakably to a radically revised canon of what is morally expected; Jesus proclaims nothing less than a thoroughgoing transformation of ethical valuation. This revised valuation does not disparage the ninety-nine righteous any more than the prodigal son's father despises his elder son, but it dignifies the repentant return of the one as worthy of celebration, not merely sulking acceptance.

But this celebration is won only at the price of the anxious effort of the exception, who must, as it were, force the universal to acknowledge it, rather like Jacob forced the angel to yield his blessing after a lengthy wrestling match.[47] That wrestling match also indicates that those who struggle with God to the point even of forcing heaven to speak out[48] are in turn blessed by God. The individual who struggles is indeed, Constantius says, strengthened by this very wrestling.[49] The exception develops her individual consciousness as a result of her ordeal and only redoubles her efforts as a result of the universal's resistance. Indeed, if she cannot bear this exertion, then the universal will not come to her aid, but helps her to the degree that she asserts herself as her newfound self. The reason for this is that, contrary to all expectation, the very process of her self-articulation is at the same time disclosing the true character of the universal. What could this mean other than that she shows the universal to itself as the fragile ideal that it truly is? The universal's frustration and impatience is overcome only by its own self-recognition as that which really cannot be sufficient unto itself, cannot have its own self-contained telos. It is thus that "the exception explains the universal and himself," such that to truly understand the exception is also to understand the limits that the exception marks to the universal. When faced with the passion of repentance, the zeal of renunciation, the determined will to forgive, the ethical as universal proves itself incapable of countenancing such excesses. In the end, "a new order of rank results," such that the exception is able to win esteem once again, but the exception, of course, does not know that this will be the outcome of her struggle. Indeed if the outcome were foreordained it would not be a struggle. The new order of rank is nothing less than the rejoicing of heaven over the one lost and found, the elevation of the exception, the paradox that the single individual really is higher than the universal.

At the same time, the universal is clearly not the universal as classically understood. It clearly cannot be a literal universal in the sense that is stipulated at the outset of the three Problemata, as already indicated. This universal is one that is susceptible to warping by the extraordinary exceptions, who, to quote a journal entry from 1850, "are the ones who introduce what is new."[50] What is new in this conception of the ethical that is suspended by the knight of faith? Viewed with respect to form, we might say that the sense of universality that is dispensed with here is any that would view the individual as being merely a member of a species, interchangeable with any other instance of the same universal qualification. In the course of his initial argumentation in *The Concept of Anxiety*, Haufniensis asserts that "man is *individuum* and as such simultaneously himself and the whole race, and in such a way that the whole race participates in the individual and the individual in the whole race."[51]

Because of this reciprocal relationship between individual member and universal species, the lives of individual human beings *matter* to all human beings. In a footnote to that same sentence, he clarifies what he means by contrast to the case of the beast: "If a particular individual could fall away entirely from the race, his falling away would require a different qualification of the race. Whereas if an animal should fall away from the species, the species would remain entirely unaffected."[52] Because the human individual has this character, both her individual life and the life of the race as a whole can be said to have a history, and further that "every individual is essentially interested in the history of all other individuals, and just as essentially as in his own."[53] This coimplication of individual to race stands as a corrective to any conception of the universal as other or more than the refraction of the individuals who are not its members precisely but more like its facets, each one disclosing something of a whole. If there were only one single individual, this whole would be neither more nor less than that very individual. Most thinking about the individual tacitly assumes that the individual is nothing but an instance or example of a type. This sort of reductionism Kierkegaard routinely lampoons in his journal as "the specimen-men."[54] If each individual were only a specimen, then indeed, it would be only right that heaven should rejoice more heartily over ninety-nine than over one, since ninety-nine specimens are surely to be preferred to just one.

Revelation thus proclaims a new way of understanding the relationship of one to many. A journal entry from 1854 develops this conceptuality: "To be a specimen is the easiest kind of life, a life shielded against direct relationship to the idea, which would be as fatal as sunstroke. The individual relates himself to the idea. In the New Testament to be a Christian is presented in such a way that one cannot be a specimen but must be an individual—'Christendom' has only specimens."[55] A marginal note to the same entry reads "But, according to the New Testament, everyone can be the single individual. Therefore Christianity ought to be proclaimed to 'all.'"[56] That it is proclaimed to all, however, does not entail that what Christianity enjoins can be discharged by all in the same way. The substance of the Christian imperative is not reducible to a general "requirement," and if it were, the human being would be nothing but a specimen, each of whom would have the same general responsibility to discharge, and each of whom could do so by meeting the same requirement. A much later journal entry puts the matter baldly but nonetheless instructively: "On the whole, and I cannot stress this enough, the extraordinary has nothing to do with the ethical. Ethically there is nothing extraordinary, for the highest is simply the requirement; it is unjust and usurious to want to have the profit of the esteem of the extraordinary by doing what is required . . . The 'extraordinary' is not connected with ethical fulfillment of what is commanded but is connected with the singular relationship to God."[57]

If there is the legitimate possibility of being an exception or the extraordinary (as Constantius stipulates), then also implied is the nonultimacy of the ethical as universal, which can lay down only a general requirement, or as Haufniensis says in the introduction to *The Concept of Anxiety*, "What is said of the law is also true of ethics: it is a disciplinarian that demands, and by its demands only judges but does not bring forth life."[58] In short, the ethical as universal is fit only for specimen-men and not for individuals. Thus what we have discovered is that the teleological suspension of the ethical is a formula for the question of whether there is a legitimate form of individuality that is answerable to more than a general requirement entailed by a humanly constructed notion of the good and, by the same token, whether there is a definitive limit to what a humanly constructed notion of the good can encompass.

Characteristic of this coupling (and in contrast to the concrete identity of the Good and conscience, according to Hegel's account) is the mismatch between the effortful striving of the knight of faith and the promised "reward" of that effort. The realm of the ethical as universal is clearly demarcated in terms of what one is entitled to in return for their doings: crime merits certain punishment, and nobility merits esteem. Part of what makes the tragic heroes who they are is the fact that they are entitled to certain consolations, chiefly admiration and sympathetic tears. The familiar examples of Agamemnon, Jephthah, and Brutus, which will not be discussed much herein, are nevertheless valuable for the fact that they highlight the basic transparency of the ethical as universal, even when the limits of that intelligibility are strained. As readers of *Fear and Trembling* are aware, in each case the tragic father figure sacrifices, or at least is prepared to sacrifice, a child in the name of a higher ethical demand: the imperative of the state or obedience to the divine speaking as a function of the state (the logic of tragic heroism assumes there is no specific duty to God that is distinguishable from duty in general).[59]

One observation that might be worth making is that the pages dedicated to the tragic heroes again return to a rhapsodic and elegiac mode of expression. Silentio holds forth without restraint on Agamemnon's "daughter's tears" and the "blush with enthusiasm" that colors the cheeks of the Greek maidens. Rather implausibly, he asserts that "if the daughter was engaged, her betrothed will not be angry but will be proud to share in the father's deed,"[60] but again the questionable character of this assertion is regarded as a consequence of the rhetorical overload that attends these descriptions. What the shift in tone again signals is that the tragic hero is precisely tragic, that there is an aesthetic dimension that has to be attended to here. The tragic hero is an interesting case not just because it lies at the borders of the ethical but because it also cues a particular and particularly well-understood aesthetic response of sorrowful identification. The tears that the tragic hero earns are correlated to the intelligibility of his act—we can understand why Brutus prefers to uphold the law over his duties as a father, though of course his preference is not an easy one to enact—as well as to the aesthetic fittingness of the tragic hero's deed and the appropriate reaction it elicits in the eye of the beholder.

This correlation between intelligibility and aesthetic gratification is in fact typical of the ideal, which finds expression both ethically and aesthetically. The tragic hero's realm is not just the ethical as universal but also the tragic as artistic construct, and both appear as manifestations of an ideal, the very nature of which is commensurability between nobility of deed and entitlement to awestruck admiration. That this ideal "within its own confines" admits of "various gradations" is clear from the examples of Agamemnon, Brutus, and Jephthah, but equally clear is that in every case the tragic hero does not move beyond "the teleology of the ethical" as such.[61] One more passage on the tragic hero offers a clue to understanding the fundamental incommensurability between the good and reward of it, between the deed and its deserts, that is definitive of the teleological suspension of the ethical. Silentio writes, "The tragic hero needs and demands tears . . . but where is the soul so gone astray that it has the audacity to weep for Abraham? . . . One cannot weep over Abraham."[62]

The teleological suspension of the ethical dispenses with an intelligible correlation between what has been done and how that deed is to be rewarded. The tragic hero, operating within the bounds of the ethical as universal, is entitled to recognition and sympathy, but Abraham's deed thwarts any clear appraisal of its worthiness. Something like the very idea of just deserts in recognition of greatness seems to be dismissed in the case of a knight of faith. Similarly, the aesthetic consolations of the tragic conventions are disposed of. One cannot weep over Abraham, there can be no tragic retelling of his story.

This is why Silentio contends that Abraham

> transgressed the ethical altogether . . . For I certainly would like to know how Abraham's act can be related to the universal, whether any point of contact between what Abraham did and the universal can be found other than that Abraham transgressed it. It is not to save a nation, not to uphold the idea of the state that Abraham does it . . . Abraham's act is totally unrelated to the universal, is a purely private endeavor. Therefore, while the tragic hero is great because of his moral virtue, Abraham is great because of a purely personal virtue.[63]

This phrase, "personal virtue," does not recur in the text, and its precise meaning is therefore difficult to establish with certainty, but the reading that follows proposes a defensible speculation. What "personal virtue" here means is arguably a form of action that exhibits this incommensurability between deed and its recompense; personal virtue is exemplarily illustrated by the revealed logic of the "hard sayings" of Jesus and the exhortation they provide to forgive sins, to sacrifice all. Personal virtue is displayed in joyful adherence to these difficult and demanding moral counsels.

Climacus seems to adopt this view as well in *Concluding Unscientific Postscript*. Commenting on Matthew 19, Climacus says, "The whole chapter speaks of the difficulty of entering the kingdom of heaven, and the expressions are as strong as possible."[64] He goes on to cite the words of Jesus in verse 12 that "there are eunuchs who have castrated themselves for the sake of the kingdom of heaven," and in verse 24 that "it is easier for a camel to go through the eye of a needle than for a rich man to enter the kingdom of God," and finally mentions "those who have left houses and brothers or sisters or father or mother or wife or children or lands for the sake of Christ's name—all of them terrible expressions of the collisions in which a Christian can be tested. Consequently, the entrance into the kingdom of heaven is made as difficult as possible, so difficult that even teleological suspensions of the ethical are mentioned."[65]

So why would Climacus call these verses from Matthew 19 "teleological suspensions of the ethical?" It seems to me that the difficulties that Jesus puts before his disciples are exemplary of what is being asked of those who would undertake the teleological suspension and embrace the life of faith. It is not just a matter of violation of the laws and customs of the people or trespassing against a specific norm but a matter of entirely revaluating what the natural man values in such a way as to strain to the breaking point the connection between merit and reward as conceived by conventional justice. The obstacles to salvation are so difficult that even the disciples despair, asking Jesus who then, if this is the ethical demand before them, who then could possibly be saved. Jesus's reply, one that figures in many of Kierkegaard's writings: "With men this is impossible; but with God all things are possible."[66]

If the test is ethical perfection, then indeed no one can be saved. This is also the message of the parable of the rich young man,[67] already remarked upon, but worth mentioning once more, as it too occurs in Matthew 19. The rich young man claims he has satisfied all the commandments, and it is in response to this profession of ethical fidelity on his part that Jesus issues the specific, individual mandate that he sell all he has and give the proceeds to the poor. This incident is an excellent encapsulation of what is involved in the teleological suspension.[68] The rich young man is ethically perfect: He has kept all the law and the prophets. He has followed the rules. The life of faith, though, requires more; it requires something individual, something that only this rich young man is asked to do. It requires discarding what the world values—in this case, his material possessions. Such an act will appear to be at once radically extravagant and dangerously immoral (isn't it grossly irresponsible to liquidate all your assets to the benefit of others, leaving nothing to yourself and your family?). Similarly, Jesus seems to give no acknowledgement of the rich young man's erstwhile moral achievements. His keeping of the law seems to have earned him no benefits under the law itself. The teleological suspension sets aside this entire mode of evaluation.

It does so too in the name of a reward, though as always, what such a reward could entail is ambiguous and not clearly correlated to what is resigned. In response to this onslaught of "hard sayings" Peter protests: "Behold, we have forsaken all, and followed thee; what shall we have therefore? And Jesus said unto them, Verily I say unto you, That ye which have followed me, in the regeneration when the Son of man shall sit in the throne of his glory, ye also shall sit upon twelve thrones, judging the twelve tribes of Israel. And every one that hath forsaken houses, or brethren, or sisters, or father, or mother, or wife, or children, or lands, for my name's sake, shall receive an hundredfold, and shall inherit everlasting life."[69] It seems safe to assume that Peter cannot really know what this means. Like Abraham, he resigns the life he has known and the conventional goods that are a part of it, and he does so with the expectation of receiving them back again, but what this will look like or how it will happen is never clear until it actually takes place. We can speak of treasure in heaven, of the church as a new and expanded family, and the pilgrimage through this world to the true spiritual home of heaven, and all of these themes retrospectively make sense of the resignation and faith of the disciples of Jesus, but for all those who undertake such faith, for all those who teleologically suspend the ethical, the move remains a risky one, undertaken in uncertainty, and for the sake of rewards that at first, at least, are only dimly intimated.

The Virgin Mary's Purely Personal Virtue

A final textual example will support my conclusions on the teleological suspension, and that is the meditation Silentio provides late in Problema I on the Virgin Mary. Like Abraham, there is a mismatch in her life. It is "unfair" from the point of view of the ethical as universal that she is singled out for divine favor. Furthermore, it seems that being singled out does not have an obvious reward but entails an unfair degree of suffering. Yet there is a reward for her, according to Silentio, though once again this reward is ambiguous and is not clearly correlated to just deserts.

"Who was as great in the world as that favored woman, the mother of God, the Virgin Mary?"[70] Silentio asks aloud, and he immediately questions the basis of her greatness as it is customarily understood: "That she was the favored one among women does not make her great,"[71] and he contrasts her situation again with the condition of the ninety-nine sheep who were never lost and the elder brother of the prodigal son, who are spokespersons for the outraged condition of natural justice and fairness. "Every young girl might ask," he points out, "why am I not so favored?" a question he says cannot be dismissed out of hand, since, after all, "viewed abstractly, vis-à-vis a favor, every person is just as entitled to it as the other."[72] As is the case with so many superficial treatments of Abraham, though, in this case as well, "we leave out the distress, the anxiety, the paradox."[73] Once again, according to the codes of fairness ensconced in the ethical as universal, everyone is equally deserving, so the ethical as universal could very well ask with some justification why Mary should be honored at the expense of all other eligible women. What Silentio reminds his reader of, though, is that the favor itself is not the basis of Mary's greatness nor is the favor an obviously unalloyed good. "To be sure, Mary bore the child wondrously, but she nevertheless did it 'after the manner of women,' and such a time is one of anxiety, distress, and paradox. The angel was indeed a ministering spirit, but he was not a meddlesome spirit who went to the other young maidens in Israel and said: Do not scorn Mary, the extraordinary is happening to her. The angel went only to Mary, and no one could understand her."[74]

While Mary's pregnancy is a miraculous one, it is still borne with all the sufferings and inconvenience that pregnancy involves in any ordinary circumstance. To all appearances, her situation is a quite ordinary one, not extraordinary at all, and the news of the miraculous situation in which she willingly places herself is not shared with anyone else, so Mary is not helped to explain the situation in a way that would make sense to others. Indeed, like Abraham, she cannot help but seem to be a flagrant sinner. As a result, the blessing or favor of God is at the same time a kind of curse: "Has any woman been as infringed upon as was Mary, and is it not true here also that the one whom God blesses he curses in the same breath?"[75] There is something terrible about being blessed, a horror that it conceals. Mary's greatness, then, does not consist in simply being favored, a condition that seems to the standards of justice to be arbitrary, but in the courage with which she accepts the blessing that is also the curse. "When, despite this, she said: Behold, I am the handmaid of the Lord—then she is great . . . She needs worldly admiration as little as Abraham needs tears, for she was no heroine and he was no hero, but both of them became greater than these, not by being exempted in any way from the distress and the agony and the paradox, but became greater by means of these."[76] Essential to Mary and Abraham's greatness, then, is their willingness to undergo an inexplicable suffering; they both accept a divine favor that will make them exceptional as well as pariahs in the eyes of their contemporaries.

In journal entries on Mary, Kierkegaard frequently highlighted a verse in the Gospel account of the infant Jesus's recognition in the temple by Simeon that he does not mention here, though it would be appropriate. In the words of Luke 2:35: "(Yea, a sword shall pierce through thy own soul also,) that the thoughts of many hearts may be revealed." This passage is referred to by Kierkegaard a handful of times in connection with the prophesied suffering of the mother of Jesus. "These parenthetical words, which were spoken in the context of the statement about Christ's being a sign which shall reveal the thoughts of many hearts, should certainly not be interpreted simply as pain at the sight of her son's death—no, it must be interpreted to mean that the moment, the moment of pain, the moment of agony, will come to her when, at the vision of her son's suffering, she will *doubt*—was not the whole thing a dream, a delusion, the whole affair of Gabriel being sent by God proclaiming her to be the chosen one, etc."[77] The prospect that Mary embraces is not just that of beholding her own son's suffering and death but the test that this horror will impose upon her own courage and humility as the means of belief: when all seems lost, can she go on finding blessing in what looks to all the world to be a curse? "A sword will pierce through your soul—and reveal the thoughts of your heart, yours also, if you still dare believe, are still humble enough to believe, that you truly are the chosen among women, the one who has found grace before God."[78] The life of faith on which Mary embarks will have its price: "You will live your life scorned by other maidens, treated as a frivolous, conceited wench or a poor, half-crazy wretch or a loose woman, and so on—after that you will be exposed to all possible suffering, and finally, because it seems as if God, too, has deceived you, a sword will pierce your own heart—this is the glad tidings."[79]

The drama and difficulty of faith is to see glad tidings where the world sees only persecution and pain. Mary's proclamation of herself as blessed in the Magnificat hymn suggests her readiness to endure these trials. In another journal entry, Kierkegaard turns to these words: "Henceforth all generations will call me blessed. O my God, this is quite different from being able to speak perfectly all the living and dead languages (as our educated girls do); this is speaking in tongues."[80] Like Abraham in his prophetic utterance, whom Silentio will say in Problema III also speaks in tongues, Mary affirms the blessing within suffering. She cannot know in what way she will suffer or what difficulties she will have to face; she does not know what a sword piercing her heart can mean exactly, just as Abraham cannot know what future will be entailed by the gift of a son, but both count the divine favor as a blessing even and amid the apparent curse that is concealed by the blessing. As Kierkegaard puts it in brief in a marginal note to one of his journal meditations on the Virgin Mary, "The true religious existence is to be as if demolished for this life—but still to consider oneself blessed."[81]

A Tentative Analogy to the Teleological Suspension: Forgiveness of Sins

With respect to the content of the reconfiguration of the relationship of individual conscience to the good that is made possible by the teleological suspension of the ethical—both in the direction of faith and the demonic—we must return to the conjoined revelations of the possibility of sin and salvation, more specifically, salvation procured by the forgiveness of sin. The very possibility of living a form of individuality that is answerable to more than what is ethically required or to refuse this form of life by rejecting what is ethically required simply *is* what is meant by either being forgiven of sin or refusing forgiveness of sin. To be forgiven (and to forgive in turn) or to spurn forgiveness (the hallmark of the demonic) are the two most obvious content-rich descriptors of what is formally signified by teleological suspension of the ethical.

This is one of the more pressing issues on which the issue of Silentio's limitations becomes most relevant. Because Silentio takes no account of sin, there is a definite impairment when it comes to the extent to which he can envision the sort of act that would qualify as one of personal virtue. The best he can identify himself with is the stoical resolve of the tragic hero, as he admits, and while he admires even more so the ability of the knight of faith to continue on not just resignedly but happily, he has no grasp of what would be required as an exemplary act of faith to make the knight's happiness possible. The argument that follows, then, must reach beyond what Silentio is able to directly assert with clarity; it has the advantage of being in conformity with what Kierkegaard's entire corpus argues about the close link between sin and atonement as the twin foundational doctrines of Christianity (and indeed the priority of guilt-consciousness as both a prelude and aid to the embrace of faith).

What has been shown, therefore, is that the teleological suspension entails the conjoined possibilities of demonic sin and faith. Because both of these possibilities are at stake, the implication of *Fear and Trembling* is that any moral system failing to take both into account is in jeopardy, if only because any such system cannot really be consistently lived. Everyone will fail, and everyone is thus an "exception" of sorts, the one to the ninety-nine. The only direct textual engagement with Hegel that Silentio undertakes confronts him on the alleged concrete identity of the good and conscience as the ultimate stopping point on the itinerary of consciousness. Yet Constantius's argument about the exception suggests that it is insufficient to simply oppose Hegel on this point but that a more thoroughgoing reevaluation of the relationship of the universal to the exception needs to take place. Such a reevaluation introduces "second ethics" as a dogmatically inspired region that belongs neither to Hegel nor to any ethics dependent only on categories that the Greeks had but has altogether different categories in reserve. Recall that Silentio says that once sin has been affirmed by ethics, then at the same moment ethics has "*eo ipso* exceeded itself."[82] The teleological suspension of the ethical is another way of phrasing this exceeding of itself to which the ethical is subject when it affirms sin. It can do this either in a negative mode of despairingly and demonically retrenching the reality of sin and refusing its forgiveness, or in a positive mode of recognizing the actuality of sin and rebuilding itself as a religious ideal with the help of the forgiveness of sin. Either way, the ethical as Haufniensis teaches is the realm of the ideal, and to teleologically suspend it is either to insist perversely on the brokenness of the ideal in the face of the actuality of sin and thereby remain in demonic despair, or humbly to rebuild the admittedly broken ideal by patiently, day by day, piecing it back together with the actuality. Suspending the ethical as universal is tantamount to conceding that the condition is not given, that virtue cannot be realized. The difference between the knight of faith and the demoniac is how they have responded to this concession. The crucial point to keep in mind is that the teleological suspension of the ethical is the explosion of the strictly ideal character of an ethics that has only standards to impose and cannot bring forth life.

Silentio says of the teleological suspension of the ethical, "There is no dearth of keen minds and careful scholars who have found analogies to it."[83] His words have become even more true in the over 150 years since they were written. The analogies are manifold, inventive, often instructive, and often completely off the point. The analogy offered here may be just as precarious as others; I leave it to the reader to decide. On December 18, 2003, Gary Ridgway, the confessed Green River Killer, who raped and murdered at least forty-eight women over the course of approximately twenty years, faced the families of his victims in court. Many heaped abuse upon him, calling him a monster, a coward, an animal, a parasite, a piece of garbage, and a son of a bitch; some said he belonged in hell. But Kathy Mills, the mother of Opal Mills, one of Ridgway's victims, addressed him directly in these words: "Gary Leon Ridgway, I forgive you. I forgive you. You can't hold me anymore. I am through with you." Robert Rule, father of sixteen-year-old victim Linda Rule, spoke in a similar vein: "Mr. Ridgway, there are people here who hate you. I'm not one of them. I forgive you for what you've done. You've made it difficult to live up to what I believe, and that is what God says to do, and that is forgive, and he doesn't say to forgive just certain people, he says forgive all. So you are forgiven."

This is the teleological suspension of the ethical brought to life. The court and its proceedings are the very procedures of *Sittlichkeit*, the laws and customs of the people at work. The court is powerless to even ask the question of forgiveness. Robert Rule and Kathy Mills cannot be ordered to forgive; they cannot even be asked to forgive. They freely do so without encouragement or permission by the bar of justice. The bar of justice can only furnish a time and place for the aggrieved to vent their feelings, which they are entitled to do. Their forgiveness does not mean that Gary Ridgway will be allowed to go free. On the contrary, Ridgway is currently spending the rest of his life in prison and, one could add, rightly so. If their act of forgiveness suspends the ethical, it certainly does not do so in the sense of overruling its legitimate demands. It does so by refusing the ethical the right to the last word. But the ethical judgment—that Gary Ridgway *really is* a piece of garbage—stands, and his punishment is not lifted. Forgiving him means that those who forgive him renounce the right to remind Gary that he is a piece of garbage. But there is a return of that which is resigned as well, and that is as Kathy Mills says, she can be "through with" Ridgway. Forgiveness, as Silentio says, "breaks the witchcraft of sorrow"[84] and frees the forgiver from being continually in the power of the one who has offended against the forgiver.[85]

The forgivers are surely anguished in the way Abraham was anguished. Their anxiety is not that of a specific situation or circumstance but is that which afflicts the very issue of how to respond to the actuality of one's own existence as a whole: Do I retain my rights as a specimen-person and hold to the ethical? Or do I resign those rights and get my life back in some unimaginably renewed and enlarged sense? Can this question even be resolved by asking whether it is "right" or "wrong" to forgive? It's not a matter of negotiating within the moral territory but whether by leaving it altogether I can come back home to it again.

Forgiveness is an outrage to the ethical as universal. There may be people in Robert Rule's and Kathy Mills's lives who object strongly on legitimate moral grounds to the very idea that they could forgive Ridgway; the case could be made that such forgiveness is a travesty to the lost lives of Linda and Opal, whose blood cries out from the ground. "How could you forgive him?" is a question that has no obvious answer. It becomes difficult to speak intelligibly about Rule's and Mills's *reasons* for forgiving Ridgway; perhaps, unlike for the tragic heroes, there are, in this case, no demonstrable reasons that would be valid in the eyes of the court and the laws it upholds. But this too would be consistent with the inexplicable character of the teleological suspension.

Notice too that Rule says God "says to forgive all," not "just certain people." Kierkegaard refers to "all" as being the proper object of the Christianly ordained duty to love, "all" as the object of the preaching of the gospel message. We are obligated to "all" where all is not an abstract totality like the universal, not a collection of specimen-persons but an assembly of individuals. So why should forgiveness of sins be regarded as a paramount example of what is meant by the teleological suspension of the ethical? We are looking for a distinctive moral attitude that needs to be admirable and shocking, that defies humanly conceived notions of what is good and right and fair, that can only be discharged personally, not by any abstract "someone," not a specimen-person, and that entails the power to reconfigure the relationship of individual to universal, to transform the ethical as universal as a result of its being exploded from within. Forgiveness counts as an act of "purely personal virtue" because it can be exercised concretely only between two, a sinner and one sinned against. Only *I* can forgive a wrong done against *me*. When I forgive I open myself to an uncertain future; risk is involved in forgiveness, inasmuch as the one forgiving has to be prepared for the possibility that she will be wronged again. The rhythm of forgiveness and sin, sin and forgiveness, is the rhythm of the contemporary knight of faith's footfalls on his way home in the evening; it is the music of the sublime in the pedestrian.[86]

The main issue at stake in the teleological suspension of the ethical is something like the forgiveness of sins: what the teleological suspension of the ethical means is not the outrageous countenancing of a morally reprehensible action by the fig leaf of faith; it is the equally outrageous countenancing of a morally reprehensible action by the retrospective absorption by faith of the morally reprehensible into its own body. Typically, interpretations of the teleological suspension vacillate between underscoring the scandal of the demand that is imposed upon Abraham, and trying to allegorize or in some way "soften" the demand by rendering it more plausible. My interpretation insists on both: the way to make the demand more plausible is to refresh the sense in which the plausible is actually outrageously demanding. We, and Kierkegaard's original readers, are used to the notion that forgiveness is a morally praiseworthy thing to do, but we have forgotten how outrageous such a demand is; we have forgotten even that such a demand could be, and has been, considered obscene. Conversely, my reading insists that the outrageous nature of the religious demand, whose offensiveness we must be schooled to appreciate anew, must also be absorbed into a new spontaneous way of thinking that fully accepts the obscenity of the religious revelation and puts it to work in ordinary living.

Forgiveness, in a powerful and positive sense, "breaks the law" antipodal to the sense in which demonic sin breaks the law. It overcomes its binding power, restoring relationship and fostering spiritual development beyond the wreckage of moral failure. By the power of forgiveness, all things become new. Forgiveness entails surmounting the "rules" that would regard retribution for wrongs done against one to be perfectly in order, defensible, and even praiseworthy. One who has been wronged, after all, is *entitled* to exact at the very least a proportional recompense for the offense. By enacting forgiveness or love for an enemy, there is then the requisite element of resignation. What one gives up is one's just deserts, one's right to press one's suit against an offender. And there is a commensurate return as well in the form of renewed and intensified relationship. This way of reading the teleological suspension (or the aspect of it that opens onto faith) does shed light on Abraham. "Insofar as the universal was present, it was cryptically in Isaac, hidden, so to speak, in Isaac's loins, and must cry out with Isaac's mouth: Do not do this, you are destroying everything."[87] The worldly wisdom that advises acting for the state, the nation, making that the measure of all righteous doings, cannot countenance such reckless disregard for justice, but forgiveness does flaunt the rules of the universal. Abraham puts in jeopardy the whole apparatus of nation and state by striking at the very foundation of these ethical structures.

The real nub of teleological suspension of the ethical thus is, on my reading, not much to do with an allegedly divine command that would trump in some way the established rules of wrong and right but refers to the way in which the imperatives of "second ethics" (most especially as given expression in the "hard sayings" of Jesus) demolish the placid and calmly rational notions of the Good inherited from Greek culture and any modern way of thinking that proves itself more indebted to classical thinking than the religious spirit of forgiveness. *Fear and Trembling* teaches that the life of faith requires much more than what the natural human being would be persuaded was rational to give, but it also teaches that the life of faith promises more in terms of happiness and gratification than the natural human being would regard as normal to expect.

7 Absolute Duty

Problema II tends to be read as a sort of restatement of the key themes of Problema I, admittedly the more famous and more often excerpted section on the celebrated and controversial teleological suspension of the ethical. Everyone admits that the topic of Problema III is different from the focus of the first two Problemata, but no one seems to feel that it is necessary to account for why Silentio chooses to more or less repeat himself in Problema I. It is my view that the first two Problemata do have related foci, but I would also argue that Problema II is not merely a retread of Problema I; if Problema II were wholly superfluous to the argument of Problema I, then I take it a separate question would have to be answered regarding why Silentio chooses to repeat himself. On my reading of the text, Problema I establishes the plausibility of a morally significant sphere of human concern that is not reducible to the universality of humanly contrived ethical norms, the realm of the ethical ideal. This is not the same as proving that there is an amoral sphere of human concern; that there is such a sphere is assumed by Silentio under the auspices of the aesthetic. It is also not the same as proving that there is an absolute duty to God, which is the specific, and importantly different topic of Problema II; in fact, I think a complete understanding of the text demonstrates that the teleological suspension of the ethical encompasses more than just the prospect of having faith. There is more than one way to teleologically suspend the ethical, as we have seen. This formula is not equivalent to having faith. It is equivalent to relating absolutely to the absolute,[1] which can be done not only in faith but also in its dialectically opposite expression: the demonic.

The teleological suspension of the ethical is accomplished not only in faith but also in the most extreme form of sin. What is at stake, then, is not just the danger to Abraham's faith but in fact the entire apparatus of the Judeo-Christian understanding of both sin and faith. Problema I establishes the possibility of an opening of ethical universality to possibilities outside itself, the possibilities of both sin and faith. We could say more specifically that since Problema I is concerned primarily with the prospect of the single individual's being higher than the universal, it is to that extent interested in the possibility of a form of subjectivity that could live its life in the shape of faith or demonic sin, both incapable of being anticipated by forms of ethical thinking and living that are closed to the revelation of sin and the forgiveness of sin. Only if one reads Problema I as having only to do only with the possibility of faith can one then read Problema

II as if it were merely restating the same point. It is not. Instead, it is enlarging upon the conclusion of Problema I in the positive direction of more deeply exploring the form of faith that the teleological suspension of the ethical makes possible. Recalling the question of Problema II—"Is there an Absolute Duty to God?"—will serve as a reminder that the more particular interest of this section is not about the possibility of adding one more duty to a roster of many but about whether the duty to God is absolute and thus transformative of all else in the sphere of the ethical as universal.

Problema II then introduces the question (though it does not fully answer it) of what might become of the ethical if it is transformed and deepened in the positive direction that Problema I simply makes conceivable. As is clear from the previous chapter's discussion, the teleological suspension of the ethical explodes the ethical ideal, causing it to exceed itself in such a way as to make possible both the demonic despair of extreme sin and the forgiveness of that sin and the bringing forth of life that only the religious ideal can inaugurate once the ethical ideal has been shattered on the rocks of the actuality of sin. The teleological suspension thus puts an end to first ethics and institutes the possibility of a second ethics. Problema II, at least to some extent, explores what that second ethics might look like; it is therefore a deepening of the question of Problema I in the positive direction (while Problema III in its way and in part is a deepening of the question of Problema I in the negative direction).

"Is there an Absolute Duty to God?"[2] therefore is not a question that restates the question of Problema I but seeks to ask and, to a limited degree, explore whether and how faith can emerge from the ethical as universal in such a way as to transform the ethical as universal by overcoming it. As readers are aware, the issue at hand, in its more precise formulation, is that according to the ethical as universal, "it is proper to say that every duty is essentially duty to God, but if no more can be said than this, then it is also said that I actually have no duty to God."[3] In other words, if every duty is in some attenuated sense a duty to God, then no duty is a duty *specifically* to God. "For example, it is a duty to love one's neighbor. It is a duty by its being traced back to God, but in the duty I enter into relation not to God but to the neighbor I love. If in this connection I then say that it is my duty to love God, I am actually pronouncing only a tautology, inasmuch as 'God' in a totally abstract sense is here understood as the divine—that is, the universal, that is, the duty."[4] Notice this way of looking at the ethical as universal is wholly consistent with the picture I have painted of it as primarily being defined by its complete security in the pagan or spiritless supposition of a humanly crafted vision of the good life that owes nothing to revelation. "God" here functions in a nonrealist way or as a nonoperative complement to moralistic humanism.

On such terms, "the whole existence of the human race rounds itself off as a perfect, self-contained sphere, and then the ethical is that which limits and fills at one and the same time. God comes to be an invisible vanishing point, an impotent thought; his power is only in the ethical, which fills all of existence."[5] The phrasing here is reminiscent of Haufniensis's claim that "either all of existence comes to an end in the demand of ethics, or the condition is provided and the whole of life and of existence begins anew."[6] If the ethical as universal really "fills all of existence," then either ethics has the last word, or a new condition is provided (the forgiveness of sin, perhaps), and "the whole of life and of existence begins anew" in a transformed and expanded manner. This would be the paradox of faith as it applies to the opening up of the possibility of an absolute duty to God: "The single individual is higher than the universal, that the single individual . . . determines his relation to the universal by his relation to the absolute, not his relation to the absolute by his relation to the universal."[7] If the single individual transcends the ethical as universal in faith, then her relation to the universal is rearticulated in terms of her new absolute relation to the absolute (in a manner consistent with Constantius's discussion of the logic of the exception and universal discussed in the prior chapter). Duty does not define God, rendering "God" a mere phantom that adds only a rhetorical veneer to the impermeable bounds of the ethical as universal; on the contrary, God limits duty.

That there can be a duty to God of some sort is not the most salient challenge to Hegel or any humanly constructed vision of the good life. A duty to the divine could conceivably be added to an extant table of duties or could, as the opening paragraphs of Problema II suggest, be simply a way of reinterpreting the basis of all duties. The real challenge is whether the duty to God can be an absolute one (and Problema II, as we will see, traces out the implications of what such a relation would mean). On the Hegelian hypothesis that Silentio is testing, "God" would be another name for the absolute as totality, "that which limits and fills at one and the same time." On such a view, "there is nothing incommensurable in a human life, and if the incommensurable . . . is present [it] is there only by an accident from which nothing results."[8] Such is Silentio's summarization of Hegel, for whom, he continues to argue, "*das Äussere* [the outer]" or "*die Entäusserung* [the externalization]" is "higher than *das Innere* [the inner]."[9] The child, for instance, is the inner, the adult, the outer, "with the result that the child is determined by the external and, conversely, the adult as *das Äussere* by the inner."[10]

Notice here on Silentio's recap of Hegel, the outer is higher than the inner, inasmuch as externalization is the meaning of the absolute, which realizes itself in its own self-externalizing, but this Hegelian self-externalizing remains within a limit that fills at the same time. The child is determined by the external because the child becomes an adult by unfolding itself, but the adult too is determined by the child inasmuch as the adult, in the end, is nothing but this self-unfolding of the child. That there is instead, Silentio suggests, an incommensurability within the development itself, is an implication that extends not only to the structure of subjectivity—the child who grows up to be an adult—but also to the absolute and indeed to the absolute subject. The incommensurability here is, crucially, "a new interiority," not the first interiority, which is the realm of "feelings, moods, idiosyncrasies" and other "vagaries."[11] The new interiority, therefore, is not a residuum of unexhausted immediacy; the new interiority, or second immediacy as Kierkegaard often calls it, is an excrescence of the absolute's self-giving. It is the generation within the absolute of the absolute's own possibility of return to itself via a genuine giving of genuine otherness, for only an other can render true return via its own denial of itself in the face of the absolute. Such a return is made possible by resignation, which allows the prospect of faith to break through. That resignation is already an advance on feeling and first immediacy is proven by the example of Socrates, who made in "an intellectual sense" "the movement of infinity" through the deployment of ignorance. By renouncing any pretense to divine wisdom and claiming ignorance for himself, Socrates "emptied himself in the infinite"[12] by resigning a fixed ideal of himself as divinely wise, a goal he had pursued assiduously at the beginning of his career. If Socrates is not then eligible for faith, at least part of the reason is that he has no notion of a God in whom one could have faith, a God that would be transcendent even to the Good.[13] "The paradox of faith, then, is this: that the single individual is higher than the universal, that the single individual . . . determines his relation to the universal by his relation to the absolute, not his relation to the absolute by his relation to the universal. The paradox may also be expressed in this way: that there is an absolute duty to God."[14] That there is a difference at all between the universal and the absolute is in fact already an innovation on Socrates and Hegel.

A vital caveat: "From this it does not follow that the ethical should be invalidated; rather, the ethical receives a completely different expression, a paradoxical expression, such as, for example, that love to God may bring the knight of faith to give his love to the neighbor—an expression opposite to that which, ethically speaking, is duty."[15] In light of some prevalent ways of interpreting *Fear and Trembling*, this sentence may be one of the most important in the entire book. If it is not clear by now from the preponderance of the critical literature that Silentio does not intend anything like the discarding of the ethical, then this passage alone should clinch the point. The ethical, according to Silentio, even when subjected to teleological suspension, is at most relativized, never invalidated. More important, I would argue, it is transformed in its very relativization. The most sophisticated commentators on *Fear and Trembling* have taken on board this point, that at no time does Silentio advocate the demolishing or wholesale discounting of the ethical as universal, but it's a point that bears repeating. A married person sets aside the preferences and tastes in which she freely indulged as an unattached person, but she does not thereby refuse herself these preferences and tastes entirely. It would be more accurate to say that she enjoys them anew as a function of her love for her spouse, who may demonstrate his love in return by bequeathing her preferences and tastes as gifts of love. She does not insist on them but relates to them in a freer and more rewarding way. Similarly, the knight of faith does not dispense with the ethical as universal but still gives her love to her neighbor, only now in a mode "opposite to that which, ethically speaking, is duty."

So what is the opposite of duty? We are left to speculate here, but we can make some reasonable conjectures about what the opposite of duty might look like. One can surmise that if duty is the realm of moral compulsion, then the opposite of duty is an area of action that is free, spontaneous, and generous. If duty is something I have to force myself to perform against my inclinations, then the opposite of duty is what flows from me happily and readily. If duty is what I must do, the opposite is what I will do willingly. The very idea of duty as a moral category, fairly or not, would have had for Kierkegaard's readers and probably still has for his readers today an unmistakably Kantian flavor. Our duty is what we must do, not what we are at all inclined to do; it is a matter of compulsion more than happy cooperation.

Further evidence for this reading is available in Silentio's remarkable discussion of one of the "hard sayings" of Jesus.[16] "As we all know, Luke 14:26 offers a remarkable teaching on the absolute duty to God: 'If any one comes to me and does not hate his own father and mother and wife and children and brothers and sisters, yes, and even his own life, he cannot be my disciple.' This is a hard saying. Who can bear to listen to it? This is the reason, too, that we seldom hear it. But this silence is only an escape that is of no avail."[17] Because this saying is indeed so hard to bear, Silentio says it isn't often repeated, and when it is, it comes with a reassuring caveat provided by amateur Greek exegesis to the effect that here the word "hate" does not mean what it seems like it means but instead means "love less, esteem less," or "honor not."[18] The effect, then, of the saying is much softened so that hearers of this particular word need not be too bothered by it. However, Silentio is not having any of this false consolation, and he points out that in the very same chapter of Luke, immediately after this hard saying, Jesus goes on to point out that anyone embarking on a project like building a tower counts the cost before beginning in order to determine her own ability to finish the job. On Silentio's reading, the close proximity of this advice to the declaration that one must hate one's own family and indeed one's own life in order to be Jesus's disciple indicates that part of the message of the hard saying is a call to be wary of beginning a project of discipleship that one cannot see through to the end. In fact, the verse that separates the two vignettes, which Silentio does not refer to, though he might have done so profitably, reads, "And whosoever doth not bear his cross, and come after me, cannot be my disciple,"[19] a caution that supports Silentio's suggestion that if one is not prepared to be crucified then one should not follow Jesus down the path that takes him to that very fate. In light of the tower metaphor, Silentio exhorts his readers to at least be "sufficiently honest" to admit that this is the summons of faith, to not water it down, even if one lacks the courage to respond positively to it.

The course of action of the prideful but honest person who holds herself back from taking up the cross because she knows herself well enough to know that she cannot carry it all the way up to Calvary is certainly to be preferred to the course of action followed by "that pious and accommodating exegete."[20] Indeed if the scripture is allowed to be sugarcoated, Silentio says, one can only hope that anyone forced to swallow that pill will be thereby convinced that "Christianity is one of the most miserable things in the world."[21] Indeed it would be so, Silentio argues, if at the very moment it tried to preach "something terrible" it ended up "slavering" instead, offering up a milquetoast counsel to the effect "that one should be less kind, less attentive, more indifferent."[22] Desirous of spewing forth this sort of lukewarm reading and teaching, Silentio instead forcefully asserts that "it is easy to see that if this passage is to have any meaning it must be understood literally."[23] A reading not "literal" enough would seem to be one, in Silentio's mind, that allows for too much comfortable distance from the text and its message. This explains why in his subsequent commentary upon Luke 14:26, Silentio offers his readers an interpretation of the hard saying that is not particularly literal but rather designed to maximize the force of the passage and educe its teaching, which actually turns out to entail not a duty to hate but a duty to love all the more.

Immediately after he states his requirement that the passage at hand be understood literally, Silentio affirms that it is indeed "God . . . who demands absolute love," but he right away qualifies what must be meant by "absolute" with a particularly helpful and appropriate example.

> Anyone who in demanding a person's love believes that this love is demonstrated by his becoming indifferent to what he otherwise cherished is not merely an egotist but is also stupid, and anyone demanding that kind of love in the same moment signs his own death sentence insofar as his life is centered in this desired love. For example, a man requires his wife to leave her father and mother, but if he considers it a demonstration of her extraordinary love to him that she for his sake became an indifferent and lax daughter etc., then he is far more stupid than the stupid. If he had any idea of what love is, he would wish to discover that she was perfect in her love as a daughter and sister, and he would see therein that she would love him more than anyone in the kingdom. Thus what would be regarded as a sign of egotism and stupidity in a person may by the help of an exegete be regarded as a worthy representation of divinity.[24]

Now there are a number of points worth observing here. First, we must underscore that God indeed, according to Silentio, demands absolute love, but what that precisely means he at first shows us, as he so often does, negatively. What does absolute love *not* demand? It does not demand that love be shown to the demander by the lover becoming indifferent to who and what the lover already loves. And it does not insist upon this because to do so would be egotistical—"You must love only me, not anybody or anything else"—and it would be stupid inasmuch as if the demander really lives in and for the beloved, then treating the beloved in this way constitutes a signing of the demander's own death sentence. If I demand that my beloved love only me, I sign my own death sentence, and I think I do this in two ways. First, the person I love is who she is at least in part because of her relationships with others. She is her mother's daughter, her friend's friend, her brother's sister, and so on. If I insist she break off these relationships altogether then I am in effect asking her to be someone else, which is stupid, because presumably I love her for who she currently is, not a fantasy of who I imagine she could be once I get her to change in a variety of ways I am secretly planning for her. As we have seen from the example of the lad and the princess, genuine love is reconciled to a living, breathing person, an actuality, not an idealized object. Second, if I insist on less love for others from my beloved, I do harm, it seems to me, to her ability to love in general, which in turn I would think inevitably does harm to her ability to love me in particular. This point about genuine love follows from the discussion of absolute duty, which clearly does not trump other duties but results in their intensification and transformation.

The marital imagery is quite fitting of course: "A man requires his wife to leave her father and mother," a pronouncement that is itself a sort of hard saying, though it does not often strike us as such. We do forsake our parents, the ones who loved us from birth, before anybody else would, for a comparative latecomer, a partner in our adult lives. Fairness would seem to militate against such an obvious travesty. Isn't it unjust that we do so little to return the gifts that our parents lavished on us from the beginning of our lives? This again is the voice of the prodigal son's elder brother speaking, and his voice does speak a truth of some importance. But what exactly do we mean by "leaving"? Again, Silentio is clear that what we definitely do *not* mean is that the new wife is entitled to become an indifferent daughter to her parents, the new husband a lax son to his parents. So when a would-be wife leaves her parents, in some sense of course she is leaving them, but she certainly does not leave them in the sense of abandoning them altogether. If the new spouses really love one another, Silentio says, each would hope to find that the other is perfect in his or her attendance to prior obligations. In fact, the beloved's observance of their ethical duties to others with whom they had relationships prior to their meeting one another should be itself *evidence* of their love for each other.

That can be so, it seems to me, only if the participants in the exclusive relationship of the marriage partnership are prepared to take delight not just in the love that each has for the other but in the general expansiveness of love as it is shared preeminently, of course in the marriage but, by extension, to others as well. In fact, let me push this point a little further here than the letter of the text specifies. Is it the case that a husband or wife is content to see their partner *being* a *good* daughter or sister or son or brother? Or is it the case that a husband or wife wants to the see their partner *becoming* a *better* daughter or sister or son or brother? I am inclined to think the latter. I suspect that partners to a priority relationship like marriage want to be able to honestly say "I am a better person now thanks to this relationship" and "The one I love is a better person because of our shared love, better than they were when we first met." In point of fact, a wife leaves her parents, therefore, not by forsaking them, and not even by being just as dutiful a child to them as she was before she got married, but by precisely becoming a *better* child to them. That improvement naturally does not happen in continuity with the prior relationship; of necessity, there is a change in the relationship between the grown child and her parents. The grown child no longer lives in the parents' home, she no longer has to do whatever they tell her, and so on. But I think if we really take Silentio's logic through here to the end, we have to say that across such changes, what we hope for the beloved is a general improvement in their love for all and that such an improvement we would regard as being attributable to the love we ourselves bear for the beloved. We want, in short, to be able to say that our relationship has had a transformative effect on all else.

The worst thing of all, of course, would be to expect that the beloved would not love anybody else at all. The fundamental error that underlies such a possessive, bullying posture is that love is somehow finite, that in order to convince me that you really love me I need to see you stop loving someone else, as if love shared with them is automatically not love shared with me. But, of course, the experience of the truly mutually devoted couple exposes this mistake for what it is; there is not only so much love to go around. Love is infinite and expansive; the more it is shared, the more there is to share. Surely this is the only right way to represent the divinity, not as a jealous control freak. So if God demands absolute love, and it would seem to be the case that God indeed does, it is demanded in such a way as to result in the expansion of love generally, both empowering lovers to love and enabling the reciprocation of love. Crucial, it seems to me, to understanding this properly, as well as to the task of repudiating a host of misreadings of *Fear and Trembling*, crucial to proper understanding here is the fact that an absolute relation is not an *exhaustive* relation.[25] An absolute duty does not relativize other duties by nullifying them in favor of itself exclusively; it relativizes them by transforming and reintensifying them from without. The absolute duty does not trump other duties; it alters them and raises them to the second power.

If I am right about this, then we might return to Luke 14:26 and ask along with Silentio, "But how to hate them?"[26] It seems to me a preliminary answer is already available: We must hate our parents in the same way a prospective bride leaves her parents. To be the disciple of Jesus means that a change will have to be imposed upon the disciple's relationships with others; the disciples in the Gospels certainly leave behind family and homes and livelihoods. But while change is involved, and the relationships that an aspiring disciple has with others will be transformed, it would seem that on the model Silentio is proposing, those relationships should not be threatened but enlarged and intensified. "The absolute duty can lead one to do what ethics would forbid," he writes, "but it can never lead the knight of faith to stop loving. Abraham demonstrates this. In the moment he is about to sacrifice Isaac, the ethical expression for what he is doing is: he hates Isaac. But if he actually hates Isaac, he can rest assured that God does not demand this of him, for Cain and Abraham are not identical. He must love Isaac with his whole soul. Since God claims Isaac, he must, if possible, love him even more, and only then can he *sacrifice* him, for it is indeed this love for Isaac that makes his act a sacrifice by its paradoxical contrast to his love for God."[27]

Abraham, we are told explicitly, cannot hate Isaac; in fact, in a line of argument that dovetails with the point I made above on the basis of the marriage example that what is really called for is not just continuation of adherence to duty but intensification of commitment, here we are told that not only can Abraham not hate Isaac but "he must, if possible, love him even more, and only then can he *sacrifice* him."[28] If Abraham does not love Isaac at all, then giving him up is not a sacrifice, just as abstaining from something you dislike during Lent is not a sacrifice. Furthermore, merely loving Isaac in a dutiful way is not sufficient to qualify the objective act of giving Isaac up to God as a proper sacrifice. This is strongly implied by a passage a couple of pages earlier in the text where Silentio argues that if Abraham were to claim that he loved Isaac more than anything in the world, which is why it is so difficult to sacrifice him, a clever hearer would have "perceived that he was manifesting feelings that glaringly contradicted his action."[29] But a conflict between feelings and action is resolvable in the mode of the tragic hero; the tragic hero, after all, does not *want* to sacrifice a beloved individual to the interests of the state, but feels he or she *must* do so out of service to a higher duty. As Silentio immediately proceeds to argue, faith thrives on this contradiction and ultimately "resolves" it only by holding the tension in place. The contradiction, note carefully, is perceived by the hearer of Abraham's confession of his love for his son as a tension between the father's "feelings" and his "action." Because of this contradiction, "the single individual simply cannot make himself understandable to anyone."[30] To Abraham's profession of love as what makes the sacrifice of the beloved so difficult, one could indeed imagine asking "Why sacrifice him, then?" But "To the question 'Why?' Abraham has no other answer than that it is an ordeal, a temptation that, as noted above, is a synthesis of its being for the sake of God and for his own sake."[31]

I take it that something like this is what Silentio means in a footnote near the end of Problema II when he again revisits the distinction between the tragic hero and the knight of faith, this time in terms of wish and duty:

> Agamemnon, for example, can say: To me the proof that I am not violating my fatherly duty is that my duty is my one and only wish. Consequently we have wish and duty face to face with each other. Happy is the life in which they coincide, in which my wish is my duty and the reverse, and for most men the task in life is simply to adhere to their duty and to transform it by their enthusiasm into their wish. The tragic hero gives up his wish in order to fulfill this duty. For the knight of faith, wish and duty are also identical, but he is required to give up both. If he wants to relinquish by giving up his wish, he finds no rest, for it is indeed his duty. If he wants to adhere to the duty and to his wish, he does not become the knight of faith, for the absolute duty specifically demanded that he should give it up.[32]

A tragic hero like Agamemnon can assure himself that he is not failing in his paternal duty because his one and only wish is to discharge his duty faithfully; but since it is his duty itself that in a higher expression obligates him to act in a way contrary to his personal preferences, then he gets both his wish and his obligation satisfied inasmuch as his wish is to do his duty, and his duty in its higher expression is what ultimately directs his action in a way that is contrary to an expression of duty he takes to be lower. For him, therefore, there is no genuine conflict. The knight of faith, however, must surrender both his wish and his duty; the knight of faith too wants nothing more than to do his duty, but in recognizing a duty as absolute he is drawn to the possibility of forsaking his duty as commonly understood and his legitimate wish to be true to it. He cannot be true to his duty or his wish to be so because in his case he cannot deceive himself into believing that he at least wants above all else to do the right thing as defined by the ethical as universal. In short, the knight of faith must give up obligation *qua* obligation. In fact, it would seem that precisely this kind of resignation is the precondition for the intensification of duty I have argued is characteristic of the life of faith.

Recall the example of the newlywed daughter. What makes it possible for her to be a better daughter than she could have before? Only the fact that she no longer *has* to be. The newlywed daughter can be a better daughter once she is not compelled to be so, though it is certainly conceivable that she would find the prospect of leaving her parents' home a sad and difficult one. Similarly, Abraham can reasonably say that his love for his son makes it difficult to sacrifice him but motivates his action regardless because he makes the sacrifice freely and not as a matter of duty in the traditional sense. On the one hand this seems like a resolution of an apparent conflict between feeling and action, but Silentio says it is a matter, actually, of achieving an absolute contradiction between them. The tragic hero does not encounter an absolute contradiction because feeling in his case can be subordinated to action, not without difficulty, but it can be so subordinated. Abraham cannot subordinate feeling to action but must hold them problematically together. Without the mediation of the ethical as universal, he has only his feeling of love for his son and the possibility of surpassing the ethical as universal. Should he embrace that possibility, his love for his son remains active in a way that is not true for the tragic hero, because Abraham has no recourse to the ethical as universal, the structure that precisely suppresses the love that Agamemnon bears toward his daughter.

Absent that mediation, there is only the feeling and the action performed out of a sense of absolute duty rather than as motivated by the ethical as universal. That there is a difference here is made clear by Silentio himself, who explains that the unmediated paradox depends "specifically on this: that the single individual is only the single individual";[33] that is to say, the individual is only who she is and is irreducible to the ethical, though she is implicated in it. Because the single individual is only the single individual, she can react in two ways to a perceived need to express absolute duty within the confines of the universal. First, such a duty can be resisted, and if it is resisted, then the "so-called absolute duty" is ignored and goes unfulfilled; second, such a duty can be fulfilled, in which case the single individual "sins, even though his act *realiter* turns out to be what was his absolute duty."[34] So the argument here is that an act that succeeds in terms of objective conformity to what absolute duty requires, fails in the end if it is discharged within the confines of the ethical as universal. If, for instance, I take it that God wants me to honor my promise to a friend, but I do honor that promise because I believe that such a mandate is in the end fully explicable and motivating as a function of Kantian moral theory, which stipulates that there is no moral duty specifically to God, then I act in a fashion that falls short of absolute duty in this case, even though honoring my promise may indeed have been the objectively right thing to do. The converse, incidentally, that acting on absolute duty in the ethical as universal is a failing, also holds true, as we can see with abundant clarity from the exordium, where Abraham fails at faithfully performing his absolute duty even though the objective deed he undertakes is exactly the one that God has asked him to perform. As we see throughout the book, the importance of the act itself cannot be separated from the importance of the accompanying mood or attitude, the "how" as correlate to the "what" of the believer's action.

Crucial to understanding the notion of absolute duty properly is the recognition that it is not essentially about the objective act but more about the "how" than the "what," as is so often the case for Kierkegaard. Absolute duty is posed to us as a possibility of acting in a certain way more than as a collection of requisite acts. In fact, in the case of the hard sayings of Jesus, absolute duty is not commanded *at all*. Jesus does not say "You must hate your parents"; he says "*If* you would be my disciple, then you will hate your parents." The disjunction is formally identical to all the questions that structure the three Problemata, which take the same shape of presenting a disjunction without resolution. No one, not even Jesus, can *command* absolute duty, for this would miss the point of absolute duty itself. The point of absolute duty is that I take it up in perfect freedom and in so doing I recommit myself, as *my self*, to all my duties with renewed alacrity.

So if the question is "how" to hate others, the answer is to love them more. Doing so affirms that my responsibilities and relationships are a constituent part of who I am and sanctifies the actuality of my life and loves as already ideal.

A Tentative Extension of the Logic of Absolute Duty: Martyrdom

Silentio's commentary on Luke 14:26 shows with special clarity the effect that the teleological suspension of the ethical has on the terrain of the ethical as universal. Far from invalidating ethics, the "second ethics" that follows upon the teleological suspension institutes a repetition of the ethical, and part of that repetition is inclusive of the possibility of an absolute duty to God. That this duty is absolute, as we have seen, entails not the evacuation of other duties but the redoubling of their force and the free, spontaneous way in which the knight of faith pursues her duties. I want to claim, then, that absolute duty to God does not just furnish one more reason to be attentive to duty or require the mere sustenance of duty but goes beyond this to change my very relationship to my obligations, provoking in me the desire to be even more faithful to them now as a matter of free commitment rather than constraint. If we think of the example of forgiveness of sins, we might call to mind another Scriptural teaching, from Matthew 18, which is a dense tangle of "hard sayings."[35] Here Jesus recounts the story of a king who commanded that a servant in his debt be sold along with his wife and children and property to settle his account. Upon hearing the servant's plea for patience, the king "was moved with compassion, and loosed him, and forgave him the debt."[36] Having done so, however, the freed servant immediately imprisons one of his fellow servants who owed him a fraction of the debt that the king had just forgiven him. When the king receives this news, he makes good on his original threat against the forgiven servant, and Jesus concludes by promising, "So likewise shall my heavenly Father do also unto you, if ye from your hearts forgive not every one his brother their trespasses."[37]

This story illustrates the power that absolute duty to God has: the experience of being forgiven should precipitate a readiness to forgive in turn. We react adversely to the uncharitable servant because his failing seems so obvious. His having been freed is gratuitous; he really does owe the money, more than he can ever pay likely enough. Being forgiven of the debt should not so easily return him to a mode of calculating his just recompense, "fair" though such a calculation may be. The second servant, after all, really does owe a debt to the first, but there is a blameworthy lack of self-awareness in the first servant, a blameworthy failure to take on board the full consequence of his status as forgiven.

I think ultimately the point of many of the "hard sayings" comes down to something like this refusal to allow the moral calculus to have the last word in our dealings with one another. Just as it would be contemptible and petty for the husband to count up the hours his wife spends with her mother and sister on one side of a ledger against the number of hours she spends with him on the other side, so too it is niggling and obsessive of the servant to insist on the settling of the debt. To embrace the logic of absolute duty is to dispense with such haggling altogether. This is, I think, the true point of Jesus's counsel to the rich young man as well, which, as we have seen, also occupies Silentio's attention.[38] Besides the reference discussed in chapter 5 above, there is also an elliptical reference in the first Danish edition to this passage and others. At the very end of Problema II, Silentio concludes this chapter by writing, "Therefore, either there is an absolute duty to God—and if there is such a thing, it is the paradox just described, that the single individual as the single individual is higher than the universal and as the single individual stands in an absolute relation to the absolute—or else faith has never existed because it has always existed, or else Abraham is lost, or else one must interpret the passage in Luke 14 as did that appealing exegete and explain the similar and corresponding passages in the same way."[39] As the Hongs point out in a footnote,[40] the "corresponding passages" Kierkegaard seems to have been thinking of are Deuteronomy 13:6–7 and 33:9; Matthew 10:37 and 19:29; and (in a parenthetical note) 1 Corinthians 7:11.

The Deuteronomy 13 passage counsels summary execution by stoning for family members who entice one another away from faithfulness to the God of Israel and commend idol worship. Interestingly, this flies in the face of the prescription elsewhere in Deuteronomy that the death penalty be applied only when a number of witnesses agree, a fact that seems to add force to the sense that we are beyond the realm of the forensic and prescriptive here and into the terrain of the absolute. This passage "breaks the law" in a way parallel to the logic of the teleological suspension of the ethical. Such is the moral seriousness of idolatry that it is raised to the level of a categorically capital offense, despite the juridical restrictions ordinarily imposed on this form of punishment. This passage can therefore be read as a companion from Hebrew scripture to the hard sayings of Jesus analyzed above.

Similarly, in the Deuteronomy 33 passage, Moses commends the zeal of Levi for the covenant, which extended to the point of disavowal of father and mother and children. This is obviously a parallel to Luke 14:26, as is the Matthew 10:37 passage, which simply reports the same hard saying in different words: "He that loveth father or mother more than me is not worthy of me: and he that loveth son or daughter more than me is not worthy of me"; and in Matthew 19:29, Jesus promises that "every one that hath forsaken houses, or brethren, or sisters, or father, or mother, or wife, or children, or lands, for my name's sake, shall receive an hundredfold, and shall inherit everlasting life."[41]

This promise, which I remarked on in the prior chapter, is the correlate to the episode of the rich young man and the conclusion that it is easier for a camel to pass through the eye of a needle than for a rich man to enter the kingdom of God. Hearing this outrageous warning, the disciples are stunned into asking Jesus, "Who then can be saved? But Jesus beheld them, and said unto them, With men this is impossible; but with God all things are possible."[42] Given perhaps that this is not the most reassuring answer conceivable, Peter presses the point, reminding Jesus that "we have forsaken all, and followed thee; what shall we have therefore?" Verse 29 just cited is the answer to Peter's question, but again, this hardly seems to be a reassuring answer, and it calls back to mind the incommensurability between sacrifice and reward that seems characteristic of the life of faith.[43]

What I want to suggest further here at the end of Problema II is that absolute duty entails the joyful acceptance of this incommensurability and promises a positive, affirmative attitude in the face of apparent unfairness. The rich young ruler could have fulfilled an absolute duty to God by obeying (cheerfully) the exhortation to sell all he had and give it to the poor. But the lesson here is not that it's bad to be rich or that the poor would be spiritually improved by being given a great deal of money. The lesson here, I think, is that we are all to regard the *difference* between being rich and being poor as itself a matter of *indifference*. This is another way of saying we should live actuality as already ideal. Presumably it is harder for the rich to do so, hence the observation that the eye of the needle is a formidable obstacle for the camel. But the logic of absolute duty does not demand something like formal equality or a state of affairs where the rich give enough to the poor so that everyone is middle-class. The logic of absolute duty demands that the knight of faith stop thinking of herself as on any kind of gradation at all: she is to stop thinking and acting on the basis of a perceived difference between "more" and "less," or your obligation on me as automatically higher than that person's over there, or time spent with a sibling as inevitably depriving a spouse of the equal amount of time that might otherwise have been his.[44]

The knight of faith instead lives a style of life where these questions of what is fair or not, who has more, who has less, are not invalidated, to be sure, but receive a relative position. Faith takes the actual to be ideal already, and does not compare the real to an unattainable ideal as a grounds for finding fault with the faithful person's real, lived situation. This is why Silentio says that "the true knight of faith is a witness, never the teacher, and therein lies the profound humanity, which has much more to it than this trifling participation in the woes and welfare of other people that is extolled under the name of sympathy, although, on the contrary, it is nothing more than vanity."[45] So it would seem that a concern with others' welfare, the sort of concern that we characteristically regard the rich young ruler as lacking, does not really capture what is at stake in absolute duty. The knight of faith is not a handwringer, not a scold who justifies her busybodying in the name of sympathy; such a "teacher" (perhaps we should say "lecturer" or "assistant professor") is in fact vain and is drawing attention to her own sense of inflated self-consciousness and moral self-importance. The knight of faith dispenses with this and all forms of calculation: "He who desires only to be a witness confesses thereby that no man, not even the most unimportant man, needs another's participation or is to be devalued by it in order to raise another's value. But since he himself did not obtain at bargain price what he obtained, he does not sell it at bargain price, either. He is not so base that he accepts the admiration of men and in return gives them his silent contempt; he knows that true greatness is equally accessible to all."[46]

True greatness is equally accessible to all, in the same way that Christianity, according to Kierkegaard, is to be preached "to all," because "everyone can be the single individual."[47] There is no room in the knight of faith for patronizing or condescension, and it is for this reason perhaps more than any other that she is alone, a fact about her that Silentio says we can detect as a sign of her condition even from the outside. Despite the emphasis on the knight of faith's elusion of detection, Silentio does make a profound admission in Problema II: "But from the paradox itself several characteristic signs may be inferred that are understandable also to someone not in it."[48] The first such sign is that the "true knight of faith is always absolute isolation; the spurious knight is sectarian. This is an attempt to jump off the narrow path of the paradox and become a tragic hero at a bargain price."[49] Notice again the language of the bargain price and recall the opening words of the preface, which decried the "clearance sale" in the world of ideas. Even the nobility of the tragic hero can be bargained down, for the tragic hero at least genuinely expresses the universal, while the sectarian pastiches even that, elevating "a few good friends and comrades" to the status of guarantors of justice itself.[50] These self-deluded are the cult of "expertise" and "worldly admiration."[51] By contrast, the knight of faith "feels the pain of being unable to make himself understandable to others, but he has no vain desire to instruct others . . . The spurious knight quickly betrays himself by this expertise that he has acquired instantly. He by no means grasps what is at stake: that insofar as another individual is to go the same path he must become the single individual in the very same way and then does not require anyone's advice, least of all the advice of one who wants to intrude."[52]

In the next chapter, the emphasis will be on the knight of faith's inability to make herself understood, but here notice that the emphasis is instead on the refusal of the knight to instruct. This refusal is in keeping with her status as witness. This recognition should attenuate our reading of Silentio's claim that "the one knight of faith cannot help the other at all. Either the single individual himself becomes the knight of faith by accepting the paradox or he never becomes one. Partnership in these areas is utterly unthinkable."[53] The reason that partnership is unthinkable is not because the one knight of faith cannot communicate to the other, but because everyone can be the single individual and everyone who becomes so does so the same way. Every knight of faith becomes one in her own way, and she does not need advice, least of all the unwelcome kind, no matter how well-intentioned.

Here at the end of Problema II, Silentio condemns the sectarians and busybodies and praises the knight of faith's "martyrdom of misunderstanding."[54] It is worth keeping in mind that "martyr" and "witness" are alternate translations of the same Greek term, so perhaps at the ultimate limit, what we are talking about when it comes to absolute duty is martyrdom. The ethical as universal cannot accommodate martyrdom, only shifting priorities and gradations of obligation, which is what even the most conscientious dutifulness boils down to. The ethical hero is great only when tragic, which is to say, only when crushed by the irresolvable conflicts that cut across the contested terrain of duty. The martyr is not tragic but joyful.[55] The martyr lives the religious ideal, accepting the actuality of her situation as ideal for her and not engaging in invidious comparison either by enviously spying out others for their putative advantages or patronizing others she imagines as being beneath her. The knight of faith goes beyond all calculation, even that good-natured calculation that with wholesome intentions wants to improve and to correct. Her greatness cannot be attained by piecemeal adjustments to the ethical as universal, elevating one priority here and directing greater attention there. It cannot even be won by pointing out flaws and campaigning for improvement. She is not a teacher, not an activist, but instead a witness to an absolute duty that imperils and sustains all duty.

8 Silence and Speech

Silence reemerges as a theme in this final major portion of the text, and it does so in the context not of the ethical but the aesthetic. The reason for this, I think, is best supplied by a remark from Climacus quoted earlier. In his "A Glance at Danish Literature" he asserts that "just as *Either/Or* had ensured that the teleological suspension would not be confused with esthetic hiddenness, so now the three pseudonymous books [*Repetition*, *Fear and Trembling*, and *The Concept of Anxiety*] ensured that sin, when it is brought up, would not be confused with this and that, with weakness and imperfection, that sorrow over it would not be confused with all sorts of things, sighing and crying as well as sniveling over ourselves and this vale of tears, that the suffering in it would not be confused with a *quodlibet*."[1] Problema III can be read as a revisiting of the effort to keep the teleological suspension from being confused with aesthetic hiddenness. As we have seen, the teleological suspension institutes the conjoined possibilities of faith and sin. Problema II explores the transformation of the ethical consequent upon the teleological suspension's opening the door to faith. Problema III distinguishes faith from aesthetic hiddenness while demonstrating the role that both aesthetic and ethical ideals play in reconstituted form within the life of faith. The first task I will explain with regard to the four vignettes—on the Delphic bridegroom, Agnes and the merman, Tobias and Sarah, and Faust and Margaret—that comprise the bulk of Problema III; the second task I will explain with regard to Abraham's declaration to Isaac that God will provide the lamb for the sacrifice.

Throughout what follows, it is important to keep in mind Haufniensis's interpretation of Silentio that he "allows the desired ideality of esthetics to be shipwrecked on the required ideality of ethics, in order through these collisions to bring to light the religious ideality as the ideality that precisely is the ideality of actuality, and therefore just as desirable as that of esthetics and not as impossible as the ideality of ethics."[2] The religious ideal has to be desirable, has to be aesthetically appealing, to offer that intimation of the timeless eternal, that so-rarely-realized perfection. And it has to be, at the same time, achievable even for sinful people. We see from the many "case studies" of aesthetic hiddenness that Silentio presents in Problema III a number of examples of how this synthesis can fail to obtain, while in the words of Abraham we see a perfect expression for the union of aesthetic and ethical ideality realized only in the religious, the ideal that is also real, the ideal that I can live, the ideal that is mine.

It is also important to keep in mind from the beginning that despite Problema III's interest in silence, a glaring fact stands out—namely, that Abraham is not silent. To anticipate here at the outset of the chapter some of what I will say at the end, I put forward two considerations. First, we have just seen at the end of Problema II that the solitude of the knight of faith is less to do with her alienation from publically available categories that would explain her situation and more to do with the fact that her adherence to absolute duty makes her a witness rather than a teacher. Abraham too is a witness, not a teacher, and when he speaks, it can be consistently claimed, I think, that his words "say nothing," as Silentio will claim, because they do not teach. They testify. In the lengthy discussion provided during Problema III there is almost no mention of the obstacle to understanding that comes up in connection with the tragic heroes, the unavailability of public categories to account for behavior in intelligible terms. That issue drops out altogether. What is at stake now, I think, is the character of a distinctive sort of communication, one that would be expressive of the religious ideal and one that is in contact with both aesthetic and ethical mandates.

The second point to keep in mind is that Abraham embroiders silence and speech in a complex manner. I have shown in the first chapter of this book, in the course of discussing Silentio's surname, that for Kierkegaard silence itself is communicative, and we will see that Abraham communicates out of a certain silence as well, but here at the end of the book we find yet more reason for rejecting the thesis that silence is mere absence of verbiage. In draft notes for *Johannes Climacus*, Kierkegaard wrote that the ancient skeptics "made a distinction between εποχη and αφασια."[3] *Epoche* is the suspension of judgment; *aphasia* is the incapacity for or refusal of speaking. Recalling Silentio's praise for Descartes and the ancient skeptics from the book's Preface, we have reason to think that the attribution of silence to Abraham here in Problema III is more a matter of *epoche* than *aphasia*. This reading is strengthened by a marginal note to the discussion of Abraham's testimony to Isaac, where Kierkegaard wrote simply "the believing εποχη."[4] It is impossible to say exactly what Kierkegaard meant by this brief note, but my suggestion will be that Abraham's words are a sort of believing *epoche*. Abraham, like all of us, has the same evidence before him that the Greek skeptics did. On the one hand he has reason to believe that God loves him and has been leading him through an extraordinary adventure of blessing upon blessing; on the other hand he has reason to believe that God is a monster who has cruelly made an unspeakable demand upon him. Like the ancient Greek skeptics when faced with a similarly unresolvable problem, in a sense he reserves judgment, because he does not *know* the answer. And yet he is believing insofar as he acts and speaks in a way that avoids demonic despair.

And this point shows us why perhaps we have to return to the aesthetic in the end; the ethical cannot discriminate between faith and the demonic, since the teleological suspension makes both possible. We have seen already that the author of *Fear and Trembling* is a communicator even though he is named "silent" and that, for Kierkegaard generally, silence can be communicative. Yet of course, as we will see too, silence can be demonic, in which case it is the absence of communication. In *The Concept of Anxiety* Haufniensis links the demonic with muteness or rejection of language. The three qualities that Haufniensis assigns to the demonic together demonstrate that it is a covert refusal of language, community, and the eternal's superintendence of time: these qualities are inclosing reserve, suddenness, and the boring. While earnestness is a kind of self-concern that is expansive and allied to the Good, the demonic is a doomed attempt to close itself off from contact with the Good.[5] The demonic "closes itself up within itself," in such a way as to refuse relationship and the medium of all relationship: language. "Inclosing reserve," Haufniensis says, "is precisely muteness. Language, the word, is precisely what saves, what saves the individual from the empty abstraction of inclosing reserve."[6] Were Abraham's silence inclosing reserve, he would be obviously demonic.

Finally, I would say it is consistent that Silentio returns to the aesthetic since this move completes the novel logic of the exception that Constantius articulates. It is not enough for the knight of faith simply to exempt herself from the ethical as universal; it is not enough for Silentio to simply elevate this exceptional status above that of the ethical as universal. The ethical as universal itself has to be transformed by the exception. So part of that transformation will include the recuperation and rehabilitation of aesthetic ideals and aspirations. The life of the knight of faith is itself a sort of artistry, and it will reflect, in conjunction with reality, the ambitions of aesthetics to eternal purity, synthetic unity, and harmonious holism. Indeed, inasmuch as the ethical as universal is itself already an overcoming of and preservation within itself of the ethical, then the wholesale reinvention of the ethical as universal will also include the reestablishment of the aesthetic.

Twofold Silence and the Triangulation of Ideals

By themselves, neither the aesthetic nor the ethical can discriminate between the silence of the divine and the silence of the demonic, both of which are made possible by the split instituted by the teleological suspension: silence, thanks to the suspension, can be either that of developed inwardness or that of self-enclosure. Silentio says, "I always run up against the paradox, the divine and the demonic, for silence is both. Silence is the demon's trap, and the more that is silenced, the more terrible the demon, but silence is also divinity's mutual understanding with the single individual."[7] The lengthy and convoluted set of studies that follows this declaration seems designed once again to achieve a largely negative purpose—namely, to show that Abraham's silence cannot be aesthetically motivated and thus must be either a function of his faith or of his demonic despair. Perhaps this is why Silentio asserts that "it would be best at this point to consider the whole question purely esthetically and to that end enter into an esthetic inquiry, to which I invite the reader to give his entire attention momentarily, while I for my part shall adapt my comments to the subjects."[8]

Nowhere in the text are Silentio's poetic gifts more in evidence than in the pages that follow, but it is equally evident from these character studies that Silentio is not a conventional poet at all. Silentio's systematic refusal to identify his project with that of the poets cannot be ignored, and it means at least that commentators cannot refer to Silentio as a poet except in the most qualified sense, as we have seen throughout this book. So why does Silentio say he is not a poet or dealing with narrative sources poetically? He is resistant to call his work poetic because he is sensitive to the limits of the aesthetic that Haufniensis marks out.[9] The aesthetic cannot cope with sin directly without making of it an object of tragedy and comedy, without turning it into an occasion for light-mindedness. So his approach cannot be straightforwardly aesthetic (neither can it be merely moralistic, since the ethical too cannot cope directly with sin).

It is also probably most evident in this part of the book that Silentio is performing the feat that Haufniensis says he is—namely, allowing an aesthetic ideal to collide against an ethical ideal in order to bring a new ideal to light. From the opening pages of Problema III it would seem that the aesthetic ideals he has in mind are of the sort we find enshrined in storytelling conventions, the "rules" that make for a satisfying narrative, particularly the element of "recognition" identified by Aristotle in his *Poetics*. Recognition is important to Silentio's discussion of the aesthetic ideal because it is the natural partner of hiddenness, and hiddenness is precisely the question of Problema III.[10] In modern drama, as opposed to Greek tragedy, the aesthetic "rules" dictate that the hiddenness of the characters be a matter of their own free choosing, not a result of fate.[11] As such, the aesthetic rules can hold a person responsible for their own choices to remain in concealment, sometimes to comic effect (as in the case of a bald man who disguises himself with a wig to make himself more attractive to women and whose subterfuge is exposed to ridicule), sometimes to tragic effect (as in the case of a girl and boy secretly in love).

In this latter example, Silentio identifies another key element of the aesthetic ideal: coincidence. "A girl is secretly in love with someone without the pair's having definitively confessed their love to each other as yet. Her parents force her to marry another (she may also be motivated by daughterly devotion); she obeys her parents, keeps her love hidden."[12] Notice that the motivation for the freely chosen concealment here is ethical in nature; the girl in love stays in secret because to do otherwise would dishonor an obligation to her family. Another example, one that Silentio brings together with the first: "A young swain has but to say one word to possess the object of his longings and restless dreams. But this little word will compromise, indeed, perhaps (who knows?) destroy a whole family. He nobly decides to remain in hiding."[13] Again the ethical ideal blocks the aesthetic ideal; everyone wants a happy ending, but such an outcome is not always possible when duty prevails over the aesthetically pleasing.

But aesthetics is not without resources of its own. "What a pity," Silentio writes,

> that here two persons, both of whom are hidden from their respective beloveds, are also hidden from each other; otherwise, a remarkable higher unity could be brought about here. —Their hiddenness is a free act, for which they are responsible also to esthetics. But esthetics is a courteous and sentimental branch of knowledge that knows more ways out than any pawnshop manager. What does it do? It makes everything possible for the lovers. By a coincidence, the respective partners in the prospective marriage get a hint of the other party's magnanimous decision. There is an explanation, the lovers get each other and also a place among authentic heroes.[14]

By recourse to a coincidence of the sort that would never take place in real life, the star-crossed lovers each discover what has been hidden by the other. Their moral resolve, as a consequence of the disclosure of their aesthetic hiddenness, only makes each *more* desirable to the other. The "higher unity" is forged from the satisfaction of the moral demands by each party and the aesthetic mandate that nobility not go unrewarded and love unrequited—everyone quite literally lives happily ever after. This is what the life of faith accomplishes. It is not just an exception to the ethical but a higher unity that preserves something of both the aesthetic and ethical within itself. What the lovers thought they had to give up for both aesthetic and ethical reasons is restored with results that end up simultaneously subverting and fulfilling the aesthetic gratification of the story and the lovers' respect for ethical norms.

The aesthetic and ethical ideals can also come into a tension that ultimately furthers the interests of both ideals when on some occasions "esthetics itself demands disclosure. When the hero, prey to esthetic illusion, thinks to save another person by his silence, then it demands silence and rewards it. But when the hero by his action has a disturbing effect on another man's life, it demands disclosure."[15] The young woman and man in the previous example elect to remain hidden out of consideration for others that is ethically motivated; they wish to avoid causing suffering to others or seek to honor obligations to others with a stake in the consequences of their decisions. But sometimes the ethical demand involves potential harm to another, and in such cases disclosure may be insisted upon not only by the ethical (which is generally true: "ethics demands disclosure")[16] but by the aesthetic as well. The reason aesthetics may insist on disclosure according to its own terms is that disclosure heightens dramatic tension and makes for a better, more satisfying story.

Silentio's example is *Iphigenia in Aulis*, wherein Agamemnon's resolve to sacrifice his daughter is put to the test (to great dramatic effect) by the disclosure of his intent to sacrifice Iphigenia to both Iphigenia herself and to her mother, Clytemnestra. On the one hand, "esthetics demands silence of Agamemnon, inasmuch as it would be unworthy of the hero to seek comfort from any other person, just as out of solicitude for the women he ought to hide it from them as long as possible. On the other hand, in order to be a hero, the hero also has to be tried in the dreadful spiritual trial that the tears of Clytemnestra and Iphigenia will cause."[17] So in this case, and it goes without saying that the case is precisely one of tragic or ethical heroism,[18] the interests of aesthetics and ethics coincide. In order for Agamemnon to be the tragic hero, he has to face his ethical duty foursquare, despite the appeals to emotion with which his loved ones will tempt him away from his duty. The spectacle of him being so tempted also makes for good drama, so the aesthetic too has an interest in disclosure, which again it engineers by means of a coincidental contrivance: an old servant shares the news of Agamemnon's plans with Clytemnestra, and "now everything is in order."[19]

The ethical demand for disclosure can be satisfied by the tragic hero through his candor with his intended victim; he has to personally take on the burden of unconcealment and expose himself to the test of his intended victim's full awareness of what is to happen to her. "The tragic hero demonstrates his ethical courage in that he himself, not prey to any esthetic illusion, announces Iphigenia's fate to her."[20] That he has to do so is a requirement of the ethical itself. But it is a requirement that is imposed upon Agamemnon in the play by means of a dramatic device and for the purpose of enhancing the dramatic power of the narrative. "Esthetics demanded disclosure but aided itself with a coincidence; ethics demanded disclosure and found its fulfillment in the tragic hero."[21] The demand is the same but realized by means that are not at the disposal of ethics, inasmuch as "ethics has no coincidence and no old servant at its disposal. The esthetic idea contradicts itself as soon as it is to be implemented in actuality."[22]

The aesthetic ideal contradicts itself as soon as it is to be implemented in actuality if only because actual life rarely works out in the same convenient way as a narrative does. In actuality, there may not be a coincidence, a deus ex machina resolution, a convenient turn of events to ratchet up the dramatic tension. The scorching irony of Greek tragedy, the inexorable force of fate to which it gives expression, are simply not often to be found in life as it is actually lived but are the product of artistic idealization of life's actuality. The machinations of fate, the twists and turns of hiddenness and recognition caroming off one another, the reversals of fortune that turn the lives of characters topsy-turvy are not a product of the actual but are imputed to the actual by the poet's idealizing work.

Life as it is actually lived is untouched by such embellishments, leaving us, in most circumstances, with just the bare demand of ethics and neither the intensification of its demands by aesthetically contrived happenstance (as is the case for Agamemnon) nor the relief of its demands by aesthetically contrived happenstance (as is the case for the star-crossed lovers). In the former sort of situation, the tragic hero rises above the enticements put in his way by aesthetic devising; in the latter sort, the aesthetic heroes prove themselves through their concealment and are happily rewarded. Roughly speaking, the former sort of situation culminates in tragedy, the latter in comedy. But life as actually lived is by turns tragic and comic and neither wholly. We can of course think of the path of our lives in terms of either tragedy or comedy or some combination thereof, but in living forward neither ideal aesthetic model necessarily helps us guide our way: when life (and particularly sin and its consequences) puts an obstacle in our path, what had hitherto seemed to be a comic development strikes us as tragic in consequence; conversely, an apparently tragic development can sometimes issue in an unexpected comic denouement. This again is the life of faith in its fullest expression. The knight of faith lives actual life as neither tragic nor comic, neither aesthetic nor ethical but both.

The remaining vignettes in Problema III complicate the triangulation of the aesthetic and ethical. How they do so will vary, but it may be helpful to consider a metaphor that Silentio introduces here that, to my knowledge, has not been remarked upon before. In the passage where he discusses Aristotle's *Poetics*, he writes, "What Aristotle develops earlier in the same chapter with regard to the various merits of tragedy, all in relation to the way περιπετεια and αναγνωρισις *carambolere*, as well as what he writes about the single and the double recognition, I cannot deal with here."[23] The salient detail we should consider for a moment before proceeding is in the word *carambolere*, which unfortunately has no ready translation into English. The Hongs, in a bracketed insertion, provide the word "converge"[24] as a translation, while Hannay renders it "clash,"[25] and Walsh chooses the word "coincide."[26] None of these is quite right, and it is perhaps no accident that opposing interpretations have been put forward—"clash" is almost opposite to "converge" and "coincide"—for what the word really implies is both collision and a fortuitous result or harmonization from collision.

When we understand this term, it will be clear that Silentio will in fact not go into what Aristotle meant by the interplay of recognition and reversal but will, in the following vignettes, enact his own interplays of the aesthetic and ethical ideals. Silentio does not recapitulate Aristotle's *Poetics*; instead he sketches his own. In Silentio's poetics, recognition and reversal are not the key terms that interact but instead the aesthetic and ethical. The key to how they interact is in the term *carambolere*, which is the Danish name for a French game of three-ball pocketless billiards called *carambole*.[27] To strike a *carambole* is to successfully shoot the cue ball in such a way as to strike both of the two other balls in one stroke, an action that requires the player to take into account the effect of the ricochet of the cue ball against the first ball as a determining factor in its movement toward the second ball. Needless to say, this is a complicated and difficult movement to execute. If in fact what follows in Problema III is Silentio's own "caramboling," then what the metaphor seems to imply is that he is not interested merely in "clashes" or "convergences" or "coincidences" but in a more elaborate sort of interplay that is in fact a wholly apposite image for what Haufniensis says Silentio is doing—the collision of one ideal against another in such a way as to "score" a point from the triangulated collisions.

The next sections of this chapter retrace Silentio's caramboling of the aesthetic and ethical. In the first vignette under discussion, we will see that the ethical and aesthetic collide in such a way that a point is not ultimately scored: the pagan context of the story, with its background assumption of the reality of fate, allows for the two ideals to come into opposition but not harmonization. In the second vignette, the ethical and aesthetic collide under the supposition of a specifically religious conceptuality that allows for a heightened tension between the two ideals that opens to the possibility at least of a religious ideal being realized. In the third and final vignettes, the ideals collide in such a way as to successfully accomplish the religious ideal.

The Delphic Bridegroom and His Bride: Either the Ethical or the Aesthetic

This metaphor should be kept in mind as an interpretive key for the examples that Silentio calls upon. The "pair of poetic individualities"[28] he immediately introduces—drawn from a reference provided by Aristotle in his *Politics*—consist of a bridegroom, who calls off his wedding because the augurs reveal that his marriage will precipitate a catastrophe, and his jilted bride. Though these are poetic personages, once again the method that Silentio deploys is not itself poetic. He first outlines the story of the doomed bridegroom in only the most schematic terms: "*The bridegroom, to whom the augurs prophesied a calamity that would have its origin in his marriage, suddenly changes his plans at the crucial moment when he comes to get his bride*—he refuses to be married. More than this I do not need. In Delphi this event could hardly come to pass without tears. If a poet were to make us of it, he no doubt could safely count on sympathy."[29]

So despite saying he needs no more than the sketch he has already provided, Silentio proceeds to embroider a rather more sentimental expansion on the story, complete with rhapsody on the beauties of the bride and the pathos of the moment wherein she realizes she is being abandoned. At its highest pitch, he breaks off with the protest: "But here I stop; I am not a poet, and I go at things only dialectically."[30] So the implication here is that the story is not being told poetically or as a poet would. He introduces it by saying "If a poet were to make use of it," as if his own usage is not poetic, and then declares openly that he is not a poet himself.

Again it would seem the best way to read this section is not as a straightforward poetic attempt to idealize an actuality but as an effort on Silentio's part to poeticize in a revised manner, to allow the aesthetic and ethical ideals to collide off one another in order to bring about a new religious ideal. In this case, however, we find that the execution of the collisions is insufficient to bring forth the religious ideal. How Silentio parses the situation of the Delphic bridegroom nevertheless contributes to a larger if indirect understanding of how the collisions must take place, and the episode speaks to one of the preeminent concerns of the text as a whole—namely, what we are to do when the ideals that guide us through life come to pieces. The bridegroom has invested all in his love for the beloved, and now he knows it cannot be. Two important considerations have to be taken into account, according to Silentio: first, "the hero obtains that information in the crucial moment. Therefore he is unstained and unremorseful";[31] and second, "he has the divine pronouncement before him, or, more correctly, against him; thus he is not directed by self-opinionated sagacity as fickle lovers are."[32] The point of these reminders is that the would-be groom receives the news of the curse against him in the nick of time, so to speak, prior to his having committed himself to the ethically paradigmatic expression of marriage. He can, and must, act in the face of the devastation of his imagined ideal and has to do so for nontrivial reasons; he is not merely "backing out." Indeed, his unhappiness is assured, perhaps even to a greater degree than the unhappiness of his intended bride, since, after all, "he is the occasion"[33] for their unhappiness.

What can we do when faced with such a setback? The story has no happy ending. Ethics enjoins upon us certain responsibilities that cannot be shirked. In this case, Silentio entertains three possible reactions. First, the bridegroom could "remain silent and get married" on the supposition that the promised disaster may not happen immediately and that it might be best to enjoy whatever happiness he and his bride can before the hammer falls. On this course of action an ethical prohibition arises. If he remains silent and does not tell his intended bride of what the augurs have prophesied, then he implicates her in his fate, "for if she had known of the prophecy, she certainly would never have given her assent to such an alliance," whereby her "righteous anger"[34] at the eventual disclosure of the pronouncement against him would have been fully warranted.

Second, he could remain silent and not get married. "Esthetics perhaps would sanction this."[35] Why would such a resolution garner the sanction of aesthetics? Because it's such a satisfying tragic conclusion: the doomed lover nobly assumes his burden of silence, longingly gazes into his beloved's tearful eyes, and declares that their love cannot be. To really complete the effect, Silentio asserts, "the esthetic point of view requires that he die," because, after all, what better way could the story end than for him to confess the truth, and his love, with his final breath? This scenario, though, despite its obvious narrative appeal, is also "an offense against the girl and the reality of her love."[36] So there are ethical objections against both the bridegroom remaining silent and marrying the bride, and remaining silent and not marrying the bride. There is no contradiction here, for the rationale that seems to unite both objections to both scenarios is that in neither does the bridegroom afford the bride the opportunity to choose for herself what she will do: marry or not marry. Ethically speaking, she is entitled to know what she is letting herself in for, and the decision has to be her own as to whether she proceeds or not. It may be dramatically interesting for him to stay silent, but it is not right to do so.

This is the gist of the third scenario, wherein the bridegroom speaks, and this is indeed what "ethics demands."[37] What the groom and bride decide to do, however, as a result of his speaking is, in a sense, a matter of indifference. "Since heaven does not use any visible force to separate them but leaves it up to them, it is conceivable that they would decide together to defy heaven along with its disaster."[38] That this option remains open to them is a function of the context in which the story is told and especially with respect to the publicity of the augurs' pronouncement. "Everything depends upon the relation in which the bridegroom stands to the augurs' pronouncement, which in one way or another will be decisive for his life."[39] It is undeniably decisive, but one might say only relatively decisive, for no new ideal results from the collision of the aesthetic and the ethical in this particular case. The choice of what to do, as long it is shared between the two of them, becomes somewhat arbitrary, for the terms on which the doomed couple share their decision are not fundamentally altered. The terms are simply that fate has spoken against them, or more precisely against him,[40] and nothing the two of them decide to do will change those terms. "Thus the augur's pronouncement is intelligible not only to the hero but also to all and does not eventuate in any private relation to the divine. He can do what he wants; whatever has been predicted will happen. He does not enter into a closer relation to the divine either by doing it or by not doing it; he does not become the object of the divine's mercy or wrath."[41]

In the absence of any deeper (or less deep) relationship with the divine, nothing fundamental changes as a result of whatever course of action the lovers adopt. The reason for this is, in brief, that they are in the grip of fate.[42] If the groom and bride choose to marry in apparent defiance of fate and a disaster does befall him, then they will simply accept the inevitability of their fate and credit themselves with having done what they willed regardless of the consequences. If the groom and bride choose to marry in apparent defiance of fate and a disaster does not befall him, then they will credit themselves with having vanquished fate through the force of their own will and commitment to one another. If the groom and bride choose not to marry in apparent acceptance of their fate, they will credit themselves with having abided by the dictates of fate and content themselves with whatever peace can come of having submitted themselves to the inscrutable. This is the fundamental ambiguity of fate, that whatever one chooses in the face of it is self-vindicating: marry and anything that seems conceivably like a disaster—illness, childlessness, tragic death in the groom's family, any eventuality that life may offer—could be construed as the promised catastrophe; do not marry and anything that seems conceivably like a disaster avoided—new love, prosperity, peaceable old age—could be construed as the reward of a life lived out of respect for the will of the gods. In any case, what they do does not matter in an absolute sense. Either they choose a happy ending come what may, or they choose to do what they think is right, however they understand that.

This is why Silentio concludes that this sketch, with its pagan presuppositions, gets him "no further than the tragic hero."[43]

> But if the will of heaven had not been declared to him by an augur, if it had come to his knowledge quite privately, if it had entered into a purely private relation to him, then we are in the presence of the paradox . . . Then his silence would not be due to his wanting to place himself as the single individual in an absolute relation to the *universal* but to his having been placed as the single individual in an absolute relation to the *absolute*. Then, as far as I can see, he would also be able to find inner peace therein, whereas his noble silence would always be disturbed by the demands of the ethical.[44]

As long as the pronouncement is a pronouncement of publicly interpretable fate, then he enters at the most into an absolute relation with the universal, which would seem to be different from where Agamemnon stands. Agamemnon, like all tragic heroes, has to subordinate one ethical commitment, to his family, to one he takes to be higher, to the nation. Recall, though, that the bridegroom has entered into no entangling ethical relationship with the bride, for they are not yet married. He subordinates the realm of the aesthetic, the realm of his desires and preferences, to the ethical mandate in general, the will of the generally revealed divine as mediated by the augurs, not to the privately revealed divine that calls him to a deeper relationship with itself.

Had he chosen silence, then the demand of the ethical would have nagged him; haunting whatever happiness he may have had with his bride would be the insistence that he should have spoken, should have made her aware of the consequences of accepting his hand. He is not, then, quite an ethical hero. In fact, "his heroism, then, essentially consists in abandoning the esthetic magnanimity, which *in casu*, however, cannot easily be imagined to have any infusion of the vanity that is implicit in being concealed, since it certainly must be clear to him that he is making the girl unhappy."[45] For him, one ethical duty does not trump another; the ethical trumps the aesthetic altogether. On the very next page, Silentio writes, "It would be altogether desirable if esthetics would sometime attempt to begin where for so many years it has ended—in the illusion of magnanimity. As soon as it did this, it would be working hand in hand with the religious, for this is the only power that can rescue the esthetic from its battle with the ethical."[46]

The aesthetic and ethical are at war with each other of course because they represent fundamentally divergent modes of life and existence; the triumph of one is by definition the defeat of the other. The religious alone can rescue the aesthetic from this battle because by denying both supremacy, each is retained in its respective place. The story of the Delphic bridegroom gets us right up to the point where a real aesthetics, as Silentio understands it, would begin: The Delphic bridegroom abandons the illusion of magnanimity, the consoling falsehood that by resolutely remaining hidden from his beloved he takes the nobler path. He knows the nobler path is the ethical one, but he is unable, without the help of the religious—which thinks in terms of providence and the good, of private, intimate relationship with God, rather than fate—to resolve the war between the aesthetic and the ethical. Such a resolution can be more closely approximated by the next tale, that of Agnes and the merman.

Agnes and the Merman: Neither the Ethical nor the Aesthetic

The Danish folk tale of Agnes and the merman is invoked by Silentio specifically in terms of providing an insight into the demonic.[47] This is a category that is not available to the pagan and involves a deeper insight into what is at stake in the collision between the aesthetic and ethical as well as a deeper insight into how that collision might give birth to a new religious ideal. A similar disavowal of the role of the poet accompanies the story of Agnes and the merman, which Silentio alters in order to distance his own retelling from a poetic one. He recites, "The merman is a seducer who rises up from his hidden chasm and in wild lust seizes and breaks the innocent flower standing on the seashore in all her loveliness and with her head thoughtfully inclined to the soughing of the sea. This has been the poets' interpretation until now. Let us make a change."[48] Again, once his version of the tale has been told, in which the merman's lecherous intent is thwarted by the perfect innocence of Agnes, who gives herself to him in willing trust, Silentio admits, "I have taken the liberty of changing the merman somewhat, and essentially I have also changed Agnes a little, for in the legend Agnes is not entirely without guilt, since generally it is pure nonsense and game-playing and an insult to the female sex to imagine a seduction in which the girl is utterly, utterly, utterly innocent."[49]

So Silentio is forced to make Agnes wholly innocent, which is required to highlight the merman's demonic self-enclosure, or as *The Concept of Anxiety* calls it, his anxiety about the good.[50] As Haufniensis explains it in that work, the demonic is the opposite of innocence[51] and in fact is provoked to manifest itself fully only by contact with innocence, as the merman's anxiety about the good is roused by Agnes's innocence (not in the original legend but in Silentio's retelling) and as "the demonic in the New Testament first appears when it is approached by Christ."[52] The demonic, then, wants nothing more than to close itself off within itself, to be left in self-imposed exile from the love of others.[53] It is on this score that we get a kind of negative analogy to the knight of faith. "With the assistance of the demonic, therefore," writes Silentio, "the merman would be the single individual who as the single individual was higher than the universal. The demonic has the same quality as the divine, namely, that the single individual is able to enter into an absolute relation to it. This is the analogy, the counterpart to that paradox of which we speak. It has, therefore, a certain similarity that can be misleading."[54] The merman's self-enclosure courts the worst form of despair: defiance.[55] The Delphic bride and groom could also have elected for a kind of "defiance" had they married despite the augurs' pronouncement, but that defiance would only have been defiance of fate, and demonic defiance, which requires a private relationship with the divine, is defiance of the good.

In this modified version of the folk tale, Silentio stipulates that the merman is repentant for his attempt to seduce Agnes. The alternatives he delineates are that the merman is either in repentance alone, which opens the door to the demonic, or he is in repentance with Agnes.[56] The first option will make them both unhappy, and the merman will in particular be burdened with "a new guilt,"[57] as he condemns himself to a lifetime of self-recrimination, bound forever to despise himself for his own wickedness. The merman's self-laceration is provoked by Agnes's trusting innocence, and on this scenario he remains hidden because he cannot admit to Agnes his original sinful intent. Trapped by his refusal to repent, "the demonic in repentance probably will explain that this is indeed his punishment, and the more it torments him the better,"[58] for surely in his guilt he decides he deserves to be alone and unloved, he is unworthy of Agnes and her faith in him. He has seen something of himself in the mirror of her innocence, and what he sees is indeed loathsome; he concludes from this, though, that his loathsomeness is unforgiveable and becomes, in his demonic rage, perversely attached to this image of himself as tortured and stricken, beyond all saving. This is the very opposite of faith, and yet "in a certain sense there is ever so much more good in a demoniac than in superficial people."[59] This can be so only if demoniacs see more clearly what superficial people do not—namely, that they are sinners, and hand in hand with that recognition, they see what it takes to be healed of sin, that it means the end of who they are, the surrender of their sinfulness and their willingness to humbly accept another's trust and love for them precisely in their wretchedness.

It is in this sense that the demoniac and the faithful are misleadingly alike. Both the demoniac and the hero of faith are absolutely related to the absolute; in defiant despair, the demoniac absolutely relates to the absolute in a negative mode, the mode of total refusal of the claims of the absolute upon oneself, refusal to be loved, just as the merman refuses to accept Agnes's love,[60] refusal to be transformed into the image of the good.[61] This posture can be called an absolute relation to the absolute inasmuch as this way of relating to the absolute has a total transformative effect on the whole of the defiant person's life. All of the merman's experience is seen through the lens of this mania; his cutting off of himself from Agnes is a result of it; his withdrawal from life follows from it. For these reasons it can be said that the merman has—and again this is the sense in which he is like the knight of faith—teleologically suspended the ethical.

The only way a positive analogy can be drawn between Abraham and the merman is if the merman's movement of repentance is followed by the movement of the absurd.[62] "If he becomes disclosed, if he lets himself be saved by Agnes, then he is the greatest human being I can imagine, for it is only esthetics that thoughtlessly supposes it is praising the power of love by having the prodigal be loved by an innocent girl and thereby saved; it is only esthetics that perceives mistakenly and believes that the girl is the heroic figure instead of the merman."[63] The merman, should he open himself to the love of another, is the real hero, but understanding him at all requires both an awareness of the passion that is sinful defiance as well as the passion that is faith. Indeed, the merman, at this point of suspense, stands for anyone who has flirted with the demonic; the choice to be made is either in offense to remain defiant or to return to the ethical in repentance, a gesture that now can be undertaken only with the help of faith. Self-tormenting repentance is possible in human powers, but without faith, the merman will never be able to "grasp actuality again"[64] and never be able to reconcile the ideal and the actual in the way that a knight of faith alone can.

In a footnote near the end of his discussion of Agnes and the merman, Silentio writes, "Esthetics sometimes treats a similar situation in its usual game-playing way. The merman is saved by Agnes, and the whole thing ends with a happy marriage! A happy marriage—that is easy enough . . . Esthetics just sees to it that the lovers find each other and does not concern itself about the rest. If only it would see what happens afterwards, but it has no time for that and promptly proceeds to slap a new pair of lovers together. Of all the branches of knowledge, esthetics is the most faithless."[65] There is a superficial way of understanding the conclusion to the story of Agnes and the merman on Silentio's retelling of it that would content aesthetics: the lovers get married and live happily ever after. Such is the aesthetic ideal, and we know that the ideal is inapplicable to reality precisely because people never live happily ever after, at least not in the way they imagine they will.

Aesthetics is content to get the happy couple to the altar, and there it leaves them. But marriage is not what happens to you and your beloved on the day you get married; it is what happens every day after that. Marriage is the lifelong process of loving another person and opening yourself in humility and trust to being loved by that person, in the full knowledge that your trust will be betrayed and you will have to forgive and be sinned against again and sin against your beloved in your turn and be forgiven again and again. It is the lifelong process of learning patience and gratitude and forbearance, and aesthetics is not ordinarily up to the task of giving us a complete, coherent, and serious account of just such a life. At the very least, it is harder to realize the potential aesthetic appeal of a narrative that goes deeper than the obvious "high points" of life. Everyone has expectations of and hopes for what their life will be like going forward, and everyone finds those expectations and hopes disappointed. Faith transforms them, showing us that it is true, life will not be what we expect or hope for, but that it can be, if we are open to it, better than what we expected or hoped.

This is what I think Silentio means when he says that it is a given on any scenario that the merman can no longer be a seducer after being defeated by Agnes's innocence. "He can be saved by Agnes. This must not be interpreted to mean that by Agnes's love he would be saved from becoming a seducer in the future (this is an esthetic rescue attempt that always evades the main point, the continuity in the merman's life), for in that respect he is saved—he is saved insofar as he becomes disclosed."[66] The "main point" is not that he is delivered from being a seducer in the future but that he now must navigate the future in conversation with his past; he becomes a new man not in the moment that he abandons his past but every day thereafter, preserving the continuity of his self by every day becoming a new self.[67]

Tobias and Sarah: Both the Ethical and the Aesthetic

What would it mean for the merman not merely to be married but to go on being married, to go on being the self that he was, with all the ethically objectionable elements thereof, and paradoxically to go on becoming the self he is becoming? How can he be who he is in a transformed manner? In partial answer to these questions, Silentio advances another "even more moving" tale specifically because in this story "the passion of repentance was not set in motion."[68] This story is that of Tobias and Sarah from the deuterocanonical book of Tobit. Again, Silentio finds it necessary in this tale to do some editorial work. In the story, Sarah receives the love of Tobias even though seven of her prior husbands have been killed by a demon on each of her seven wedding nights. This detail is a bit too unintentionally comic for Silentio's purpose and perhaps also a bit too melodramatic in its emphasis on "Tobias's magnanimity" and the "appalling aspect" of the story that is underscored by the fact that Tobias is the only son of his parents.[69] "Consequently, this must be put aside."[70]

As a result of Silentio's revision, "Sarah, then, is a girl who has never been in love, who still has a young girl's beatific treasure . . . [the capacity] to love a man with all her heart. And yet she is unhappier than anyone else, for she knows that the evil demon who loves her will kill her bridegroom on the wedding night."[71] Her unhappiness is indeed superlative, for the source of it lies not in external determinations to which she is subject but within herself. If unhappiness comes from without, according to Silentio, consolation is still possible, but not for Sarah. Indeed, her situation is not only superlatively unhappy but paradoxically so. "Many a girl has become unhappy in love, but she nevertheless did *become* that; Sarah *was* that before she became that. It is grievous not to find the person to whom one can give oneself, but it is *unspeakably* grievous not to be able to give oneself. A young girl gives herself, and then it is said: Now she is no longer free. But Sarah was never free, and yet she had never given herself."[72]

Once again, however, Silentio changes the story to realize his purposes, and he does so expressly in a direction divergent from that of the "poets." "If a poet read this story and were to use it," writes Silentio, "I wager a hundred to one that he would make everything center on the young Tobias . . . this heroic courage would be the subject. I venture to propose another."[73] Granted that "Tobias behaves gallantly and resolutely and chivalrously,"[74] and his actions certainly appeal to the reader's aesthetic sensibilities, but Silentio deems any man unwilling to rise to his level of exemplary courage for the sake of love "a milksop who does not know what love is or what it is to be a man or what is worth living for; he has not even grasped the little mystery that it is better to give than to receive and has no intimation of the great mystery that it is far more difficult to receive than to give."[75] For the same reason that it is the merman, not Agnes, who is the true hero, so it is Sarah, not Tobias, who is the real hero; the reason is that it is harder to receive another's love in humility than it is to give love. This is something "the poets"[76] should know already and concern themselves with in their work, but Silentio has to retell the story in order to place Sarah's heroism in the proper light.

It is Sarah who has the courage to accept the love of another even though without being guilty of anything she is nevertheless cursed to be the death of the one who loves her. Sarah is clearly meant to be a mirror image of the demonic merman, and ethics, Silentio says, can only make sport of her, "just as it would be a taunting of Sarah for ethics to say to her: Why do you not express the universal and get married? Natures such as those are basically in the paradox, and they are by no means more imperfect than other people, except that they are either lost in the demonic paradox or saved in the divine paradox."[77] The demand of ethics, that each express the universal, is shattered on the almost comic extremity of Sarah's situation, but her situation is again, like the merman's, illustrative of the human situation itself. There are only two options for her or for anyone like her: first, the demonic, like the merman or Richard III, also mentioned in this context as one set apart and defiantly unwilling to be healed; or second, an absurd salvation, a stroke of genius touched with madness.[78] "What love for God it takes," Silentio writes, "to be willing to let oneself be healed when from the very beginning one in all innocence has been botched, from the very beginning has been a damaged specimen of a human being!"[79] Sarah's faith makes her well, even though by receiving another's love she may very well be the death of him. In this sense her story fulfills the ethical demand: Like the Delphic bride, Tobias knows what he is getting into. He knows her love may kill him. Indeed, anyone who marries pledges to remain with his or her beloved "until death do us part," which is a straightforward but certainly not simple way of saying the lover is prepared to endure the death of the beloved or to ask the beloved to endure his or her own death. If one thought carefully about these words, the demonic possibility would surely be a temptation: Why bother to love another at all? We're both just going to die anyway.

The story of Tobias and Sarah fulfills the aesthetic demand as well, inasmuch as the happy ending we all long for is attained. It is not a sentimental tearjerker to be sure, but it has a serious consolation won by an act of faith. On the wedding night, Sarah and her mother give voice to their passion for the absurd, their conviction that with God all things are possible. "Edna prepared the chamber, and she escorted Sarah into it and wept, and she received her daughter's weeping. And she said to her: My child, take heart. The Lord of heaven and earth may exchange your sorrow for joy!"[80] Tobias's prayer is likewise answered: the happy couple are delivered from their doom.

Silentio specifically says this is a story that ethics cannot comprehend, and it is one that aesthetics cannot deliver on its own terms either. There may be other moments in *Fear and Trembling* when Silentio allows the desired ideality of aesthetics to collide with the required ideality of ethics, but perhaps this one is the most significant. In aesthetics, things turn out just the way we want; like a good theater production, events play out to maximum effect. Two lovers hide a secret from each other, but a coincidence exposes them and everyone lives happily ever after. What aesthetics, the most faithless of the sciences,[81] prescribes can never be made actual.[82] But neither can ethics be made actual. With no room for coincidence and no patience for sentimentality,[83] ethics insists on things being not the way we find most satisfying but the way they must be. In the new ideality, the ideality of actuality, which is the religious, the desirability of aesthetics is preserved: things turn out for Tobias and Sarah just the way we want. And the rigors of ethics are softened, the purity of its ideal made attainable.

Marriage remains the paradigmatic example of the ethical relation, but Tobias and Sarah's marriage is forged on the terms of the religious: born in and sustained by faith. This marriage is likewise the marriage of beauty and justice, though both beauty and justice, as we spontaneously understand them, must be overcome and reshaped in order to be harmonized. The aesthetic is transformed but ultimately satisfied by the blessed beginning of Tobias and Sarah's story and the promise of their greater joys to come. The ethical is transformed and satisfied, having been endangered by the curse of Sarah's situation and rebuilt on the basis of Sarah's trust in God and willingness to accept Tobias's love. Do Tobias and Sarah get what they want? In a sense surely they do, but they also get more than what they wanted, for they cannot imagine the way in which their desires will be fulfilled, particularly once it seems that those desires cannot be fulfilled in the straightforward way they imagine. They get what they want in the end, but they do so in a way they could not have wanted, such that in a way they get what they did not want as a more satisfying replacement for what they did want.

The story of Tobias and Sarah, to a greater extent than the stories of Agnes and the merman and the Delphic betrothed, gives the reader of *Fear and Trembling* an illustration of what Haufniensis means by second ethics in *The Concept of Anxiety*. Recall that there Haufniensis claimed that aesthetics cannot properly treat sin without making it either tragic or comic. This is the state of affairs attained by the Delphic betrothed: their story will be either tragic or comic, depending on what they choose, what eventually does or does not befall them, and how they respond to that eventuality. The story of Agnes and the merman likewise could be either tragic or comic depending on whether the merman chooses the demonic or the divine, whether he repents alone in self-recrimination or with Agnes in a relationship that can be renewed only if it goes forward on terms different from those on which it began. In this story, though, the tragedy or comedy are not defined narrowly, according to the classical terms of fate: the merman's choice is one that the intrusion of sin, as understood according to revelation, both complicates and makes possible in a higher register. Finally, the story of Tobias and Sarah is clearly a comedy and one that would not make sense in classical terms but is a specifically religious comedy.

That Silentio changes each story in such a way as to distance it from mere "poetry" suggests that he is trying to stretch the tales to accommodate phenomena that are not inherent to aesthetics: he is trying to reconceive the very parameters on which these stories are possible by allowing the classical aesthetic ideal to come into collision with an ethical ideal. The gods demand that you not go through with your desire; your sinfulness prevents you from being happy; the certainty of death prevents you from asking another for his love. In escalating order of clarity, these three stories enact, then, on altered terms the possibility of the new religious ideal, the ideal of actuality, coming to the fore. Life rarely works out in the same way that a good story does. Life rarely allows us to overcome the difficulties imposed by our failures to be the people we must be morally. Faith recognizes that fate, our own sinfulness, and death stand in the way of our own ideals of happiness and that no ideal worthy of our aspiration can fail to acknowledge these very real hindrances. But faith also holds out a new ideal, one that grants sin and death their due and nevertheless promises a happy ending to our story. Not a happy ending that we can imagine for ourselves but one beyond our imagining.

Faust and Margaret: Both the Ethical and the Aesthetic Revisited

The same points are discernible in Silentio's brief and somewhat tacked-on treatment of the Faust legend. "To take yet another case, let us imagine that an individual, by being hidden and by remaining silent, wants to save the universal."[84] In

Faust's case there is perhaps a coincident fulfillment of the aesthetic and ethical ideals inasmuch as Faust observes aesthetically mandated silence for the sake of the preservation of the ethical, in order to protect the ethical as universal. Faust's doubt would appear to threaten the integrity of the ethical—he "sees through," so to speak, the flimsiness and instability of the ethical as universal but holds his peace so as not to undermine the faith of others in that ideal. In this final case too, however, Silentio avowedly distances his treatment from one that would be expected of the poets. "Faust is a doubter, an apostate of the spirit who goes the way of the flesh. This is the poet's interpretation, and although it is repeated again and again that every age has its Faust, nevertheless one poet after the other undauntedly walks this beaten path. Let us make a little change."[85]

So despite the fact that everyone agrees every age has its own Faust, Silentio wryly observes that no poet has really introduced a change into this succession of unvarying interpretations of the Faust legend. In particular, Silentio regards even Goethe's version as lacking in the psychological complexity of "doubt's secret conversations with itself," which would be enriched if we consider the possibility of Silentio's proposed change of attention to Faust's "sympathetic nature" while retaining his status as "the doubter par excellence." Silentio goes on to lament once again that the poets should have introduced this insight and considered the ramifications of it for Faust's story, but "in our age, when indeed all have experienced doubt, no poet as yet has made any step in this direction."[86]

Keeping in mind Silentio's early discussion of the nobility of Descartes's doubt, we might read the proposed change to Faust's legend as picking up on some of the personal depth of Descartes's project and the way in which Descartes's doubt can yield a sort of intellectual double movement of resignation and faith. Silentio's counsel to the poets along these lines is, "Only when one turns Faust into himself can doubt take on a poetic aspect; only then does he actually discover within himself all the sufferings of doubt. Then he knows that it is spirit that maintains existence, but he also knows that the security and joy in which men live are not grounded in the power of the spirit but are easily explained as an unreflected bliss."[87] When Faust's doubt becomes inward, then his self-knowledge becomes a lens by which he understands something of humanity in general. For Faust, as for Vigilius Haufniensis, it is true that "unum noris omnes," where the "unum" is one's self:[88] "know yourself and you know everyone." What Faust knows when he turns inward is that only the spirit sustains existence, and what ordinary people call happiness is only comfort and good fortune. "As doubter, as the doubter, he is higher than all this,"[89] for he sees the fragility of the ordinary person's so-called happiness, the wretchedness of their contentment and ease.

Just as Silentio felt called upon to torment the merman and Agamemnon a bit, put them to the test of the aesthetic and ethical demands, so too does he repeat his confidence that "I am very inventive when it comes to tormenting heroes" and subjects Faust to the test of Margaret. Once again, Silentio puts his hero of choice in Problema III into relationship with another, and this time yet again a romantic relationship. At the same time, he yet again differentiates this encounter from others extant in the literature. "Faust sees Margaret, but not after having chosen lust, for my Faust does not choose lust at all; he sees Margaret not in Mephistopheles's concave mirror but in all her adorable innocence."[90] Like the merman, Silentio's Faust meets himself in the mirror of his beloved's innocence. Since Silentio's Faust retains his sympathetic nature, his "love for people," he conceals both his doubt and his love for Margaret. Faust can "very easily fall in love with her. But he is a doubter; his doubt has destroyed actuality for him, for my Faust is so ideal that he is not one of these scientific doubters who doubt one hour every semester on the podium but otherwise are able to do everything else."[91] This Faust is the ideal of doubt, not a dabbler like those Silentio ridicules at the beginning of *Fear and Trembling* by contrast to the Greek skeptics and Descartes. His ideal purity has robbed him of actuality, for he cannot, by reason of what he knows about himself and about the flimsiness of human happiness, be reconciled to the realm of existence in its lived actuality. The lad in resignation idealizes his beloved; Faust idealizes *himself*: "He holds to his resolution and remains silent and does not tell anyone of his doubt, nor does he tell Margaret of his love."[92]

Once more, such an ideal figure will have no part of half measures or bargaining: "Faust is too ideal a figure to be satisfied with the nonsense that if he spoke he would prompt a general discussion, or that the whole affair would pass without any consequences, or perhaps this or perhaps that . . . He remains silent in order to sacrifice himself—or he speaks in the awareness that he will throw everything into disorder."[93] Faust, then, has the same choice to make as the Delphic bridegroom or the merman. Ethically his mandate is to speak "even though by speaking he brings every misfortune possible down upon the world."[94] Still, Silentio claims such a person should be preferred to the dilettante in doubt, who half questions and half consoles. Like Abraham, such a speaker cannot make his choice based on "the outcome," which "cannot help a person either in the moment of action or with respect to responsibility."[95] If he keeps silent, he "will add a little spiritual trial to his other agonies," for he will have the same guilt as the merman could or the bridegroom would if he were to marry without informing his bride of the curse against him. In this case, he will be forever nagged by the ethical with the question "How are you going to be sure that your resolution was not prompted by cryptic pride?"[96]

The only other alternative is one that is clearly comparable to the condition of the truly repentant merman, the one who repents with Agnes out of a willingness to receive her love and a repentance over his own condition paired with faith in his own forgiveness and ability to go forward. Faust "the doubter can become the single individual who as the single individual stands in an absolute relation to the absolute . . . he can get authorization for his silence. In that case, he must make his doubt into guilt. In that case, he is within the paradox, but then his doubt is healed, even if he may have another doubt."[97] The only way out for Faust is the only way out for the merman, which is to admit his sinfulness to himself and be ready to have it forgiven. Faust's doubt is not an intellectual pose, but it must be deepened even further into a matter for which he must take personal responsibility, not as an inevitable conclusion of his own intellectual supremacy. It is not just unfortunate that given his more profound insight Faust sees truths that others keep hidden from themselves; it is an anxiety-inducing realization for which Faust is responsible, not just ethically—as if his doubt were a matter primarily of shielding others from their own vulnerabilities (indeed, a faithful Faust might be called to "wound from behind," to name the disease of despair that he sees in others in order to delude them into the truth, like a Kierkegaardian psychologist)—but religiously, for the effect his doubt has not so much on others but on *himself*. For as we have seen, Faust's doubt cuts him off from both the world and his love for Margaret. Were he to open himself to the actuality of existence and of his love for Margaret, his doubt would be healed, even while he would be open to "another doubt," which can only be the doubt that is sin-consciousness, the sober self-awareness that never leaves the faithful person.[98]

Abraham's Final Utterance

Having canvassed, then, the various triangulations that Silentio explores in Problema III, I think we can perceive clearly that Abraham's faith cannot be confused with aesthetic hiddenness. The last major topic to explore, then, is Abraham's own profession of faith: "God himself will provide the lamb for the burnt offering, my son." I argue that these words both in form and content encapsulate one of the key features of Abraham's faith. They give voice to a trust *that* God will provide while remaining completely indeterminate with respect to *how* God will provide. The final utterance of Abraham, therefore, is a model of all communication about faith, including the text of *Fear and Trembling* itself. Insofar as Abraham speaks words about faith that are both true and beautiful, and insofar as he himself does not fully grasp the meaning of his own words, or his own words gesture toward a truth that eludes his grasp and the grasp of any traditional discourse, philosophical or poetic, he provides the paradigm for not just faith itself but for all intelligible talk about faith.[99] Abraham's words are then the culmination of *Fear and Trembling* as well as my study of it.

Silentio sets Abraham's inability to speak against two other forms of non-utterance: the withholding of speech in defiance of ethical responsibility and the withholding of speech in deference to aesthetic fittingness. As we have seen, the whole cavalcade of characters introduced in Problema III is trotted out by Johannes in order to demonstrate their dissimilarity to Abraham. All the "aesthetic heroes" maintain silence in order to save or protect another person, and they do so in such a way as to fulfill an aesthetic imperative: their silence is not a matter of ethical accountability alone, but it aims at the realization of an aesthetic ideal. Silence viewed aesthetically can intensify drama, holding the audience in suspense; can heighten irony, as when the viewer knows something vital the characters don't; and can deepen the observer's admiration for a character who faces her fate with heroic determination.

Sometimes, Johannes writes—and these are interesting cases—both the aesthetic and the ethical ideal demand disclosure. We know why the ethical does, because responsibility to others requires that we give an account of ourselves, our intentions, and our justifications for our actions. The aesthetic sometimes does as well, again because the dramatic force, the quality of a story as a story, is enhanced. Here we see how the life of faith and the language that describes such a life reappropriate aesthetic integrity on the far side of the suspension of the ethical. I intend to show in this section how words of faith stretch themselves to address both a chastened ethical demand and a reassertion of an equally fragmented aesthetic requirement. In faith, the ethical and aesthetic are both overcome but also transformed in such a way as to put redoubled pressure on the person of faith and her way of speaking. In the case of successful speech about faith, a case that I would say typifies what Kierkegaard means by *communication*, the good and the beautiful reunite in a way that will be open to question by the suspicious but life-giving to one ready for faith. If these are the parameters within which Johannes is working, what they imply is that he judges Abraham's final utterance to be the only one that does justice to the ordeal in which Abraham finds himself *and* to the faith that is guiding him through it. This is why Johannes claims that Abraham's "total presence"[100] is discernible in this word: this is, as it were, the message of his life, the consummation of his character.

This is clearly seen by way of comparison to the case of Agamemnon from *Iphigenia in Aulis*, discussed above. Recall that at first it would seem that Agamemnon is both aesthetically and ethically justified in maintaining his silence; for his heroism to be what it is, he must keep the terror to himself without seeking comfort from another and prevent the relevant parties to his intended deed from finding out what he has in store, to protect them, as it were, for as long as he can. But they do find out his plan by a coincidental aesthetic contrivance and thus bring ethical pressure to bear on the tragic hero. The drama is also heightened, of course, by the tears and pleas of the king's wife and daughter. I think it is useful to read Abraham against Agamemnon once again, here in Problema III, just as Johannes had his reader do in Problemata I and II. The primary point of disanalogy between Agamemnon and Abraham is that the former can speak but does not, while the latter "*cannot* speak."[101] Now it should be abundantly clear that by this Johannes does not mean Abraham is physically incapable of issuing forth language (*aphasia*); the dilemma is that he cannot in speaking make himself *understood* (*epoche*): "Even though I go on talking night and day without interruption, if I cannot make myself understood when I speak, then I am not speaking. This is the case with Abraham . . . Now, Abraham can describe his love for Isaac in the most beautiful words to be found in any language. But this is not what is on his mind; it is something deeper, that he is going to sacrifice him because it is an ordeal."[102] Now Johannes the playwright, the dramatist, the imitator of Euripides, imposes upon Abraham's silence.

This imposition may indeed be one of the more substantial innovations of Problema III, since throughout the text Silentio has emphasized Abraham's alienation from communication and community, but the argument of *Fear and Trembling* ends up in a more interesting position. We should not assume the exact correlation of the ethical as universal and the realm of community. As we have seen, the ethical as universal makes room only for specimen-people, not the togetherness of single individuals. The ethical as universal may be the space of a sort of public rationality and responsibility, but this would not exhaust all possible forms of communication and togetherness. The ethical as universal is, in my view, the contested realm of *political* transparency, a site where the only possible community would be an unhappy one, that of the collectively resigned. This point is clarified once again by comparison to the situation of Agamemnon and Iphigenia. Speaking of the possibility that the daughter would come to comprehend the father's intentions, Silentio writes, "Iphigenia submits to her father's resolve; she herself make the infinite movement of resignation, and they now have a mutual understanding."[103] But surely this so-called mutual understanding is only the false companionship of two persons in simultaneous despair, not shared harmony.

The religious is the only site of genuine community and communication, in the religious and conventional sense of that word.[104] The religious, not the ethical as universal, is the place where we might expect communication to take place, on the other side of the shipwreck of the aesthetic and the ethical. If Abraham is compelled to speak by Silentio, it is then because, like Agamemnon, he is now under the renewed pressure of both ethical and aesthetic concerns, which reassert themselves in new cooperation within the life of faith, where genuine community and communication are made possible. "I shall now consider in more detail these last words by Abraham," writes Johannes. "Without these words, the whole event would lack something; if they were different words, everything perhaps would dissolve in confusion."[105] I submit that the "something" that would have been lacking in the incident is an *aesthetic something*, a quality that, if it were missing, would diminish the artistry and the perfection of the narrative *qua* narrative. Abraham's story is after all *a story*, and as such it recovers something of the ideals that faith transforms in their overcoming: as story it must be ethically demanding and aesthetically satisfying in order to transform the self.

Johannes says he has often wondered to himself whether a tragic hero should have "last words" to say, and he says further he has decided it comes down to what sphere of life such a hero belongs to, whether or not his deed is oriented to spirit. That a tragic hero can say "a few appropriate words" is not in question, only "how appropriate it is for him to say them."[106] Again, notice the emphasis on the language of aesthetic fittingness. Later on the same page, again by way of contrast to Agamemnon, Johannes contends that a tragic hero like the Greek king, whose deed is not oriented to spirit, would undercut the integrity of his consummating act, the sacrifice of his daughter, if he were to speak about it before, during, or after actually doing it himself. Johannes explains, "tragic conventions enjoin him to complete his task in silence."[107] Once more, it is an aesthetic imperative that enters into this prefatory consideration of Abraham's last words: Are they appropriate? Do they fulfill the conventions that the genre demands be observed?

Closer to Abraham's situation is Socrates, since he is an intellectual hero whose deed is oriented to spirit, unlike Agamemnon's. Hence the circumstance of his death calls for commentary. Were Socrates simply to die silently, his companions could lose confidence in his fidelity to the methods and passions of his life, which were inseparable from the art of conversation. Socrates, then, must *say something* upon the occasion of his death in order to vindicate for the last time the manner in which he spent his life. Now, according to Johannes, while all this may be valid, nevertheless,

> these brief suggestions are indeed not applicable to Abraham if one expects to be able to find by means of some analogy an appropriate final word for Abraham, but they do apply if one perceives the necessity for Abraham to consummate himself in the final moment, not to draw the knife silently but to have a word to say, since as the father of faith he has absolute significance oriented to spirit. I cannot form in advance any idea of what he is going to say; after he has said it, I presumably can understand it, perhaps in a certain sense understand Abraham in what was said without thereby coming any closer to him than in the preceding exposition.[108]

Note carefully the essential claim here that Johannes is making: What we can be sure of, based on an analogy to Socrates and others like him, is that Abraham must have something to say, but what that something is we cannot predict. Once that something has been said, then in that something we have the best opportunity we will get to understand Abraham, not that he can be understood in any conventional sense, as Johannes has consistently denied, but that if he is to be understood in any way, this is that way, through the retrospective grasp of what he said, the content of which was in no way predictable, though the occasion demanded it. What motivates the utterance of Abraham's words of faith is both an ethical demand and aesthetic expectation; that he must speak is an eventuality that is not utterly unpredictable given the argument so far, though what he will speak is utterly unpredictable. The scene has been set for this final act, inasmuch as the ethical and aesthetic collide in this moment: Abraham speaks because he is ethically required to do so and because the conventions of dramatic narrative dictate it.

So Abraham is bound to speak, though we don't know how he will, and once he does, he shows himself to be an accomplished player of *carambole*: "God himself will provide the lamb for the burnt offering, my son." This utterance fulfills—admittedly elusively—the ethical demand that Abraham not lie about what he is convinced of. "Now, if Abraham had replied: I know nothing—he would have spoken an untruth. He cannot say anything, for what he knows he cannot say."[109] Ethically, if he were going to tell Isaac what he intended, as Agamemnon told Iphigenia so they could share a "mutual understanding,"[110] "then he ought to have spoken long before this,"[111] as Johannes points out. They also express an aesthetically satisfying quality as well, whether we are content to call them "irony" as Johannes does or by some other name, the point is that they have a beauty and fittingness that is appropriate to the situation. Abraham's final word is elegant, economical, elusive, and forecasts the happy ending for which every reader longs. Faith thus has to unite the ethical and aesthetic after both have been individually surpassed on the itinerary of the faithful person's journey. As a result, words of faith will evince a sort of fidelity to both a chastened ethical requirement to speak truthfully and a fragmented aesthetic demand to speak beautifully.

Abraham, speaks "in a divine language," he speaks "in tongues"[112] or "in a strange tongue."[113] And this, I submit, is what anyone who wishes to speak about faith must do. This mode of expression reaffirms confidences and trusts—"The Lord will provide"—while conceding that even the speaker herself has no idea *how* the Lord will provide. Abraham's utterance is both in form and content the paradigmatic speech about faith. Abraham's final utterance preserves the trauma of the ordeal, in that his words at once admit the need for divine provision, and gesture beyond the trauma of the ordeal, in that they give voice to faith in that very provision. One could even say that Abraham's words have a sort of performative power, in that by expressing this trust they actually make of Abraham the sort of person who is actually possessing this trust, and they constitute a sort of pledge that Abraham makes before his son in the face of their shared uncertainty.

Faith trusts God will provide while remaining open to the unexpected ways in which that provision will express itself: This is both *what* Abraham says and *how* he says it. His wisdom is one that speaks truly and beautifully about a truth that the speaker cannot claim to possess but by which he is possessed. The one who speaks of faith in an important sense does not know what she is talking about, but her words give voice to a meaning that recedes from her grasp and from the grasp of every traditional discourse.

A Tentative Extension of Abraham's Words: Providence and Proclamations of Love

Judge William, in the second part of *Either/Or*, draws a distinction between what can be portrayed esthetically and what can be poetically reproduced, which he insists are two different categories that do not completely overlap. "Everything I am talking about here," he writes to his young friend "A," "certainly can be portrayed esthetically, but not in poetic reproduction, but only by living it, by realizing it in the life of actuality."[114] This claim accords completely with the overall argument I have been pursuing about *Fear and Trembling*. This explains why Silentio himself is not a poet classically construed and how Abraham can communicate without being a "teacher" or speaker in the sense of an ethical authority or tragic hero. This explains why *Fear and Trembling* has to return to the aesthetic, for in the life of faith, the aesthetic genuinely comes into its own; the aesthetic impulse and project is completed only when it can be lived, when it becomes the ideal of actuality. Judge William continues,

> Here I am at the summit of the esthetic. And in truth, he who has humility and courage enough to let himself be esthetically transformed, he who feels himself present as a character in a drama the deity is writing, in which the poet and the prompter are not different persons, in which the individual, as the experienced actor who has lived into his character and his lines is not disturbed by the prompter but feels that he himself wants to say what is being whispered to him, so that it almost becomes a question whether he is putting the words in the prompter's mouth or the prompter in his, he who in the most profound sense feels himself creating and created, who in the moment he feels himself creating has the original pathos of the lines, and in the moment he feels himself created has the erotic ear that picks up every sound—he and he alone has brought into actual existence the highest in esthetics.[115]

Abraham is a character in a drama that God is writing, and when he speaks he does so in this "original pathos" where the authorship of his words comes into question—whether it is the actor or the prompter who is putting words into his mouth or the other way around. This reciprocal ventriloquism, we might say, is characteristic of Abraham's utterance, and this is the very summit of the aesthetic, according to Judge William.

I would like to draw an analogy to another form of expression that we routinely accept as accomplishing this same double play between the ethical and aesthetic. Taking as an inspiration Johannes's last remark about Abraham's greatness—that it consisted in his having "remained true to his love"[116]—we might consider the possibility of comparing his words of faith with another sort of utterance: a proclamation of love. Imagine a lover proclaiming his love as a kind of act of ventriloquism; when we proclaim love we do not, in a sense, know if it is really ourselves speaking or the prompter speaking through us: our words achieve the highest possible in aesthetics, but we live them as our own. If a lover promises his beloved "I will love you always," then this declaration has to be evaluated in a distinctive way. If the beloved held the lover to such a promise in strictly ethical terms, then any lover would fail by that standard, because no one can always live up to it. At any given moment in that shared life, a lover may in fact not be particularly loving; certainly at various moments he won't feel very loving. Conversely, a beloved would be well within her rights to take it that her lover is not speaking merely aesthetically when he says "I will love you always." The lover stakes himself in the words of his pledge. He may know he can't exactly fulfill the words of his own promise even as he makes it, but he can't possibly qualify his promise with a mental or verbal reservation along the lines of "As far as I know, I will love you always."[117] This restriction prevents him from disavowing his own words.

Declaring "I will love you always" does not assume that this promise will be fulfilled in the same way; the *how* of its fulfillment remains open to future reinvention and imaginative reconstrual. It doesn't assume that we grasp at the time of proclamation the full consequence of the promise. What it means to have pledged ourselves in such a way cannot be clear at first; only living into the promise over the course of time and practicing its fulfillment (possibly even failing at fulfilling it, even repeatedly) can reveal what it meant in the first place. Finally, such a proclamation of love does not even require strict correctness every single moment of every single day. The test cannot consist in a series of occasional verifications, as if the beloved could determine whether her lover really loved her by "checking up" every day on the quality of his behavior to make sure it met her expectations. The quality of such a proclamation does not conclusively rely on any definite outcome, as if love could be utterly vitiated by an undesirable state of affairs or completely vindicated by a set of fortuitous developments. The quality of a proclamation of love instead expresses a stance that has been taken up by the lover in the face of *any* outcome, for good or ill. Indeed, such resolve in the face of any eventuality is what makes a promise what it is.

The "test" of its validity is proven in the complex repetitions of its performance, not in its susceptibility to verification or falsification. We could imagine a churlish beloved objecting to her lover's promise on the grounds that during the course of the week she felt unloved every day between breakfast and lunch. Or a pedantic beloved smugly accrediting her lover with success on the grounds that he was slavishly attentive to her every need. Both of these "standards" would suit only the one judging externally, the one relying on her own unregenerate notions of what love must look like in order to "count," as it were. And both would fail to discern that the proof of love is not fully deducible from a series of specific acts that do or do not suit her preferences. The beloved holds her lover to his promise with the recognition that how his love will be shown may differ from how she wants to be shown love and will be prepared to forgive his failures, an act that doesn't excuse him from his promise but in fact holds him to it all the more insistently.

Abraham's utterance is similar to this in that when he expresses confidence in the Lord's provision, he cannot wholly know in what sense this is true; Abraham's confidence is that the Lord will provide even when it seems like this cannot be true, or even that there is no way to test whether it is true, or even when it seems like divine provision is nothing other than what human understanding would deem a deprivation instead. Abraham and the lover, if I can put it provocatively, do not know what they are talking about. What they mean can only be lived out. What they have in common is the prophetic and performative dimensions of their promise. Indeed, the meaning of Abraham's life is that the Lord will provide, but how he has provided—through the departure from Ur, through the miraculous pregnancy of Sarah, through the renunciation and gifting back of Isaac—has been ever a surprise and ever will be. What divine provision will look like always fails to meet our expectations or deviates from the norm or defies customary ways of understanding. The faithless person will take this failure as cause for despair and designate one sort of outcome as the result of good fortune, while another she will judge as bad luck or fate. Like the lad in love with the princess, who the princess really is remains a mystery. Across the different iterations of promise and fulfillment that mark the knight of faith's path through life, our expectations as to what the fulfillment will look like, who our beloved really is, where the blessing is amid our suffering, have to be constantly adjusted. In the same way, a faithful lover could look back on a lifetime of devotion and say that through thick and thin, in sickness and in health, for richer and poorer, in times of joy and times of sorrow—despite perhaps even many failures—that he did remain true to his love.

For the person of faith, the goodness and beauty of life are fragile gifts. Silentio never mentions this, but the Genesis account says that Abraham, after sacrificing the ram, gave Mount Moriah a new name, "Jehovah-jireh," which means the place where the Lord saw, or better yet, saw to it. In Latin we would say *pro-videre*, to look ahead, to look out for. Or to use the traditional theological term that is etymologically linked to "provision," Abraham renames Moriah "Providence," because, for the knight of faith, *all* is providence. That the Lord will provide is the content of Abraham's life and faith; what that means not even Abraham really knows. But he must give voice to it, to this truth that exceeds articulation, and once he does, he passes the test. Just as Socrates really dies before he dies, with his final, consummating speech,[118] so I would argue is Abraham born again as the father of Isaac with these words—long before he raises the knife.

Conclusion

WHILE *FEAR AND Trembling*, as we saw at the outset of this book, begins at great length and with great difficulty, it ends briefly, but in a way also with great difficulty, since it argues that there is no ending, only beginning again. The text literally turns back on itself in a sort of reflexive conclusion, recapitulating its own preface. Silentio's epilogue begins by referencing the occasion on which Dutch spice merchants threw their cargo overboard in order to reinflate the price of their goods by creating an artificial scarcity.[1] A similar image opened the preface, where Silentio decried the fact that not only in the world of business but in the world of ideas also, the age is holding a great clearance sale. The knight of faith, by contrast, recall from the end of Problema II, does not win faith at a bargain price or sell it on the cheap either. Silentio asks, then,

> is this the kind of self-deception the present generation needs? Should it be trained in a virtuosity along that line, or is it not, instead, adequately perfected in the art of deceiving itself? Or, rather, does it not need an honest earnestness that fearlessly and incorruptibly points to the tasks, an honest earnestness that lovingly maintains the tasks, that does not disquiet people into wanting to attain the highest too hastily but keeps the tasks young and beautiful and lovely to look at, inviting to all and yet also difficult and inspiring to the noble-minded (for the noble nature is inspired only by the difficult)?[2]

So if the problem is that there is a clearance sale on in the world of ideas, it would seem here, at the very end of the text, that the solution is not more deception but less. The price manipulation by the spice merchants is not held up by Silentio as an example to be imitated, since the age seems to be sufficiently capable of deceiving itself, and additional deceptions are not required. Instead, the key idea of earnestness is invoked by Silentio's memorable description of children at play, an image that is far more important than the example of the Dutch merchants. "When children on vacation have already played all the games before twelve o'clock and impatiently ask: Can't somebody think up a new game—does this show that these children are more developed and more advanced than the children in the contemporary or previous generation who make the well-known games last all day long? Or does it show instead that the first children lack what I would call the endearing earnestness belonging to play?"[3]

Recall that the preface focused, in its early paragraphs, on the interplay of *stasis* and *dynamis*, movement at the spot, or what Silentio comes to call in

Problema III—with his treatment of Agnes and the merman—the "continuity" in the merman's life. Only aesthetics can be satisfied by the consoling thought that the merman simply and instantaneously changes into another sort of person; the life of faith is the one that allows me to go on being me while also being the me who I was in the past. The point of this anecdote is again to unify the notions of change and permanence, and by returning to this theme at the end of the book, *Fear and Trembling* performs its own lesson on movement at the spot, making the epilogue a sort of chiastic counterpoint to the preface. The point of the life of faith is not to create a false impression of exception or superiority or to artificially inflate one set of ethical or aesthetic priorities over others but to keep the tasks young and beautiful and inviting to all, since everyone can be the single individual, and this has to happen, it would seem, in a way that soberly appraises the risks but does not scare people off entirely (despite the apparent shock value of Abraham's story, which by the time we reach the end of *Fear and Trembling* we would have to say has been significantly blunted). The trick is, like the inventive children, to make the same old game last all day, and this is a matter of honest earnestness, not trickery or scare tactics. Part of what we gain by the long perambulation through Problema III, in fact, is this restored sense of aesthetic attraction; the difficulty of the life of faith is retained, but it is dramatized for us in an arguably more intuitive and attractive fashion by Sarah's gentle courage, by the sympathetic Faust who conquers doubt, by the merman who repents with Agnes. These heroes of faith will need earnestness, for each begins where aesthetics usually leaves off, on the threshold of a life that calls for commitment and recommitment again and again.

The point of "earnestness" is not to invent possibilities from whole cloth or to mechanically reenact the same old possibilities but to revivify the old, to move at the spot. The children do not show off their maturity or progressiveness by calling for a new game; they betray their lack of imagination and dedication to the task of playing the same game afresh. As any devotee of a sport knows, the rules of the game are never restrictive of new possibilities for play; they are, in point of fact, the conditions for the possibility *of* possibility. Only the uninitiated and the uncreative fail to see the potential for innovation within the established or that the established is precisely what calls for innovation and makes it permissible.

For a useful illustration of how earnestness accomplishes this feat, let us turn one last time to Haufniensis, our guide through these pages. Haufniensis refuses to define earnestness, but he does insist that it is no mere personality trait or settled aspect of character. Earnestness is the means by which action can be kept original rather than mechanically habituated.[4] Earnestness is neither unfeeling habit nor immediate feeling, which Haufniensis calls enthusiasm. Earnestness builds necessarily on feeling but does so by relativizing enthusiasm. "To make everything as concrete as possible," Haufniensis writes, "I shall use an example.

Every Sunday, a clergyman must recite the prescribed common prayer, and every Sunday he baptizes several children. Now let him be enthusiastic etc. The fire burns out, he will stir and move people etc., but at one time more and at another time less. Earnestness alone is capable of returning regularly every Sunday with the same originality to the same thing."[5] It is surprising, perhaps, that Haufniensis's example is liturgical, but it is also highly appropriate. One cannot repeat the same ritual, or like the children in Silentio's example, play the same game, on the basis of enthusiasm alone, for this waxes and wanes. One has to be committed to the repetition for its own sake, since each time the Sunday service, each time the afternoon's game, is in one respect the same, while in numerous other respects it is different. Earnestness allows me to repeat the same old thing in a new way, but that is possible only because in every case the same old thing is *mine*, and my own self is, Haufniensis argues, the true concern of earnestness. In fact, if earnestness is directed to any specific field of endeavor or interest, and presumably this holds for liturgy and sports, then it degenerates into pedantry.

The earnest person is first and foremost in earnest not about anything in particular but about herself. As Haufniensis asserts, "This same thing to which earnestness is to return with the same earnestness can only be earnestness itself," such that earnestness is wholly self-reflexive: "To do anything with earnestness requires, first and foremost, knowledge of what the object of earnestness is," and that is nothing other than one's own self.[6]

It is likewise significant that Haufniensis points to earnestness as the only appropriate mood for sin. We have seen that the argument of *Fear and Trembling* is indirectly structured around a strategic omission of sin, and I have tried to construct (perhaps too inventively, some readers might say) an interpretation that leads us into the text's implications as well as direct indications. We have seen that Haufniensis rejects both tragic and comic attitudes toward sin, but his reason for commending the fitness of earnestness, I think, is clarified by the contrast to enthusiasm. Just as some Sundays the parson wakes up without much enthusiasm for leading worship or baptizing babies and will need a deeper resource to draw upon for him to artfully and wholeheartedly commit himself to his tasks for the day, we cannot vanquish sin merely by the strength of any specific resolve, simply because some days we just do not feel like doing what is right or resisting what is wrong. Earnestness keeps in view the sort of self as a whole I am striving to become and allows that to be the guide, not an unstable passion for avoiding what is wrong.

What the age needs, then, is not an exercise in deception but an exercise in seriousness that directs the reader's attention back onto herself and puts her tasks in the proper light of sober joy, the "endearing earnestness belonging to play." This is the mood fitting for Sarah's incipient marriage to Tobias, for the merman on his way to repentance with Agnes, for Faust as he humbles himself before Margaret, for Abraham on his way to Moriah, for Mary as she welcomes the miraculous birth; it is the mood of faithful life.

Finally, at the very end of the book, Silentio laments the fortunes of Heraclitus, the paradigmatic thinker of change, who was outdone by his follower. "Heraclitus the obscure said: One cannot walk through the same river twice. Heraclitus the obscure had a disciple who did not remain standing there but went further—and added: One cannot even do it once. Poor Heraclitus, to have a disciple like that! By this improvement, the Heraclitean thesis was amended into an Eleatic thesis that denies motion, and yet that disciple wished only to be a disciple of Heraclitus who went further, not back to what Heraclitus abandoned."[7] Again we see here a recapitulation of the preface and its indictment of the age and its characteristic demand to "go further." The impetus to go further results in the unexpected but stultifying inversion of the position that was meant to be abandoned. Thus movement away from the spot results, rather than movement at the spot. This makes it clear that Silentio is not valorizing movement for the sake of it nor arbitrarily privileging stasis, but attempting to think them together. The reference to the Eleatics is itself repeated in the opening lines of *Repetition*, published the same day as *Fear and Trembling*, which tell the story of Diogenes's gestural refutation of the Eleatic denial of movement. Heraclitus, the Eleatics, and Heraclitus's disciple all unwittingly fail to solve the problem of movement by emphasizing one pole over the other, while Kierkegaard seeks to solve the problem by reference to repetition, another name for movement at the spot. This is true of not only the text entitled *Repetition* but also of *Fear and Trembling*. In both the example of Heraclitus and the children at play, what is at stake is continuity, which is Silentio's attempt to capture something of both *stasis* and *dynamis*, movements and positions.

The reason both have to be brought into consideration is that Silentio, consistent with the whole course of his treatment, claims that "the highest passion in a person is faith, and here no generation begins at any other point than where the previous one did. Each generation begins all over again; the next generation advances no further than the previous one, that is, if that one was faithful to the task and did not leave it high and dry."[8] So part of the paradoxical character of the belonging together of *stasis* and *dynamis* is that the highest pitch of passion, which is nothing other than faith, is one that, by definition, goes no further than what came before. Faith is not ever an advance on anything, since it is a product of earnestness and thus is only a reflexive co-opting of its own basis. For the earnest "progression" of faith there can be no advance, only a repetition.

This dynamic is written not just at the individual level but across the generations. If the whole task of each generation is nothing other than the effort of repetition, then all of history is nothing but repetition, nothing but the recapitulation in its own terms of each generation's task.[9] History is nothing other than the children who repeat the same old game in a new way, nothing other than the parson who performs the same ritual in a new way on a new Sunday that is nevertheless like all the other Sundays in the calendar. As Silentio cautions, though, "That it should be fatiguing is, of course, something that one generation cannot say, for the generation does indeed have the task and has nothing to do with the fact that the previous generation had the same task, unless this particular generation, or the individuals in it, presumptuously assumes the place that belongs to the spirit who rules the world and who has the patience not to become weary."[10]

It is only from an abstract third-person perspective that one might judge the task of the present generation as "fatiguing," since there is no sense in which the current generation can regard its task as tiresomely the same as the prior generation's except by such an abstract third-person perspective. If such a perspective could genuinely be taken up, then the current generation could regard itself as burdened or bored or dismayed by the fact that its task was substantially the same as that of every other generation. And perhaps this is indeed the difficulty that Kierkegaard thinks the current generation faces, that it is all too apt to regard its own circumstance as distinctively bored and distanced from the task of every generation. This age thinks it is in need of a new deception, a new distraction, but in fact it is truly in need only of a reminder of where it belongs in the grand scheme of human history and what earnestness, real human feeling for the specific tasks of the human being, enjoins upon it. Inattentiveness to the call of earnestness, failure to adhere to the genuinely human task, results in a whole generation being "wrong, and no wonder, then, that all existence seems wrong to it, for there surely is no one who found existence more wrong than the tailor who, according to the fairy story, came to heaven while alive and contemplated the world from that vantage point."[11]

The story Silentio refers to, "The Tailor in Heaven,"[12] collected by the Grimm brothers, rewards attention, for it is a religious version of the Orpheus myth mentioned in the preliminary expectoration. There, Orpheus is condemned by Silentio[13] (following the interpretation given by Phaedrus in Plato's *Symposium*) for attempting to cheat his way into the underworld by entering in without bravely being prepared to die. "The Tailor in Heaven" is also a parable that parallels in message Jesus's condemnation of the unforgiving servant discussed in the coda of chapter 7. In "The Tailor in Heaven," Saint Peter is under orders from the Lord not to admit anyone to heaven during his stroll in the celestial garden. The tailor knocks at the gate and presents himself as an honest tradesman appealing for entry. Saint Peter, though, condemns the tailor as a filcher of cloth and blocks his way at first. The tailor appeals to Saint Peter for mercy, which he receives. Once in heaven, the tailor admires a golden chair with a matching footstool.[14] When he succumbs to the temptation to sit in the chair, he realizes that sitting here in the Lord's chair affords him a view of what is going on below on earth. The tailor, from this divine perch, espies an elderly woman secreting away two veils from her washing.

"The sight threw him into such a rage that he seized the golden footstool and hurled it through the sky at the thieving old woman on earth." When the Lord returns and finds his footstool missing, Saint Peter admits that he allowed the tailor to enter heaven.

> The Lord told the tailor to come forward and asked him if he had taken the footstool and what he had done with it. "O Lord," the tailor answered joyfully, "I saw an old woman down on earth steal two veils while washing clothes, and in my wrath I hurled the footstool at her." "You scoundrel!" said the Lord. "If I were to judge like you, what do you suppose would have happened to *you* long ago? And besides, all my chairs, benches, tables, even my fire tongs, would be gone; I'd have thrown them all at sinners. We can't keep you in heaven. It's out through the gate with you, then you can go where you please."[15]

The tailor in the fantastical tale has of course achieved a perspective that is impossible for any existing human being, a view from nowhere. Only by such an impossible view, though, could a human being regard herself as absolved of her definitive task and thus exhausted, bored, like the children who plead for someone to think of a new game. Furthermore, it would seem that the same impossible viewpoint engenders the sort of unforgiving spirit condemned by Jesus's final teaching in Matthew 18. The tailor has the same defect as the forgiven servant who in turn refused to forgive his debtor. Despite being shown mercy himself, he shows none when given the power to judge others. So according to Silentio's use of the Grimm tale, both boredom and spite are fostered by the impossible view from nowhere; from that vantage point all of existence looks "wrong."

By contrast, "as long as the generation is concerned only about its task, which is the highest, it cannot become weary, for the task is always adequate for a person's lifetime."[16] A human life, as actually lived, has enough to do by fearlessly and lovingly drawing attention to the task, and that task is nothing other than to live its own real possibilities, to make its ideals actual. That this is a task for each generation is a function of the fact that no individual can claim for herself to have realized the ideal in a merely abstract way—that is to say, in the way that any prior individual or generation has realized it. Each individual must earn the ideal of actuality on her own terms, not at a bargain price, not in the fashion that any other individual has done so, though again, the call to do so is incumbent upon all, not upon some.

This is why we must, as readers of *Fear and Trembling*, take to heart some of Silentio's final words of wisdom (and warning): "Whatever one generation learns from another, no generation learns the essentially human from a previous one."[17] Much has been learned from Kierkegaard's masterpiece in the more than 170 years since it was written, but no text can teach the essentially human, which is "passion," Silentio says, and what is more, "faith is the highest passion in a person."[18]

To learn that, Kierkegaard's readers will have to begin all over again. Since the book teaches this lesson by ending in such a way as to return to its own beginning, we can surmise that a major part of its teaching on faith is that faith cannot be sustained by repeating in a mechanical or exact fashion the achievements of any exemplar, even one as estimable as Abraham himself, because no one can simply be Abraham or directly appropriate his example. To live the life of faith is to be like Abraham while being unlike Abraham, and as Haufniensis suggests, this can be accomplished only by triangulating the aesthetic against the ethical to let a new ideality come forward, an ideal that can actually be lived.

That it can be lived is the key to its power to make me happy, for the aesthetic ideal will only disappoint: it contradicts itself as soon as it is to be applied to reality because it cannot be consistently lived on its own terms and for its realization asks more than what lived life can deliver. The ethical ideal too can only disappoint, since no one can actually abide by its restrictions and demands: I cannot help, it would seem, but fail to live by what it asks. The religious ideal alone has the desirable quality of the aesthetic and its attraction to an eternal perfection that actual life rarely affords, and the softening of the ethical such that its demands can be met even by an imperfect individual. The aesthetic alone will fail me, and I will fail the ethical alone, but the life of faith is one that is ideal for me. To live as Abraham did is to live freely and joyfully, not the perfect life in an abstract sense (always illusory anyway), but the life that is perfect for you. As Kierkegaard quipped in *The Concept of Irony*, "In no way is the true ideal in the beyond—it is behind insofar as it is the propelling force; it is ahead insofar as it is the inspiring goal, but at the same time it is within us, and this is its truth."[19]

This lived ideal is not possible if faith is nothing more than an exceptional condition vis-à-vis the ethical as universal. Living the new ideal of actuality is possible only if faith is the shipwreck of both the ethical and the aesthetic. Life is not conformable to the aesthetic alone, as we have seen, but if something of the aesthetic cannot be preserved, then religious life remains wholly divorced from the timeless unspoiled beauty of the aesthetic ideal. The knight of faith is able to transform her actual existence in such a way as to capture some of the ideal qualities of a work of art. Across its transformative leaps, her life holds to a kind of unity and integrity that cannot be sustained by commitment either to the aesthetic ideal alone or the ethical ideal alone. Similarly, she remediates the intractable difficulties of meeting ethical obligation, in earnestness conquering sin, loving others and being loved with abandon, returning again and again to her duties with joyful freedom. Spurning the juvenile consolations of fate, rather than being merely grudgingly reconciled to life, in resignation she acknowledges the impermanence and pain of living but in faith celebrates its essential goodness. Finally, she stands alone before God and thereby becomes the one she uniquely is and is called to be. Such is the task, for each and for all.

Notes

Introduction

1. Søren Kierkegaard, *Søren Kierkegaard's Journals and Papers*, ed. and trans. Howard V. Hong and Edna H. Hong, assisted by Gregor Malantschuk, 2nd ed., 7 vols. (Bloomington: Indiana University Press, 1999), 6491.

2. On this point I feel a special kinship with the view of Kevin Hoffman developed in his "Facing Threats to Earthly Felicity: A Reading of Kierkegaard's *Fear and Trembling*," *Journal of Religious Ethics* 34, no. 3 (2006): 439–59.

3. Søren Kierkegaard, *Fear and Trembling* and *Repetition*, ed. and trans. Howard V. Hong and Edna H. Hong (Princeton, NJ: Princeton University Press, 1983), 59.

4. A fascinating study could be undertaken of all such moments in the Kierkegaardian authorship, though again such a study could hardly yield the conclusion that Kierkegaard's "own" voice is distinguishable in such moments. In keeping with the conviction that *Fear and Trembling* cannot be successfully read in isolation from other sources, I will throughout what follows also draw on the journals, again not because these citations offer an undisputed privilege in ascertaining Silentio's meaning but because they offer an ongoing commentary by Kierkegaard himself on his own evolving thoughts on the issues that inspired the text.

5. The reference is to Saint Paul, in 2 Corinthians 5:17, (King James Version).

6. Søren Kierkegaard, *The Concept of Anxiety*, ed. and trans. Reidar Thomte (Princeton, NJ: Princeton University Press, 1980), 17n.

7. Ibid., 3.

8. Ibid., 12.

9. Ibid., 14.

10. Ibid.

11. Ibid., 16.

12. See especially the end of chapter 2 and the entirety of chapter 3.

13. *The Concept of Anxiety*, 16.

14. Ibid., 19.

15. Ibid., 22.

16. Ibid., 16.

17. Ibid., 16–17.

18. Ibid., 17.

19. Ibid.

20. Ibid., 19. The deeper this presupposition is pressed, in fact, the more it verges toward the dogmatic terrain of hereditary sin.

21. Ibid., 17.

22. Ibid., 19.

23. Ibid.

24. Haufniensis frequently in this work associates paganism with spiritlessness, which is a sort of neopaganism that has departed from revealed inspiration. See sections 1 and 2 of chapter III. See also Anti-Climacus's associations of spiritlessness with paganism in *The Sickness*

unto Death, ed. and trans. Howard V. Hong and Edna H. Hong (Princeton, NJ: Princeton University Press, 1980), 44–47 and 100–104.

25. *The Concept of Anxiety*, 17.

26. Ibid., 19.

27. Ibid., 23.

28. Ibid., 20.

29. There is an elegant and insightful discussion of second ethics in John Hare, *The Moral Gap: Kantian Ethics, Human Limits, and God's Assistance*, repr. ed. (Oxford: Clarendon Press, 2002), 216–21.

30. *The Concept of Anxiety*, 20.

31. Ibid., 14–15.

32. Ibid., 149.

33. Ibid.

34. Ibid., 150.

35. There may be a parallel here to Anti-Climacus's discussion of the difference between "annihilated possibility" and "consummated possibility." See *The Sickness unto Death*, 15. See also Climacus's discussion of possibility in Søren Kierkegaard, *Philosophical Fragments* and *Johannes Climacus*, ed. and trans. Howard V. Hong and Edna H. Hong (Princeton, NJ: Princeton University Press, 1985), 72–75.

36. *The Concept of Anxiety*, 15.

37. *The Sickness unto Death*, 16–17.

38. For more on this point and on Kierkegaard's use of narrative to make his readers capable of an appropriate reaction to the actuality of sin that would be neither comic nor tragic see my "Holy Hypochondria: Narrative and Self-Awareness in *The Concept of Anxiety*" in *Kierkegaard Studies Yearbook 2011*, ed. Heiko Schulz, Jon Stewart, and Karl Verstrynge (Berlin: De Gruyter, 2011): 239–61.

39. George Pattison, "Kierkegaard: Aesthetics and 'The Aesthetic,'" *British Journal of Aesthetics* 31, no. 2 (1991): 140–51, 140.

40. Ibid., 141.

41. My thanks to Wojciech Kaftanski for this phrasing.

42. Pattison, "Kierkegaard: Aesthetics and 'The Aesthetic,'" 142.

43. Ibid., 143.

44. As Pattison points out, "since God is acknowledged to be the ground and guarantor of reality, it follows that what is merely a product of human imagination will have no claim of itself to be 'real.' Indeed, its 'reality' may turn out to be sheer illusion. This is indeed the case (according to Kierkegaard) with the exponents of Romantic irony and in such fictional characters from his own authorship as Johannes the Seducer and Quidam, in whom are depicted the emptiness of a life based solely on imaginative possibility" (143). Indeed for Kierkegaard a life based solely on imaginative possibility is hopelessly impoverished and despairing, but I will show that the imagination nevertheless has a relative role to play in the life of faith.

45. Pattison, "Kierkegaard: Aesthetics and 'The Aesthetic,'" 142–43.

46. Ibid., 143.

47. Ibid., 143–44.

48. Pattison mentions tragedy as well, and his remark dovetails with a point I have already made above: "Even in tragedy the aesthetic form persuades us to see suffering sympathetically, contemplatively and disinterestedly" (144).

49. Pattison, "Kierkegaard: Aesthetics and 'The Aesthetic,'" 144.

50. Ibid., 145.

51. Ibid., 146, Pattison's uses own translation, altered from the quote I have provided from Søren Kierkegaard, *Either/Or II*, trans. Howard V. Hong and Edna H. Hong (Princeton, NJ: Princeton University Press, 1987), 135, 136.

52. Pattison, "Kierkegaard: Aesthetics and 'The Aesthetic,'" 147–48.

53. I endorse Pattison's conclusion: "As Kierkegaard understands it art is thus inherently limited in its ability to deal with transcendence, suffering and time, three of the key features of a religious existence. This does not necessarily mean that all art is immoral or irreligious, but since Kierkegaard does tend to reduce all questions to the religious question and to regard every life as 'planned religiously' anything which falls short of a fully religious attitude is liable to be seen as a form of despair. In particular art comes to be seen as a kind of compensatory wish-fulfilment—in much the same way, in fact, in which Nietzsche and Freud were to regard religion . . . It is in the light of this diagnosis that art comes to serve Kierkegaard as a model for all forms of life outside faith, aesthetics becomes the basis for 'the aesthetic.' In this way even the bourgeois philistine (whose lack of aesthetic sensitivity was no virtue in Kierkegaard's eyes) can be described as 'aesthetic.' For bourgeois religiosity proclaims peace where there is no peace and shrugs off the challenge of existential temporality. By obscuring suffering and transiency the bourgeois avoids a full consciousness of his situation 'before God'" (147, 148). But I leave aside Pattison's final criticism of Kierkegaard's conception of art, mainly because whether the Dane's understanding of the character of art is accurate or complete or not is not my concern; all I need to show is how his understanding of the aesthetic ideal and the life of the aesthete are linked and share the same limitations, limitations that the religious life overcomes and transforms within itself.

54. Because these ideas are only fully explored in Problema III, a complete treatment of them will have to be postponed to the appropriate place in the argument of this book, but the preliminary indications I have already made in this direction should be kept in mind throughout.

55. *The Concept of Anxiety*, 17n.

56. Faith comes up as an example of a way in which concepts can be illicitly appropriated by a branch of science that should only presuppose them; in this case Kierkegaard surely has Hegel in mind. Haufniensis writes, "Thus when in dogmatics *faith* is called the *immediate* without any further qualification, there is gained the advantage that everybody is convinced of the necessity of not stopping with faith . . . The loss is quite obvious. Faith loses by being regarded as the immediate, since it has been deprived of what lawfully belongs to it, namely, its historical presupposition. Dogmatics loses thereby, because it does not begin where it properly should begin, namely, within the scope of an earlier beginning. Instead of presupposing an earlier beginning, it ignores this and begins without ceremony, just as if it were logic" (10). While only an example, the use of faith in this context further cements the connection between this text and *Fear and Trembling*, especially with reference to the latter's indictment of those who insist on "going further" than faith found in the Preface and with the discussion of faith and the immediate in Problema III.

57. *The Concept of Anxiety*, 17. It is to this sentence that Haufniensis's footnote is appended.

58. From the beginning of Problema I: "As soon as the single individual asserts himself in his singularity before the universal, he sins [*synder*], and only by acknowledging this can he be reconciled again with the universal" (54); from the beginning of Problema II: "Every time the individual shrinks from it, every time he withholds himself in or slips down again into the qualifications of feeling, mood, etc. that belong to interiority, he trespasses [*forsynder*], he is immersed in spiritual trial" (69); and from the beginning of Problema III: "Every time he desires to remain in the hidden he trespasses [*forsynder*] and is immersed in spiritual trial from which he can emerge only by disclosing himself" (82).

59. *Fear and Trembling*, 98.
60. *Journals and Papers*, 1030.
61. Catherine Pickstock grasps this point well in her *Repetition and Identity* (Oxford: Oxford University Press, 2013), 90: "Kierkegaard spoke of this recollection as 'repetition backwards.' He suggested that, in the modern, Christian era, recollection must philosophically cede place to repetition. However, that he did not thereby mean to derogate or abandon the Platonic gesture is indicated by his inverse naming of repetition as 'recollection forwards.' Indeed, in order to repeat, or to develop a flexible *habitus*, one must both remember and anticipate."
62. My argument, then, has something in common with John E. Hare's in his *The Moral Gap*, where he too has recourse to Kierkegaard to avail himself of the resources required to address the fact that morally speaking, we are on our own power incapable of discharging our obligations. Hare does not discuss *Fear and Trembling* much, but I think some of what I say in this book might be compatible with his argumentative agenda.
63. Eph. 3:20 (KJV).
64. I take it this is what Silentio has in mind when he says in connection with Abraham that "no doubt he was surprised at the outcome, but through a double-movement he had attained his first condition, and therefore he received Isaac more joyfully than the first time" (36). How could Abraham have received Isaac back *more* joyfully than the first time? Only if he had an original expectation in mind, something to the effect of "I would like to have a son," and then had that expectation thwarted by the apparent requirement from God that his son be given up, and then additionally had the faithful expectation that he would nevertheless still have a son (as he originally wanted) on different terms than he originally imagined (as a gift from God not once but twice or as a gift rather than what he was owed on the basis of God's promise). In this sense Abraham gets what he wanted in a different way than he possibly could have imagined. He wants a son, and he has a son, but he gets his son on a condition that is itself granted to him by God, not once but twice and is doubly demanding of gratitude because it is doubly beyond all human expectation.
65. I thank Sarah Kohrs for having powerfully suggested to me this way of putting the matter: I think she is right that the issue at stake is nothing less than the harmonization of beauty and justice.
66. I have in mind the fascinating but ultimately misguided interpretation of Stephen Mulhall in his *Inheritance and Originality* (Oxford: Oxford University Press, 2001), 364–80. I do not recapitulate Mulhall's argument in total in these pages, but I do engage him directly in my "'He Speaks in Tongues': Hearing the Truth of Abraham's Words of Faith," in *Kierkegaard's* Fear and Trembling: *A Critical Guide*, ed. Daniel Conway (Cambridge: Cambridge University Press, 2015), 229–46. Hoffman too touches on this in a way that is highly illuminating: "Johannes de Silentio seems aware of two characteristic responses to the binding of Isaac: naïve, unreflective acceptance and knee-jerk offense. Each of these reactions are [sic] inappropriately distracted, one by the knife and the other by the happy outcome. Focusing on the outcome fosters pious but Sunday-schoolish sentiments, while focusing on the knife confirms good old-fashioned moral humanism" (440).
67. In chapters 2, 3, and 4, I will argue that each of the styles adopted by Silentio is intended to show how this effect cannot be realized by the deployment of various strictly delineated genres.
68. Patrick Stokes, *Kierkegaard's Mirrors: Interest, Self, and Moral Vision* (Basingstoke, UK: Palgrave Macmillan, 2010), 123.
69. It would be unwise to place too much weight on an unfinished work, but Stokes effectively demonstrates that the fundamentals of this early incomplete account found in *Johannes*

Climacus are taken up and expanded in *The Sickness unto Death* and *Concluding Unscientific Postscript*. See Stokes, *Kierkegaard's Mirrors*, 29–60.

70. Stokes's treatment of this material is excellent (*Kierkegaard's Mirrors*, 29–46), and I will not attempt to provide the full discussion he does, only to show how his reading is relevant to establishing the importance of the dynamic interplay between actuality and ideality.

71. Stokes, *Kierkegaard's Mirrors*, 29–30.

72. Søren Kierkegaard, *Philosophical Fragments* and *Johannes Climacus*, ed. and trans. Howard V. Hong and Edna H. Hong (Princeton, NJ: Princeton University Press, 1985), 166.

73. Ibid.

74. *The Concept of Anxiety*, 74.

75. George Willis Williams, "Too Much Coffee and Not Enough Walking: Kierkegaard on the Ambivalence of Experience" (unpublished article). See also Stokes, *Kierkegaard's Mirrors*, 33: "But while Climacus does take the concept of raw sensibilia seriously, he nonetheless holds . . . that *experience* is not *prior* to our conceptualization but rather that experience *is* conceptualization; *all* our experience is always already conceptually structured."

76. *The Concept of Anxiety*, 159–60.

77. See my "Holy Hypochondria: Narrative and Self-Awareness." See also Williams, "Too Much Coffee and Not Enough Walking" (Unpublished).

78. *Johannes Climacus*, 166.

79. Ibid.

80. Ibid., 166, 167.

81. Ibid., 167.

82. Ibid.

83. Ibid., 168.

84. *The Concept of Anxiety*, 45. It should be noted though that for Haufniensis innocence is by no means immediacy, since these two categories belong to different sciences: ethics and logic respectively (35). For Kierkegaard we never "have" the immediate because it is mediated the moment it is acknowledged as the immediate; but because innocence is not the immediate, innocence is both possessed and lost (not by reflection but by choice) and indeed recoverable in the life of faith.

85. Ronald L. Hall, "The Origin of Alienation: Some Kierkegaardian Reflections on Merleau-Ponty's Phenomenology of the Body," *International Journal for Philosophy of Religion* 12, no. 2 (1981): 111–22, 116–17.

86. *Johannes Climacus*, 168.

87. Ibid.

88. Ibid.

89. Ibid.

90. Ibid., 169.

91. The notoriously baffling opening paragraph of *The Sickness unto Death* (13) seems to outline a similar structure by which the dualities that compose the human being—infinite and finite, temporal and eternal, freedom and necessity—when simply posited in their togetherness, do not yet define a self. Just as in that latter text a "third" is required to make the human being a self, so too as we will see shortly, *Johannes Climacus* argues that dichotomies are sufficient for reflection but the categories of consciousness will have to be trichotomous.

92. Stokes, *Kierkegaard's Mirrors*, 36.

93. Ibid.

94. *Johannes Climacus*, 169.

95. Stokes, *Kierkegaard's Mirrors*, 38.

96. "If, however, the relation relates itself to itself, this relation is the positive third, and this is the self." *The Sickness unto Death*, 13. What Anti-Climacus here calls "the positive third" he contrasts to the merely "negative unity" that obtains when the two are posited together without being explicitly related to in an interested way, as *involving me*.

97. "And if there is no third factor, there really is no synthesis, for a synthesis that is a contradiction cannot be completed as a synthesis without a third factor." *The Concept of Anxiety*, 85.

98. Or, to use the word that Stokes goes on to explain in his book, I am always interested. See also Stokes, *Kierkegaard's Mirrors*, 42: "Consciousness both encompasses ideality/language and actuality, yet is not reducible to them."

99. *Johannes Climacus*, 169.

100. As Stokes observes, "But—and here Climacus raises his standard against Idealism—reflection is *not the same thing* as consciousness, but is rather a necessary *but not sufficient* condition for the relation between the elements of a dichotomy to occur" (36).

101. *Johannes Climacus*, 170.

102. Ibid., 169–70.

103. Ibid., 170.

104. Stokes, *Kierkegaard's Mirrors*, 37.

105. *Fear and Trembling*, 53. This sentiment is obviously not a celebration of fideistic irrationalism. See Stokes, *Kierkegaard's Mirrors*, 40: "Belief cannot emerge from the opposition of reflection unless the elements of the oppositions are reflected upon by something that is necessarily always beyond the reflective process, something capable of calling that process to a halt in resolution. Doubt, therefore, can never be overcome by reflection, and becomes, as Climacus set out to show, not an intellectual problem but a personal one. In the experience of doubt I am referred back to the necessity of *choosing* to believe something."

106. *Johannes Climacus*, 171.

107. Since *Repetition* was published on the same day as *Fear and Trembling* we will have occasion to refer to it in the course of what follows, but we cannot undertake a systematic treatment of this idea.

108. *Johannes Climacus*, 171.

109. Ibid.

110. Certainly Catherine Pickstock seems to think so in her *Repetition and Identity*. See also John Milbank in "The Sublime in Kierkegaard," *Heythrop Journal* XXXVII (1996): 298–321, 319n25: Milbank's suggestion that "while 'the religious' for Kierkegaard exceeds the scope of the three philosophic transcendentals [the true, the good, and the beautiful], it is also the true condition for their integration: the religious alone completes the ethical, and does so by 'bringing back' the poetic/aesthetic in a higher guise" is one that this book aspires to develop.

111. *Johannes Climacus*, 171.

112. Ibid., 167. Stokes makes an important relevant observation here in *Kierkegaard's Mirrors*, 42: "We might ask an important question at this point: if all conscious experience is always mediated/conceptualized, why am I speaking of consciousness as trapped *between* immediacy and reality? Why can't we just say that we are *alienated* from the immediate? The answer, I think, is precisely the immediacy and 'closeness' with which the 'residue' left over from our imperfect conceptualizations imposes itself upon us. Most of the time—almost *all* of the time, in fact—the generality of the concepts by which we schematize the world presents no difficulty; the 'slippage' between our concepts and the world is rarely even noticeable and only occasionally problematic." My understanding of *Fear and Trembling* is that it concerns itself with one of those exceptional, problematic situations.

113. If I am right about this then Pattison's account of the aesthetic would have to be qualified to show that Kierkegaard is not merely in complete accord with the Romantic account of

the ideal qualities of art insofar as he regards the aesthetic ideal as already implicated with the actual. We can read Kierkegaard on this point as offering not just a rejection of Romanticism but a specifically Christian form of Romanticism.

114. *Journals and Papers*, 6511.

115. *The Sickness unto Death*, 77–79.

116. Ibid., 77.

117. Ibid., 77–78.

118. Kierkegaard links forgiveness with faith and sin-consciousness in his *Works of Love*, trans. Howard V. Hong and Edna H. Hong (Princeton, NJ: Princeton University Press, 1995), 294–95: "Forgiveness takes the forgiven sin away. This is a wonderful thought, therefore also faith's thought, because faith always relates itself to what is not seen. I *believe* that what is seen has come into existence from what is not seen; I see the world, but what is not seen I do not see; that I believe. Similarly, in *forgiveness—and sin*—there is also a relation of faith of which we are rarely aware. What, then, is the unseen here? The unseen is that forgiveness takes away that which does indeed exist; the unseen is that what is seen is nevertheless not seen, for if it is seen, it obviously is unseen that it is not seen. The one who loves sees the sin he forgives, but he believes that forgiveness takes it away. This cannot be seen, whereas the sin can indeed be seen; on the other hand, if the sin did not exist to be seen, it could not be forgiven either. Just as one by faith *believes* the *unseen* ***into*** what is seen, so the one who loves by forgiveness *believes* ***away*** what is seen. Both are faith."

119. *Works of Love*, 17–90.

120. Ibid., 336.

121. Ibid.: "Who is it, then, who is in need of forgiveness, the one who did wrong or the one who suffered the wrong? Certainly it is the one who did wrong who needs forgiveness, but the loving one who suffered the wrong needs to forgive or needs agreement, reconciliation, words that, unlike the word 'forgiveness,' which reminds us of right and wrong, do not make such a distinction but lovingly make a mental note that both are in need." See also Kierkegaard's powerful discussion of Matthew 6:14 at *Works of Love*, 380: "'*Forgive, then you will also be forgiven.*' Someone, however, might manage to misinterpret these words in such a way that he imagined that it was possible to receive forgiveness himself although he did not forgive. Truly this is a misinterpretation. Christianity's view is: forgiveness **is** forgiveness; your forgiveness is your forgiveness; your forgiveness of another is your own forgiveness; the forgiveness you give is the forgiveness you receive, not the reverse, that the forgiveness you receive is the forgiveness you give."

122. *Fear and Trembling*, 59.

123. Ibid., 70.

124. That we can understand Abraham in a qualified sense is affirmed throughout the text and repeated at the end as well: "I cannot form in advance any idea of what he is going to say; after he has said it, I presumably can understand it, perhaps in a certain sense understand Abraham in what was said without thereby coming any closer to him than in the preceding exposition" (117–18) and again, "But a final word by Abraham has been preserved, and insofar as I can understand the paradox, I can also understand Abraham's total presence in that word" (118).

1. Titular Matters

1. Quoted in *Fear and Trembling*, xxxvi.

2. Søren Kierkegaard, *The Point of View*, ed. and trans. Howard V. Hong and Edna H. Hong (Princeton, NJ: Princeton University Press, 1998), 37.

3. The relationship of Kierkegaard's thinking to kenotic theology is fully explored in David R. Law, *Kierkegaard's Kenotic Christology* (Oxford: Oxford University Press, 2013).

4. Phil. 2:2 (KJV).

5. Phil. 2:3 (KJV).

6. Phil. 2:4 (KJV).

7. Phil. 2:5–8 (KJV).

8. Phil. 2:9–10 (KJV).

9. Phil. 2:13 (KJV).

10. My understanding of the importance of Paul's sentiment encapsulated in the title of the book cuts against one of the major interpretations of this text, that of Ronald M. Green in his oft-cited "Enough Is Enough: *Fear and Trembling* Is *Not* about Ethics," *The Journal of Religious Ethics* 21, no. 2 (1993): 191–209. Green argues that the text gives expression to the Lutheran doctrine of justification, but Philippians 2:12 is arguably the single most troublesome verse from Paul's pen for Luther's doctrine of justification. I can't completely vindicate this intuition in this book, but I would at least suggest (partly provocatively perhaps) that *Fear and Trembling* is ultimately more about sanctification than justification.

11. Quoted in *Fear and Trembling*, xxxvi.

12. Climacus, in his "A Glance at Danish Literature," writes that in *Fear and Trembling* "the inability to become open, hiddenness, is here a terror, compared with which esthetic hiddenness is child's play. To represent this existence-collision in an existing individuality was impossible, since the difficulty of the collision, although *lyrically* it extorts the utmost passion, *dialectically* holds back the expression in absolute silence." *Concluding Unscientific Postscript*, ed. and trans. Howard V. Hong and Edna H. Hong (Princeton, NJ: Princeton University Press, 1992), 261–62.

13. *Journals and Papers*, 5660.

14. *Fear and Trembling*, 7.

15. Ibid., 244.

16. Once in the journal does Kierkegaard himself refer to Silentio as a poet, but he does so in such a way as to imply that this term in the immediate context is equivalent to "pseudonym." *Journals and Papers*, 6327.

17. *Fear and Trembling*, 241.

18. *Journals and Papers*, 6511.

19. *Fear and Trembling*, 7.

20. *Journals and Papers*, 10.

21. I think there is certainly no reason to believe that Silentio is engaged in a conspiracy against his readers to mislead them or to subvert a more-or-less traditional and orthodox (at least from within the broadly Augustinian-Lutheran tradition) account of faith.

22. *Journals and Papers*, 6598.

23. Ibid., 4301.

24. Ibid.

25. I have treated the question of silence in *Fear and Trembling* with greater detail in "The Phenomenon of the Good: Reconstructing Religion in the Wake of Deconstruction," in *Reexamining Deconstruction and Determinate Religion: Toward a Religion with Religion*, ed. J. Aaron Simmons and Stephen Minister (Pittsburgh, PA: Duquesne University Press, 2012), 131–54.

26. *Point of View*, 37.

27. Søren Kierkegaard, *The Concept of Irony with Continual Reference to Socrates* and *Notes of Schelling's Berlin Lectures*, ed. and trans. Howard V. Hong and Edna H. Hong (Princeton, NJ: Princeton University Press, 1989), 258.

28. *Journals and Papers*, 3983.
29. Ibid., 6896.
30. Ibid., 3404.
31. The most important aspect of silence that I am leaving out in this introductory discussion is demonic silence, which is yet another dimension of this important theme. That discussion will have to await the chapter on Problema III. Suffice it to say for now that silence is far from a univocal concept in *Fear and Trembling.*

2. A Philosophical Preface

1. *Fear and Trembling*, 245.
2. Ibid., 9.
3. Søren Kierkegaard, *Fear and Trembling*, ed. C. Stephen Evans and Sylvia Walsh and trans. Sylvia Walsh (Cambridge: Cambridge University Press, 2006), 7.
4. Søren Kierkegaard, *Fear and Trembling*, trans. Alastair Hannay (London: Penguin, 1985), 44.
5. *Fear and Trembling*, 15.
6. *Fear and Trembling*, trans. Alastair Hannay, 49.
7. *Fear and Trembling*, 27.
8. *Fear and Trembling*, trans. Alastair Hannay, 57.
9. *Fear and Trembling*, 250.
10. D. C. Schindler observes of Plato's *Republic* that it too starts in fits so to speak. He suggests this is because "Plato resists the absolutization of any starting point, and thus effects the note of drama, precisely by repeatedly *starting over.* This gesture immediately relativizes the various points of departure, showing them to be exactly that." *Plato's Critique of Impure Reason: On Goodness and Truth in* The Republic (Baltimore, MD: Catholic University of America Press, 2008), 46. Since Kierkegaard was perhaps one of the greatest readers of Plato of the modern age, he may have appreciated something of this point. Many of Schindler's observations about how *The Republic* operates as a text are applicable to *Fear and Trembling* as well. Like Plato, Kierkegaard too rejects the illusion of the "'pure' or absolute beginning" aspired to in German Idealism (Schindler, *Plato's Critique of Impure Reason*, 42), and he writes with the logic of drama, which entails the need to start and start again to get to the end of a journey, a journey that makes sense only at the end but must be begun at the beginning, or even series of beginnings that in turn make sense only once the end demonstrates that they were partial or relative approaches in the first place (Schindler, *Plato's Critique of Impure Reason*, 44–45).
11. *Fear and Trembling*, 5.
12. Ibid.
13. Ibid. The economic metaphor returns in the Epilogue, which I will eventually argue recapitulates the preface. To some extent, then, we cannot even understand the first beginning of the book without getting to the end, a feature of what we might call the dramatic logic of *Fear and Trembling*, as indicated in footnote 10 above. Some have succumbed to the temptation to see in this opening picture of a conceptual clearance sale a hint that Silentio intends to "drive up the price of faith" so to speak, but the Epilogue actually militates against this conclusion, substituting an appeal to earnestness (the essentials of which we have already seen elaborated in the introduction above) for the language of price manipulation. It is true that Silentio will contrast the risk of faith, the need to take a gamble on the life of faith by investing all in its possibility, with the security of bet-hedging and living life with one's investments so to speak—one's passions and commitments and attachments to others in relationships of

love and devotion—comfortably spread out in a diversified portfolio, never loving too much, never committing too much, never allowing one's self to be fully involved with another, but he does so because this timidity is not a close cousin to faith but its contemptible counterfeit. We have already seen that Kierkegaard likens the inveterate gambler to the fatalist rather than the knight of faith. The knight of faith is not addicted to fortune but is more like the children in the Epilogue who manage to make the same old games new through their earnest commitment to play. I will eventually argue that the right response to the clearance sale in ideas is not to artificially inflate the cost of faith but to redeem the time, lingering with the task of a lifetime with creative fidelity.

14. *Fear and Trembling*, 5.

15. Ibid.

16. Ibid., 243.

17. Ibid., 88n.

18. *The Sickness unto Death*, 36. See also *Fear and Trembling*, 78, where Silentio says that a so-called knight of faith who cannot sustain the passion of love "never moves from the spot"—that is, never even meets the initial requirements of faithfully becoming oneself by moving *at* the spot.

19. Søren Kierkegaard, *Fear and Trembling* and *The Sickness unto Death*. Trans. by Walter Lowrie. First paperback edition. (Princeton, NJ: Princeton University Press, 1968), 169.

20. *Journals and Papers*, 891.

21. Ibid., 2283.

22. That the notion that one is a sinner has to be revealed is a constant theme of the authorship (see for one particularly important discussion *The Sickness unto Death*, 89–95), though it comes up only very briefly (but I would argue with decisive significance) in Problema III of *Fear and Trembling*.

23. Perhaps there is no better passage on the togetherness of these two themes, awareness of one's own sin and awareness of one's own forgiven state, in all of Kierkegaard's writings than the first principal section of "On the Occasion of a Confession." *Upbuilding Discourses in Various Spirits*, ed. and trans Howard H. Hong and Edna V. Hong (Princeton, NJ: Princeton University Press, 1993), 7–24. For a solid discussion of how Cartesian/Hegelian conceptuality undergoes a "practical or existential transformation" at Kierkegaard's hands, see Anders Moe Rasmussen, "Rene Descartes: Kierkegaard's Understanding of Doubt and Certainty," in *Kierkegaard Research: Sources, Reception and Resources: Volume 5: Kierkegaard and the Renaissance and Modern Traditions: Tome I: Philosophy*, ed. Jon Stewart (Aldershot, UK: Ashgate, 2009), 11–21.

24. Rasmussen, "Rene Descartes: Kierkegaard's Understanding of Doubt and Certainty," 14.

25. *Fear and Trembling*, 5.

26. Ibid., 6.

27. Ibid., 5.

28. Ibid., 6.

29. Ibid.

30. Ibid.

31. As Rasmussen argues, institutionalized Cartesianism is here certainly also another guise for Hegelianism. Rasmussen, "Rene Descartes: Kierkegaard's Understanding of Doubt and Certainty," 14.

32. *Fear and Trembling*, 8.

33. Ibid., 340.

34. *Journals and Papers*, 6434.

35. I thank Adam Correll Rutledge for inspiration on this point.

36. Sources for deeper understanding of Kierkegaard's debt to the skeptics include Jose R. Maia Neto, *The Christianization of Pyrrhonism: Scepticism and Faith in Pascal, Kierkegaard, and Shestov* (Dordrecht, NL: Kluwer, 1995) and Anthony Rudd, "The Skeptics: Kierkegaard and Classical Skepticism" in *Kierkegaard Research: Sources, Reception and Resources: Volume 2: Kierkegaard and the Greek World: Tome II: Aristotle and Other Greek Authors,* ed. Jon Stewart (Aldershot, UK: Ashgate, 2010), 165–82.

37. *Fear and Trembling*, 6.

38. Ibid., 6–7.

39. Ibid., 7.

40. Ibid.

41. Ibid.

42. Ibid.

43. Ibid., 33.

44. Ibid., 7.

45. Ibid., 8.

46. Ibid., 53.

3. A Narrative Approach

1. *Fear and Trembling*, 9.

2. Much of what I say in this chapter is indebted to John Lippitt's *Routledge Philosophy Guidebook to Kierkegaard and "Fear and Trembling"* (London: Routledge, 2003). Lippitt does not seem to insist that the man is Silentio, but he advances two reasons for why the man might be Silentio himself; neither, however, is conclusive. "First, just as Johannes has described himself as 'no philosopher,' so this man is described as 'no thinker.' Second, exactly that dimension of the Abraham narrative which obsesses this man is that on which Johannes' book concentrates" (22). Both of these are true, of course, but just because the man is not a thinker does not mean he is Silentio, and the ostensible narrowness of their shared interest in just this vignette within the Abraham epic was stipulated from the outset; the man is said to have been impressed from childhood by the story of Abraham and his temptation in particular, not the story of Abraham *in toto.*

3. *Fear and Trembling*, 9.

4. Ibid.

5. Ibid.

6. Jacques Derrida's encounter with this section of the text in his "Literature in Secret" is one of the now rare treatments that seems to betray no awareness of the very likely fact that Silentio meant these versions to be indirectly and negatively communicative, casting light on Abraham by narrating what must *not* be the case about him for his story to effectively illustrate the true form of faith. See Jacques Derrida, *The Gift of Death*, second ed., trans. David Wills (Chicago: University of Chicago Press, 2008).

7. *Fear and Trembling*, ed. C. Stephen Evans and Sylvia Walsh, xi.

8. *Fear and Trembling*, 10.

9. Ibid.

10. Jean-Luc Marion, *Being Given: Toward a Phenomenology of Givenness*, trans. Jeffrey L. Kosky (Stanford, CA: Stanford University Press, 2002), 300: "Every child is born naturally from its mother, but strictly speaking, it always remains of unknown father; there is no child who is not a foundling, that is to say, received. As a result, it has been admitted since time immemorial that the sole proof of paternity resides in the juridical recognition of the child by the father; paternity is accomplished symbolically, not first of all or always biologically. The

father becomes one, in all cases and not only in adoption, only by his decision to recognize, ask for, and claim as his own the foundling and natural child."

11. *Fear and Trembling*, 11.
12. Ibid., 255.
13. Ibid.
14. Ibid., 10.
15. Ibid.
16. Ibid.
17. I must thank my former student Alexander Kim for pointing this out to me. To my knowledge no commentator has noticed this fact. Evans is unintentionally imprecise when he writes in a footnote to the Exordium that "Hagar, an Egyptian slave-girl belonging to Sarah, bore a son to Abraham named Ishmael; both mother and son were driven into the desert at Sarah's request after the birth of Isaac." (10). It would be more exact to say that they were driven into the desert after the weaning of Isaac. Finally, I would stress that while it is the case according to scripture that Sarah asked Abraham to drive Ishmael and Hagar into the desert, he complies only when he is assured by God that they too will be taken care of by him and that he will make Ishmael the father of a great nation as well.
18. This shift of emphasis from the masculine to the feminine portends a general move in this direction that Silentio undertakes later in *Fear and Trembling*, at the end of Problema I and in Problema III. We will see that there is something stereotypically "feminine" about faith, but that association is anticipated here for the first time. His praise for the heroism of Mary, of Sarah (the wife of Tobias) and Agnes represent more complete developments of this feminine dimension of faith.
19. *Fear and Trembling*, 11.
20. Ibid., 12.
21. Ibid.
22. Ibid., 13.
23. Ibid.
24. Ibid., 10, 12, 13, 14.
25. Ibid., 13.
26. Ibid.
27. Ibid.
28. Ibid., 14.
29. Ibid.
30. Ibid.

4. A Rhetorical Rehearsal

1. *Fear and Trembling*, ed. C. Stephen Evans and Sylvia Walsh and trans. Sylvia Walsh, 12.
2. *Fear and Trembling*, trans. Alastair Hannay, 49.
3. *Fear and Trembling*, 77. The suspicion that Abraham's lack of faith is being strategically omitted is intensified by the fact that Silentio unfavorably contrasts Abraham with two of the other great patriarchs but neglects again to mention any likeness between Abraham and the patriarchs' shortcomings. "Moses," he says, "struck the rock with his staff, but he did not have faith (*Fear and Trembling*, 19); and "Jacob," he reminds us, "had twelve sons, one of whom he loved; Abraham had but one, whom he loved" (*Fear and Trembling*, 20).
4. Lippitt, I think, is able to successfully argue against the suspicions of Andrew Cross and Stephen Mulhall, who claim that "a focus on Abraham necessarily amounts to an evasion of one's own God-relationship. While accepting the general point that this *could* happen—just

as feeling the need to learn one more ancient language before thinking about one's relationship to God *could* happen—there is no reason to suppose that this is a necessary or even likely eventuality" (200–1). Something of Cross's concern, I think, would be more relevant to the eulogy than to the text as a whole, but Cross assumes Silentio definitely is the poet, such that reservations about poetry in general automatically indict Silentio's entire project, but this is the very identification that I question and thus the consequence that it entails. If we have no reason to think Silentio is the poet then we have no reason to think that he is subtly placing his own effort under censure.

5. *Fear and Trembling*, 23.

6. Ibid., 343.

7. We will come back to a similar point in our exposition of Problema III, where Sarah's situation is explained as the religious version of the classical sentiment to the effect that no genius is untouched by madness. There again an analogy is drawn between religious and pagan madness, and more generally, a correspondence is evidenced between the classical understanding of a certain trope that explains human affairs and its richer religious articulation.

8. *The Dialogues of Plato*, trans. Benjamin Jowett (Chicago: Encyclopedia Britannica, 1952), 123–30.

9. *Journals and Papers*, 3323.

10. *Fear and Trembling*, 16.

11. *Journals and Papers*, 4245.

12. This issue has been comprehensively studied by Jon Stewart in his *Kierkegaard's Relations to Hegel Reconsidered* (Cambridge: Cambridge University Press, 2003), 184–95.

13. *Phaedrus*, 134.

14. Ibid.

15. Ibid.

16. Ibid.

17. *Journals and Papers*, 824.

18. *Phaedrus*, 134.

19. Kierkegaard's use of this term in *Fear and Trembling* is yet another suggestion of the proximity between the writing of this text and the rhetorical backdrop presumed by at least this part of it.

20. *Phaedrus*, 134.

21. Ibid., 135.

22. Ibid., 137.

23. Ibid.

24. Ibid., 138.

25. *Fear and Trembling*, 15.

26. Clare Carlisle notices the change in mood but does not explain it the same way I do. *Readers' Guides: Kierkegaard's "Fear and Trembling"* (London: Continuum, 2010), 56.

27. *Fear and Trembling*, 15. The following sentence too, "He is recollection's genius," is also telling. As suggested in the introduction above, recollection is often associated by Kierkegaard with the necessary but incomplete work of generating ideals for ourselves based on an always imperfect and incomplete retrospective of our lives. We look back over the course of life and discern in our own past the outlines of what looks like a destined course, proceeding neatly from promising childhood to adolescent adventure to adult success and settled maturity along paths of family, career, and so forth. This process is essential to choosing how we will live in the future, but it alone cannot resolve that issue. We can live forward only by repetition, venturing into the unknown and unknowable by faith alone. The poet is the genius of recollection but not of repetition; hence a poet can help assemble an ideal, but a poet is powerless to reconstruct an ideal after it has been ruined by actuality.

28. *Fear and Trembling*, 61.
29. *Repetition*, 132.
30. *Journals and Papers*, 3794.
31. *Fear and Trembling*, 15–16.
32. Ibid., 23.
33. Edward F. Mooney notices this as well. See *On Søren Kierkegaard: Dialogue, Polemics, Lost Intimacy, and Time*, new ed. (Aldershot, UK: Ashgate, 2007), 150.
34. Lippitt, *Routledge Philosophy Guidebook to Kierkegaard and "Fear and Trembling,"* 29.
35. *Fear and Trembling*, 16.
36. Ibid.
37. Lippitt, *Routledge Philosophy Guidebook to Kierkegaard and "Fear and Trembling,"* 29.
38. To quote Lippitt's reaction to this material: "What is going on here? If this is a 'speech in praise' of Abraham by a poet, then perhaps we should not expect rigour of argument to be high on the agenda. It certainly isn't" (30). Lippitt revisits this material in his seventh chapter in relation to the question of Silentio's reliability. I think this material is less relevant to the issue of authorial reliability and more to do with the author's use of various methodological tactics in approaching his subject matter. The puzzling nature of these preliminary assertions can be explained by reference to the conventions of the genre in which Silentio is dabbling.
39. Kierkegaard would have been quite familiar with the Ciceronian framework of classical oratory and its conventions from school age; he owned numerous copies of Cicero's works, including two sets of the *Opera Omnia*, and purchased a translation as late as 1852. See Thomas Eske Rasmussen, "Cicero: A Handy Roman Companion: Marcus Tullius Cicero's Appearance in Kierkegaard's Works," in *Kierkegaard Research: Sources, Reception and Resources Volume 3: Kierkegaard and the Roman World*, ed. Jon Stewart (Aldershot, UK: Ashgate, 2009), 11–38, 14.
40. Many commentators have remarked upon the importance of context for Abraham's deed (indeed some have maintained that greater attention to the context of Abraham's ongoing relationship with God would be a salutary corrective to Silentio's intense concentration on just the events surrounding Moriah), but no commentator has recognized that this section is included in response to the demands of the form of expression that is eulogy understood in its traditional conception.
41. *Fear and Trembling*, 17.
42. Ovid is one possible candidate for the exiled individual to whom Silentio tacitly contrasts Abraham (*Fear and Trembling*, 342n6), but Alastair Hannay has also mentioned Jeremiah as a possibility. *Fear and Trembling*, trans. Alastair Hannay, 150n16.
43. *Fear and Trembling*, 17.
44. Ibid.
45. Ibid.
46. Ibid.
47. See "The Expectancy of Faith," "Patience in Expectancy," and "The Expectancy of an Eternal Salvation," in *Eighteen Upbuilding Discourses*, ed. and trans. Howard V. Hong and Edna H. Hong (Princeton, NJ: Princeton University Press, 1990).
48. *Fear and Trembling*, 17.
49. Ibid., 18.
50. Ibid.
51. More specifically, the generation that is historically contemporaneous with Christ has only the advantage of being shocked more readily than a generation at greater historical remove, but this shock lends itself as readily to the possibility of taking offense as it does to acquiring faith. See *Philosophical Fragments*, 93: "This generation has relatively the advantage

of being closer to the jolt of that fact. This jolt and its vibrations serve to arouse awareness. The significance of such awareness (which can also become offense) has already been appraised in Chapter IV. Assume that it is an advantage to be somewhat closer (compared with later generations)—the advantage is related only to the dubious advantage of the contemporary."

52. *Fear and Trembling*, 18.
53. *Fear and Trembling*, 19.
54. Ibid., 18.
55. *Philosophical Fragments*, 93.
56. Hoffman sees this as well: "Infinite resignation can result in stoic self-inclosure; but it is also the precondition of a mature moral outlook . . . As part of a mature moral outlook, de Silentio hints that such an orientation is a precondition for even recognizing, and therefore taking delight in, everyday miracles when they do happen to occur." Hoffman, "Facing Threats to Earthly Felicity," 446.
57. *Fear and Trembling*, 18.
58. Ibid.
59. *Fear and Trembling*, 19.
60. Ibid.
61. Ibid.
62. *Phaedrus*, 267c–267d.
63. *Fear and Trembling*, 19.
64. One thinks in particular of Kant's edict on Abraham's situation: "Abraham should have replied to this supposedly divine voice: 'That I ought not to kill my good son is quite certain. But that you, this apparition, are God—of that I am not certain, and never can be, not even if this voice rings down to me from (visible) heaven.'" See Immanuel Kant, *The Conflict of the Faculties*, trans. M. G. Gregor and R. Anchor, in *Religion and Rational Theology*, ed. A. W. Wood and G. di Giovanni (Cambridge: Cambridge University Press, 1999), 280. According to the basic presuppositions of *Fear and Trembling*, as indicated by this passage from the eulogy, Kant's interpretation is not even "in the game," so to speak. On the contrary, Kant's ideal rational speaker has already foreclosed the possibility of the miraculous and clearly cannot attain the eternal youth of Abraham, which prepares him for the possibility of acknowledging a marvel when it appears.
65. Hoffman, "Facing Threats to Earthly Felicity," 444.
66. *Fear and Trembling*, 21–22.
67. Hoffman, "Facing Threats to Earthly Felicity," 444. There is one concern I have with Hoffman's language here, and that is the reference to "fate." For Kierkegaard, generally, fatalism must be distinguished from faith, both within *Fear and Trembling* and elsewhere in the corpus (notably *The Sickness unto Death*, 50–60; and *The Concept of Anxiety*, 96–103).
68. Hoffman, "Facing Threats to Earthly Felicity," 441.
69. Ibid., 441–42. On the basis of this analysis, Hoffman critiques Andrew Cross and C. Stephen Evans, the former for putting too much stress on the knife and the latter for putting too much stress on the outcome. Lippitt also raises important concerns with Cross's picture (*Routledge Philosophy Guidebook to Kierkegaard and "Fear and Trembling,"* 67–75).
70. Hoffman, "Facing Threats to Earthly Felicity," 442.
71. Ibid., 444.
72. Lippitt, *Routledge Philosophy Guidebook to Kierkegaard and "Fear and Trembling,"* 75.
73. See Hoffman, "Facing Threats to Earthly Felicity," 447: "I find it important to stress, however, that to cite an especially unique trust and intimacy between Abraham and his God, as a way of explaining his faith, detracts from the central relevance of the text as a whole. Readings that do so find it difficult to coordinate de Silentio's clear assumption that Abraham

is both great and to be imitated." Both Lippitt and Hoffman are concerned at this point to combat the reading of Cross, who regards Abraham's theism as a strike against the account of faith. See Lippitt, *Routledge Philosophy Guidebook to Kierkegaard and "Fear and Trembling,"* 75; and Hoffman, "Facing Threats to Earthly Felicity,' 447.

74. Hoffman, "Facing Threats to Earthly Felicity," 441.

75. Ibid.

76. As Hoffman points out, many interpretations fall into one of two errors: either they downplay the fact that the knife is in Abraham's hand or they overemphasize it to the exclusion of other salient details. In the discussion at hand, as well as in others to come, I will try like Hoffman to steer between these two extremes. Hoffman, "Facing Threats to Earthly Felicity," 440, 442. Yes, the knife is in Abraham's hand, but at the same time, "the story is *not* about a religious legitimation of child sacrifice." Ibid., 439.

77. *Fear and Trembling*, 19–20.

78. Ibid., 20.

79. Ibid.

80. Ibid., 21.

81. Lippitt, *Routledge Philosophy Guidebook to Kierkegaard and "Fear and Trembling,"* 32. Lippitt says it is "less than entirely clear" to him why Silentio insists that this course of action is still admirable.

82. *Fear and Trembling*, 20–21.

83. Ibid., 30.

84. Ibid.

85. Lippitt speculates that this Abraham could be considered a tragic hero on the grounds that a deed of this sort could be convincingly rendered in a tragedy, but this conjecture is not likely either (Lippitt, *Routledge Philosophy Guidebook to Kierkegaard and "Fear and Trembling,"* 32). The tragic heroes all have to go through with the sacrifice of another and legitimate their deeds by recourse to publicly available categories and concepts. It is more likely that this Abraham is at best an aesthetic hero, whom Silentio says in Problema III acts to save another, not himself. "Esthetics allowed, indeed demanded, silence of the single individual if he knew that by remaining silent he could save another. This alone adequately shows that Abraham is not within the scope of esthetics. His silence is certainly not in order to save Isaac; in fact, his whole task of sacrificing Isaac for his own and for God's sake is an offense to esthetics, because it is able to understand that I sacrifice myself but not that I sacrifice someone else for my own sake" (*Fear and Trembling*, 112).

86. *Fear and Trembling*, 22.

87. Ibid., 16.

88. Ibid.

89. Ibid., 22.

90. Ibid., 23.

91. Ibid.

92. Ibid.

5. Beginning from the Heart

1. *Fear and Trembling*, trans. Alastair Hannay, 57.

2. Obviously, the expectoration is itself called "Preliminary," and so it is with respect to the other problemata sections. As the fourth section of the book, however, it can hardly be regarded as preliminary to the entire book, only to the numbered problemata.

3. *Fear and Trembling*, 27.

4. 2 Thess. 3:10 (KJV).
5. 2 Thess. 3:12 (KJV).
6. 2 Thess. 3:7–9 (KJV).
7. Silentio's reference to Orpheus contributes to this case here as well. Silentio rather sarcastically observes that "he who will not work does not get bread but is deceived just as the gods deceived Orpheus with an ethereal phantom instead of the beloved, deceived him because he was soft, not boldly brave, deceived him because he was a zither player and not a man" (27). It is interesting to observe that the version of the Orpheus and Eurydice myth Silentio has in mind must be that of Plato's *Symposium* and specifically Phaedrus's condemnation of Orpheus. Phaedrus too is contemptuous of Orpheus in the opening to his discourse on love: "But Orpheus, the son of Oeagrus, the harper, they [the gods] sent empty away, and presented to him an apparition only of her whom he sought, but herself they would not give up, because he showed no spirit; he was only a harp-player, and did not dare like Alcestis to die for love, but was contriving how he might enter Hades alive; moreover, they afterwards caused him to suffer death at the hands of women, as the punishment of his cowardliness." Plato, *Symposium*, in *The Dialogues of Plato*, trans. Benjamin Jowett (Chicago: Encyclopedia Britannica, 1952), 153. This is not Virgil's version of the tale, and this one, in keeping with my understanding of Silentio's argument at this stage of *Fear and Trembling*, emphasizes the difference between the actual (Eurydice herself) and the unreal (her phantom) and the need for risk and commitment, even in the face of death, to earn spiritual bread.
8. *Fear and Trembling*, 27.
9. Ibid.
10. Isa. 26:18 (KJV).
11. *Philosophical Fragments*, 94–95.
12. *Fear and Trembling*, 27.
13. Ibid., 28.
14. Ibid.
15. See my "Holy Hypochondria: Narrative and Self-Awareness in *The Concept of Anxiety*."
16. *The Concept of Anxiety*, 156.
17. Ibid., 160.
18. Ibid., 161.
19. Ibid., 158.
20. Ibid.
21. Ibid.
22. Ibid.
23. *Fear and Trembling*, 28.
24. Recall the discussion in the Introduction above of the prophet Nathan and King David.
25. *The Concept of Anxiety*, 158.
26. Ibid.
27. Ibid.
28. *Fear and Trembling*, 28.
29. Ibid.
30. Ibid.
31. *The Concept of Anxiety*, 16.
32. *Fear and Trembling*, 28–29.
33. Ibid., 29.
34. Ibid., 31.
35. Ibid., 30. I have already pointed out that this passage casts some doubt on the sincerity of the eulogy on Abraham, which comes quite close to asserting Abraham's prescriptive right to greatness.

36. Ibid.
37. Ibid., 31.
38. Ibid.
39. Ibid.
40. Ibid., 32. Emphasis in the original.
41. Ibid., 33.
42. Ibid.
43. Ibid.
44. Ibid., 33–34.
45. Ibid., 34.
46. Ibid.
47. Ibid., 35.
48. Ibid.
49. *The Sickness unto Death*, 77. See the discussion above in chapter 1.
50. Ibid.
51. Ibid.
52. Ibid.
53. Ibid., 78.
54. Ibid.
55. *Fear and Trembling*, 36.
56. Ibid.
57. Ibid.
58. Ibid., 36–37. As in the vignettes featured in the exordium, it should be noted that when Silentio considers how he would react if the task of sacrificing Isaac had fallen to him, he says he would have done just as Abraham did, only with an attitude entirely lacking in joy.
59. Ibid., 37.
60. Ibid., 36.
61. Ibid.
62. For a commendable development of this metaphor's significance see Sylvia Walsh, *Living Poetically: Kierkegaard's Existential Aesthetics* (University Park: Pennsylvania State University Press, 1994), 128–30; 136–45.
63. *Fear and Trembling*, 37.
64. Ibid., 38.
65. Ibid.
66. Ibid., 39.
67. Ibid.
68. Ibid., 40.
69. Ibid., 39.
70. Ibid., 40.
71. Ibid., 39.
72. Ibid.
73. Ibid., 39–40.
74. See her "What the Faithful Tax Collector Saw (Against the Understanding), in *International Kierkegaard Commentary: "Without Authority,"* ed. Robert L. Perkins (Macon, GA: Mercer University Press, 2006), 298.
75. Ibid. Hough's article is quite rich with insight in fact. I concur with her judgment for instance that missing from Silentio's portrait is any account of sin, which makes this vision incomplete and does not quite rise to the challenge of dealing with evil (305). It is only unfortunate that she chose to word the content of the knight of faith's belief as a false one, which

is highly misleading. One other weakness in wording might be the use of the terms "epistemic flexibility" (298) in connection with faith; I would prefer the language of "resiliency," or elasticity, which Constantin Constantius associates with irony (*Repetition*, 137) and asserts is required to make productive use of the mood of erotic love. I think elasticity or resiliency is a hallmark of faith as well.

76. *Fear and Trembling*, 47.
77. Ibid., 41.
78. Ibid.
79. Ibid., 40.
80. The happy marriage and all that it symbolizes does not come to the fore in the text's argumentation until very nearly the end, with Tobias and Sarah's story. The contemporary knight of faith implies this conclusion but only in the most minimal way.
81. *Fear and Trembling*, 41.
82. Ibid., 42.
83. Ibid.
84. Ibid.
85. Ibid., 43.
86. Ibid.
87. Ibid., 42n. Emphasis in the original.
88. Ibid., 43.
89. Ibid.
90. Ibid.
91. Ibid., 45.
92. Ibid., 43–44.
93. Ibid., 44.
94. Ibid.
95. Ibid.
96. Ibid.
97. Ibid., 50.
98. Ibid., 46.
99. Ibid., 47.
100. Ibid., 46.
101. Ibid., 46–47.
102. Ibid., 47.
103. Ibid.
104. Ibid., 47–48.
105. Ibid., 49.
106. Ibid. See Matthew 19:16–26 (KJV).
107. Ibid.
108. Ibid., 50.
109. Ibid.
110. Critical consensus has coalesced around a desire to reject this obviously problematic interpretation. See Lippitt, *Routledge Philosophy Guidebook to Kierkegaard and "Fear and Trembling,"* 67–68, where Lippitt quotes Andrew Cross to the same effect, from his "*Fear and Trembling*'s Unorthodox Ideal," *Philosophical Topics* 27, no. 2 (1999): 227–53, 238.
111. One might object that Abraham gets Isaac, his same son, back. But how could Isaac possibly be the *same* after the journey to Moriah?
112. Edward F. Mooney, *Knights of Faith and Resignation: Reading Kierkegaard's "Fear and Trembling"* (Albany: State University of New York Press, 1991), 58.

113. Ibid.
114. Ibid., 53.
115. Hoffman, "Facing Threats to Earthly Felicity," 445.
116. Ibid., 446.
117. *Fear and Trembling*, 20.
118. Ibid., 59.
119. Lippitt observes this as well on page 62 of his *Routledge Philosophy Guidebook to Kierkegaard and "Fear and Trembling."* For additional concerns about Mooney's account, see Lippitt, *Routledge Philosophy Guidebook to Kierkegaard and "Fear and Trembling,"* 54–59; Hoffman, "Facing Threats to Earthly Felicity," 445; and Ronald L. Hall, *The Human Embrace: The Love of Philosophy and the Philosophy of Love: Kierkegaard, Cavell, Nussbaum* (University Park: Pennsylvania State University Press, 2000), 28–33.
120. *The Sickness unto Death*, 15.
121. Hall, *The Human Embrace*, 36.
122. Hall cites a later passage where Anti-Climacus says that despair is "the first element in faith" (*The Sickness unto Death*, 116n), but this does not prove as much as he hopes either. Despair is only the first element in faith because the possibility of despair is a mark of primordial consciousness. Without the possibility of despair there is no consciousness at all and thus of course no faith. That does not prove that faith depends in a significant way on despair. Besides, Anti-Climacus is quite clear that the possibility of despair is a tremendous gift, while the actuality of despair is the worst sort of curse. He militantly opposes any confusion here between the essential value of being capable of despair and the dreadful affliction of actually being in despair. See *The Sickness unto Death*, 15.
123. Lippitt seems to endorse the "annulled possibility" reading on page 67 of his *Routledge Philosophy Guidebook to Kierkegaard and "Fear and Trembling."* Both he and Hall are rightly desirous of an explanation of the relationship between resignation and faith that makes sense of them going together rather than being separated by a temporal or logical lag, as if one resigns and then has faith. I agree with them that the "double movement" is not two discrete moments, but my interpretation shows how the two can be thought together without dubious recourse to the "annulled possibility" thesis, which in my view is unsupported by the text, requires importing an extraneous conceptual apparatus that is not analogous to the argument of *Fear and Trembling*, and construes resignation only negatively.
124. Lippitt, *Routledge Philosophy Guidebook to Kierkegaard and "Fear and Trembling,"* 67.
125. Ibid.
126. Ibid.
127. *Fear and Trembling*, 119.
128. Andrew Cross, "*Fear and Trembling*'s Unorthodox Ideal," *Philosophical Topics* 27, no. 2 (1999): 227–53, 242.
129. Cross, "*Fear and Trembling*'s Unorthodox Ideal," 246–47.
130. This point is also made by Hoffman in "Facing Threats to Earthly Felicity," 442, where he also calls Cross to account for reducing the issue of *Fear and Trembling* back to a myopic focus on "a literal sacrifice." The larger issue that Hoffman and I both want to address is the implication for human life generally on the premise of Abrahamic faith.
131. Cross, "*Fear and Trembling*'s Unorthodox Ideal," 250.
132. Lippitt, *Routledge Philosophy Guidebook to Kierkegaard and "Fear and Trembling,"* 70.
133. *Fear and Trembling*, 119.
134. Ibid., 35.
135. Ibid., 36.
136. Lippitt, *Routledge Philosophy Guidebook to Kierkegaard and "Fear and Trembling,"* 70.

137. Ibid., 72.
138. Cross, "*Fear and Trembling*'s Unorthodox Ideal," 237.
139. Ibid.
140. Lippitt, *Routledge Philosophy Guidebook to Kierkegaard and "Fear and Trembling,"* 71.
141. Ibid., 75.
142. Matt. 6:24 (KJV).
143. "But to want to serve the idea—which in regard to erotic love is not to serve two masters—is in fact a strenuous service, for no beautiful woman can be as exacting as the idea, and no girl's disapproval can be as distressing as the wrath of the idea, which above all is impossible to forget." *Repetition*, 140–41.

6. Teleological Suspensions

1. *Fear and Trembling*, 54.
2. Ibid., 30.
3. *Fear and Trembling*, 55.
4. To recall Haufniensis's terminology from *The Concept of Anxiety*, 20–21.
5. The connection is patent in Problema II: "The paradox of faith, then is this: that the single individual is higher than the universal, that the single individual—to recall a distinction in dogmatics rather rare these days—determines his relation to the universal by his relation to the absolute, not his relation to the absolute by his relation to the universal. The paradox may also be expressed in this way: that there is an absolute duty to God, for in this relationship of duty the individual relates himself as the single individual absolutely to the absolute" (70); again, "Therefore, either there is an absolute duty to God—and if there is such a thing, it is the paradox just described, that the single individual as the single individual is higher than the universal and as the single individual stands in an absolute relation to the absolute—or else faith has never existed because it has always existed." (81).
6. *The Concept of Anxiety*, 15.
7. The phrasing is used twice in Problema I (56, 62); twice in Problema II (70, 81); most frequently in Problema III (93, 97, 98, 111, 113, 120).
8. *Fear and Trembling*, 98.
9. *The Concept of Anxiety*, 19.
10. Anti-Climacus also supports this contention at length. See in particular *The Sickness unto Death*, 90: "What constituent, then, does Socrates lack for the defining of sin? It is the will, defiance. The intellectuality of the Greeks was too happy, too naïve, too esthetic, too ironic, too witty—too sinful—to grasp that anyone could knowingly not do the good, or knowingly, knowing what is right, do wrong."
11. *Fear and Trembling*, 98.
12. Lippitt again has a good discussion of this point. *Routledge Guidebook to Kierkegaard and "Fear and Trembling,"* 122–23.
13. *Fear and Trembling*, 98–99. Also from the same page, in a footnote to these words, Silentio writes, "Up until now I have assiduously avoided any reference to the question of sin and its reality. The whole work is centered on Abraham, and I can sill encompass him in immediate categories—that is, insofar as I can understand him. As soon as sin emerges, ethics founders precisely on repentance; for repentance is the highest ethical expression, but precisely as such it is the deepest ethical self-contradiction."
14. Ibid., 98.
15. *The Concept of Anxiety*, 17n.

16. This conception would be inclusive of, for example, Merold Westphal's reading of the ethical as Hegelian *Sittlichkeit*, but it would also be broader, such that exceptions to it would not constitute only a breach of "the laws and customs of my people," though they may do so, but also would include any sin in the strong, Judeo-Christian conception thereof. See Westphal, "Kierkegaard and Hegel" in *The Cambridge Companion to Kierkegaard*, ed. Alastair Hannay and Gordon Marino (Cambridge: Cambridge University Press, 1998), 107; *Transcendence and Self-Transcendence* (Bloomington: Indiana University Press, 2004), 87; *Becoming a Self* (West Lafayette, IN: Purdue University Press, 1996), 102–11; *Levinas and Kierkegaard in Dialogue* (Bloomington: Indiana University Press, 2008), 23–24, 53.

17. *The Sickness unto Death*, 87.

18. I would say that Problema III of *Fear and Trembling* does the same thing.

19. *Concluding Unscientific Postscript to* Philosophical Fragments, 268.

20. *The Sickness unto Death*, 89.

21. *Fear and Trembling*, 61–62.

22. Anti-Climacus will also argue this point at length. See in particular *The Sickness unto Death*, 89: "There has to be a revelation from God to show what sin is."

23. John Hare provides an argument about second ethics in his *The Moral Gap* that rests on a reading of *Either/Or II* but I think is just as relevant to *Fear and Trembling*. Hare builds a convincing analogy between the way in which the ethical life (as Judge William argues) preserves the interesting and attractive precisely by deemphasizing it and the way in which the religious life preserves the ethical again by relativizing it. The trick is to repeat the aesthetic within the ethical, something the Judge argues is possible when aesthetic pleasure is demoted from the place of central concern in life to a "side-effect" of a more enduringly delightful existence of responsibilities attended by their own deeper fulfillments (216). The great enemy of the aesthete, boredom, is thereby vanquished simply because the avoidance of boredom is no longer the driving (unattainable) imperative. "To apply the analogy," Hare writes, "the transition to the religious life should mean that we can now relax about the ethical life, because it no longer has the emphasis it did before; and this should mean both that we can now sustain the ethical life and that it should not matter to us so desperately when we do not" (217). The reason it should not matter so desperately is not of course because we should not take sin seriously but because we now have both the proper diagnosis for it and a remedy for it. The demonic is the maniacal obsession over one's own failures and even perverse adherence to them; to make the teleological suspension of the ethical is to be clear about the nature of the demonic and to open the door to its exorcism. Hare of course is juxtaposing second ethics with Kant, not Hegel, but if he is right, then indeed the teleological suspension is a corrective not just to Hegel but to other similarly limited ethical views as well.

24. Søren Kierkegaard, *Concluding Unscientific Postscript*, 266.

25. Ibid.

26. Ibid., 266–67.

27. Ibid., 267–68.

28. Ibid.

29. Ibid., 267.

30. *Fear and Trembling*, 99.

31. Brian Gregor, "Kierkegaard and the Phenomenology of Temptation," in *Kierkegaard as Phenomenologist: An Experiment*, ed. Jeffrey Hanson (Evanston, IL: Northwestern University Press, 2010), 129–30, 132.

32. Ibid., 131.

33. Ibid., 130.

34. *Concluding Unscientific Postscript*, 269.

35. *Fear and Trembling*, 54.

36. Ibid. Lippitt is surely right (81–82) that Silentio is not *asserting* this to be the case at the beginning of Problema I; on the contrary, as the developed disjunction that follows in the text and that we have chosen to analyze first demonstrates, the ultimacy of the ethical as universal is precisely what is being placed in question.

37. *Fear and Trembling*, 54.

38. G. W. F. Hegel, *Outlines of the Philosophy of Right*, ed. Stephen Houlgate and trans. T. M. Knox (Oxford: Oxford University Press, 2008), 136.

39. *Fear and Trembling*, 55.

40. *Philosophy of Right*, 151–52.

41. *Fear and Trembling*, 55.

42. I am borrowing here the form of an argument given by David Kangas on a different topic. He makes an analogous case for Kierkegaard's evasion of Hegel on a different point in his "The Logic of Gift in Kierkegaard's *Four Upbuilding Discourses* (1843)," *Kierkegaard Studies Year Book 2000* (Berlin: De Gruyter, 2000), 100–120.

43. With respect to this way of putting the matter, an enigmatic remark in the final pages of the preliminary expectoration should command a moment's attention. Silentio returns to the metaphor of dancing, one that has already been remarked upon as suggestive of the aesthetic dimension of the knight of faith's way of living. "If someone who wanted to learn to dance were to say: For centuries, one generation after the other has learned the positions, and it is high time that I take advantage of this and promptly begin with the quadrille—people would presumably laugh a little at him, but in the world of spirit this is considered utterly plausible. What, then, is education? I believed it is the course the individual goes through in order to catch up with himself, and the person who will not go through this course is not much helped by being born in the most enlightened age" (*Fear and Trembling*, 46). Translation modified. The Hongs have "In the world of spirit this is very plausible," while Walsh has "In the world of spirit it is highly plausible" (39). The problem with both is that they make it sound as if Silentio is endorsing this folly as inappropriate to the finite world but at home in the infinite. However, Kierkegaard is as consistently opposed to "shortcuts" in the world of spirit as he is in the world of dancing. Hannay's is a better rendering: "In the world of spirit such an attitude is considered utterly plausible" (75). The Danish is "men i Aandens Verden finder man det yderst plausibelt," so there is no exact correlate in the original for Hannay's "attitude," which is surely meant to be clarifying rather than rigidly faithful, while translating "finder man" as "is considered" is both more accurate and truer to Kierkegaard's meaning. The Hongs' and Walsh's "is" is too emphatic for "finder," which can mean both literally "find" as in "discover" or "find" in the looser sense of "regard as" or "consider" as in, "I found him a trifle pedantic." The point is that education is a sort of catching up with one's self, a marvelous expression for the development of consciousness, which necessarily has to retrace certain steps, just as a beginner in dancing has to learn the basics, even if those patterns have been well established in historical practice and mastered by thousands of the beginner's predecessors. A similar logic is found in the passage from *Repetition* below, where Constantius insists that the exception cannot "bypass the universal but has to battle *through* it.

44. *Repetition*, 226–28.

45. Luke 15:3–7 (KJV).

46. Luke 15:29–30 (KJV).

47. Gen. 32:22–31 (KJV).

48. A feat that Job too accomplishes through his suffering in chapters 38–41.

49. A similar sentiment is found in a journal entry of 1846: "It is elevating and upbuilding to consider how feeble the age is, how in fact it really works against itself. It persecutes and hounds the exceptional person, but the more it does this, the more certainly the exception becomes immortal. To be persecuted is already something noteworthy, and a completely insignificant person could become immortal merely by having been shabbily persecuted by his contemporaries" (*Journals and Papers*, 1077).

50. *Journals and Papers*, 1084.

51. *The Concept of Anxiety*, 28.

52. Ibid., n. See also *Journals and Papers*, 2986: "Each animal is only a copy or specimen [*Exemplar*]. Man, on the other hand, is the only animal species in which every specimen is (κατὰ δύναμιν) more than the race, is an individuality, intended [*lagt an*] to be spirit."

53. *The Concept of Anxiety*, 29.

54. *Journals and Papers*, 1825, 3561, 2907.

55. Ibid., 2048.

56. Ibid., n.

57. *Journals and Papers*, 1090.

58. *The Concept of Anxiety*, 16.

59. *Fear and Trembling*, 57–59.

60. Ibid., 57.

61. Ibid.

62. Ibid., 61.

63. Ibid., 59.

64. *Concluding Unscientific Postscript*, 592.

65. Ibid.

66. Matt. 19:26 (KJV).

67. Matt. 19:16–22 (KJV).

68. One fact that makes the comparison imperfect is that the law is itself revealed, not a humanly constructed notion of the good. You might call this incident a specifically Christian version of the teleological suspension.

69. Matt. 19:27–29 (KJV).

70. *Fear and Trembling*, 64–65.

71. Ibid., 65.

72. Ibid.

73. Ibid.

74. Ibid.

75. Ibid.

76. Ibid.

77. *Journals and Papers*, 364.

78. Ibid.

79. Ibid., 2674.

80. Ibid.

81. Ibid., 2671.

82. *Fear and Trembling*, 99.

83. Ibid., 56.

84. Ibid., 61. In a journal entry relevant to his reading of the legend of Agnes and the merman Kierkegaard says the religious has its name because it loosens the power of all witchcraft (*Journals and Papers*, 5668).

85. Incidentally, it was after Robert Rule's brief speech that Gary Ridgway first shed tears during his sentencing; he remained unexpressive after the abuse and invective was directed toward him.

86. The same case could be made, perhaps, for other forms of adherence to a demand that transcends the limits of the ethical as universal: selling all you have and giving the proceeds to the poor, loving your enemy, praying for those who persecute you, cutting off a hand or plucking out an eye that offends. Forgiveness to me seems to be an important instance, but it bears something in common with all of the "hard sayings."

87. *Fear and Trembling*, 59.

7. Absolute Duty

1. The connection between the absolute relation to the absolute and the subject matter of Problema II is clear: "The paradox of faith, then is this: that the single individual is higher than the universal, that the single individual—to recall a distinction in dogmatics rather rare these days—determines his relation to the universal by his relation to the absolute, not his relation to the absolute by his relation to the universal. The paradox may also be expressed in this way: that there is an absolute duty to God, for in this relationship of duty the individual relates himself as the single individual absolutely to the absolute" (70); again, "Therefore, either there is an absolute duty to God—and if there is such a thing, it is the paradox just described, that the single individual as the single individual is higher than the universal and as the single individual stands in an absolute relation to the absolute—or else faith has never existed because it has always existed." (81).

2. *Fear and Trembling*, 68.

3. Ibid.

4. Ibid.

5. Ibid.

6. *The Concept of Anxiety*, 17n.

7. *Fear and Trembling*, 70.

8. Ibid., 68.

9. Ibid., 69.

10. Ibid.

11. Ibid.

12. Ibid.

13. Climacus makes a related point in *Philosophical Fragments*, contrasting, as he does so often, faith with the intellectual posture of Socrates: "One does not have *faith* that the god exists, eternally understood, even though one assumes that the god exists." Thus "Socrates did not have faith that the god existed . . . and for him the existence of the god was by no means something historical" (87).

14. *Fear and Trembling*, 70.

15. Ibid.

16. I have already argued that the "hard sayings" are a good source of content for the teleological suspension and its ramifications. Silentio's choice of texts is thus more than appropriate, and the kinship between such passages and the exemplary quality of Abraham's faith is cemented by his direct association of the two themes in this section: "Anyone who does not dare to mention such passages [like Luke 14:26] does not dare to mention Abraham, either." *Fear and Trembling*, 75.

17. *Fear and Trembling*, 72.

18. Ibid.

19. Luke 14:27 (KJV).

20. *Fear and Trembling*, 72.

21. Ibid.

22. Ibid., 72–73.

23. *Fear and Trembling*, 73. The expression translated here (perhaps problematically) by the Hongs is *efter ordene*, which seems like a rather nonliteral way of saying "literally."

24. *Fear and Trembling*, 73.

25. I am thinking especially of Derrida's interpretation in *The Gift of Death* and those it inspired.

26. *Fear and Trembling*, 73.

27. Ibid., 74.

28. Ibid.

29. Ibid., 70.

30. Ibid., 71.

31. Ibid., 70–71.

32. Ibid., 78n.

33. Ibid., 70.

34. Ibid.

35. In this chapter we read that no one shall enter the kingdom of heaven unless they become like a little child (verse 3), that if a hand or foot is the cause of offense then it should be cut off (verse 8), that heaven rejoices more over the one lost and found than the ninety-nine (verse 13), and the exhortation to forgive others not seven times but seventy times seven (verses 21–22).

36. Matt. 18:27 (KJV).

37. Matt. 18:35 (KJV).

38. *Fear and Trembling*, 49.

39. Ibid., 81.

40. Ibid., 351.

41. Finally, the 1 Corinthians passage is Paul's counsel to divorced women that "if she depart, let her remain unmarried or be reconciled to her husband: and let not the husband put away his wife." I leave aside this passage because as Hannay reports, the Danish editors suggest that 1 Corinthians 7:9 may in fact have been the verse Kierkegaard had in mind. In the entire authorship, 1 Corinthians 7:11 is mentioned only here, whereas verse 9 gets five mentions in all.

42. Matt. 19:25–26 (KJV).

43. Also noted in the prior chapter is Climacus's association of Matthew 19 with the teleological suspension. See *Concluding Unscientific Postscript*, 592.

44. I thank Michael R. Kelly for directing my attention to a passage from Bergson that makes a similar point: "The morality of the Gospels is essentially that of the open soul: are we not justified in pointing out that it borders upon paradox, and even upon contradiction, in its more definite admonitions? If riches are an evil, should we not be injuring the poor in giving them what we possess? If he who has been smitten on the one cheek is to offer the other also, what becomes of justice, without which, after all, there can be no 'charity'? But the paradox disappears, the contradiction vanishes, if we consider the intent of these maxims, which is to create a certain disposition of the soul. It is not for the sake of the poor, but for his own sake, that the rich man should give up his riches: blessed are the poor 'in spirit'! The beauty lies, not in being deprived, not even in depriving oneself, but in not feeling the deprivation." Henri Bergson, *The Two Sources of Morality and Religion*, trans. R. Ashley Audra and Cloudesley Brereton with the assistance of W. Horsfall Carter (London: MacMillan, 1935), 45–46.

45. *Fear and Trembling*, 80.

46. Ibid., 80–81.

47. *Journals and Papers*, 2048n.

48. *Fear and Trembling*, 79.

49. Ibid.
50. Ibid.
51. Ibid., 80.
52. Ibid.
53. Ibid., 71.
54. Ibid., 80.
55. Given that the martyr cannot be accommodated by the ethical, we could envision that the demonic antipode to her (equally alien to the ethical as universal) is her dark twin, the suicide, who perfectly realizes the pernicious dream of full "autonomy."

8. Silence and Speech

1. *Concluding Unscientific Postscript*, 268.
2. *The Concept of Anxiety*, 17n.
3. *Johannes Climacus*, 261.
4. *Fear and Trembling*, 255.
5. *The Concept of Anxiety*, 123.
6. Ibid., 124.
7. *Fear and Trembling*, 88.
8. Ibid., 82.
9. *The Concept of Anxiety*, 14–15.
10. *Fear and Trembling*, 83.
11. Ibid., 84–85.
12. Ibid., 85.
13. Ibid.
14. Ibid.
15. Ibid., 86.
16. Ibid., 87.
17. Ibid.
18. Ibid.
19. Ibid.
20. Ibid.
21. Ibid., 87–88.
22. Ibid., 87.
23. Ibid., 83–84.
24. Ibid., 84.
25. Søren Kierkegaard, *Fear and Trembling*, 111.
26. Søren Kierkegaard, *Fear and Trembling*, 73.
27. "Carambole," *A New English Dictionary on Historical Principles*, ed. James A. H. Murray, vol. II.C., Part I. C-COMM. (Oxford: Clarendon, 1893), 104.
28. *Fear and Trembling*, 88.
29. Ibid., 89. Emphasis in the original.
30. Ibid., 90.
31. Ibid.
32. Ibid.
33. Ibid. John Lippitt has a good discussion of these points in his *Routledge Philosophy Guidebook to Kierkegaard and "Fear and Trembling,"* 116–17. I owe much to his analysis in his chapter.

34. *Fear and Trembling*, 90–91.
35. Ibid., 91
36. Ibid.
37. Ibid., 92.
38. Ibid.
39. Ibid.
40. Ibid.
41. Ibid., 92–93.
42. My analysis here depends considerably on Haufniensis's discussion of fate and the genius from chapter III of *The Concept of Anxiety*.
43. *Fear and Trembling*, 92.
44. Ibid., 93.
45. Ibid., 92.
46. Ibid., 93.
47. Ibid., 94.
48. Ibid.
49. Ibid., 95.
50. *The Concept of Anxiety*, 118–54.
51. Ibid., 123: "The demonic is anxiety about the good. In innocence, freedom was not posited as freedom: its possibility was anxiety in the individual. In the demonic, the relation is reversed. Freedom is posited as unfreedom, because freedom is lost. Here again freedom's possibility is anxiety. The difference is absolute, because freedom's possibility appears here in relation to unfreedom, which is the very opposite of innocence, which is a qualification disposed toward freedom."
52. Ibid., 119.
53. Ibid., 123: "The demonic is unfreedom that wants to close itself off. This, however, is and remains an impossibility. It always retains a relation, and even when this has apparently disappeared altogether, it is nevertheless there, and anxiety at once manifests itself in the moment of contact."
54. *Fear and Trembling*, 97.
55. *The Sickness unto Death*, 67–74.
56. *Fear and Trembling*, 96.
57. Ibid.
58. Ibid.
59. Ibid.
60. According to Silentio, it is much harder to accept love than to love, which is why in his examination of the story of Tobias and Sarah he will declare Sarah the hero (104).
61. Nowhere is this aspect of the demonic more pointedly described than at the close of Part One in *The Sickness unto Death*: "Figuratively speaking, it is as if an error slipped into an author's writing and the error became conscious of itself as an error—perhaps it actually was not a mistake but in a much higher sense an essential part of the whole production—and now this error wants to mutiny against the author, out of hatred toward him, forbidding him to correct it and in maniacal defiance saying to him: No, I refuse to be erased; I will stand as a witness against you, a witness that you are a second-rate author" (74). See also *The Concept of Anxiety*, 137: "The utmost extreme in this sphere is what is commonly called bestial perdition. In this state, the demonic manifests itself in saying, as did the demoniac in the New Testament with regard to salvation: What have I to do with you? Therefore it shuns every contact [with the good], whether this actually threatens it by wanting to help it to freedom or only touches it casually. But this is also enough, for anxiety is extraordinarily swift. Therefore, from such a

demoniac is quite commonly heard a reply that expresses all the horror of this state: Leave me alone in my wretchedness."

62. *Fear and Trembling*, 99.
63. Ibid.
64. Ibid.
65. *Fear and Trembling*, 97n.
66. Ibid., 98.
67. This recalls the Preface and its concern for a harmony between *stasis* and *dynamis*. Continuity is a key issue for subjective development, and it intersects with earnestness, the power by which the self achieves a sort of unity over time.
68. *Fear and Trembling*, 102.
69. Ibid.
70. Ibid.
71. Ibid.
72. Ibid., 103.
73. Ibid.
74. Ibid.
75. Ibid., 104.
76. Ibid., 106: "With regard to all such things, the poets ought to be almost the first to sound the alarm. God only knows what books the present generation of young versifiers is reading!"
77. Ibid.
78. Ibid., 106–7.
79. Ibid., 104.
80. Ibid., 103.
81. Ibid. 97n.
82. Ibid., 87.
83. Ibid., 86.
84. Ibid., 107.
85. Ibid., 107–8.
86. Ibid., 108.
87. Ibid.
88. The quote appears in the footnote on page 79 of *The Concept of Anxiety*.
89. *Fear and Trembling*, 108.
90. Ibid., 109.
91. Ibid., 110.
92. Ibid.
93. Ibid.
94. Ibid., 111.
95. Ibid.
96. Ibid.
97. Ibid.
98. John Lippitt sees this too: Faust "needs to recognise himself as guilty: for an absolute relation to the absolute (a relation to God unmediated by the ethical) to be possible, he must accept himself as a sinner . . . In which case, Johannes would mean that if Faust was to understand himself as a sinner and relate himself to Him who can forgive sin then 'his doubt is cured': that is, his sins are forgiven." *Routledge Philosophy Guidebook to Kierkegaard and "Fear and Trembling,"* 128.
99. That Abraham's speech is intelligible is in fact stipulated by the text, though its intelligibility is not that of discourses that address only objective truth. Readings of *Fear and*

Trembling that regard Abraham as hermetically sealed off from *all* intelligibility overstate the issue and neglect the final qualified assurances of Johannes that "insofar as I can understand the paradox, I can also understand Abraham's total presence in that word" (118); "it is apparent that one perhaps can understand Abraham, but only in the way one understands the paradox. I, for my part, perhaps can understand Abraham" (119); and "I presumably can understand it, perhaps in a certain sense understand Abraham in what was said without thereby coming any closer to him than in the preceding exposition" (117–18). If Abraham were *completely* incomprehensible then there would be no point in writing *Fear and Trembling.*

100. *Fear and Trembling*, 118.
101. Ibid., 113, 115.
102. Ibid., 113.
103. Ibid., 115.
104. Both valences are remarked upon by Haufniensis in *The Concept of Anxiety*, 124; in English, the use of the word "communicate" to mean "take holy communion" has become archaic but can be found, for example, in the rubrics to the older editions of *The Book of Common Prayer.*
105. *Fear and Trembling*, 116.
106. Ibid.
107. Ibid.
108. Ibid., 117–18.
109. Ibid., 119.
110. Ibid., 115.
111. Ibid., 118.
112. Ibid., 114.
113. Ibid., 119.
114. *Either/Or II*, 137.
115. Ibid.
116. *Fear and Trembling*, 120.
117. Richard Moran makes the point that there is a normative expectation that simply goes along with first-person testimony: "We also expect and sometimes insist that he take himself to be in a position to *speak for* his feelings and convictions, and not simply to offer his best opinion about them. ('Do you intend to pay the money back?' 'As far as I can tell, yes.')." Clearly this would not be a suitable form of proclamation, and we can't read Abraham's utterance as if it were akin to this. Richard Moran, *Authority and Estrangement: An Essay on Self-Knowledge* (Princeton, NJ: Princeton University Press, 2001), 26. This helpful quote appears in Anthony Rudd, *Self, Value, and Narrative* (Oxford: Oxford University Press, 2012), 14.
118. *Fear and Trembling*, 117.

Conclusion

1. *Fear and Trembling*, 121.
2. Ibid.
3. Ibid., 122.
4. *The Concept of Anxiety*, 149.
5. Ibid.
6. Ibid.
7. *Fear and Trembling.*, 123.

8. Ibid., 121–22.

9. The belongingness of the individual and historical to one another is a point repeatedly insisted on by Haufniensis. "Every individual is essentially interested in the history of all other individuals, and just as essentially as in his own. Perfection in oneself is therefore the perfect participation in the whole. No individual is indifferent to the history of the race any more than the race is indifferent to the history of the individual. As the history of the race moves on, the individual begins constantly anew, because he is both himself and the race, and by this, in turn, the history of the race." *The Concept of Anxiety*, 29.

10. *Fear and Trembling*, 122.

11. Ibid.

12. Jacob Ludwig Carl Grimm, Jacob W. Grimm, Wilhelm Grimm, *Grimms' Tales for Young and Old: The Complete Stories*, trans. Ralph Manheim (New York: Knopf Doubleday, 2011), 126–27.

13. *Fear and Trembling*, 27.

14. *Grimms' Tales for Young and Old*, 126.

15. Ibid., 127.

16. *Fear and Trembling*, 122.

17. Ibid., 121.

18. Ibid., 122.

19. *The Concept of Irony*, 305.

Index

JEFFREY HANSON is a research associate at the Program on Integrative Knowledge and Human Flourishing in Harvard University's Institute for Quantitative Social Science. He is also editor of *Kierkegaard as Phenomenologist: An Experiment* and editor with Michael R. Kelly of *Michel Henry: The Affects of Thought.*